FRATRI FIDISSIMO
IOANNI

GOD WAS IN CHRIST

An Essay on
Incarnation and Atonement

by

D. M. BAILLIE, D.D.

Professor of Systematic Theology
in the University of St. Andrews

NEW YORK
CHARLES SCRIBNER'S SONS
1948

Contents

5

CONTENTS

Preface

This book is not a treatise, but an essay for the present time. It has turned out a more controversial volume at some points than I could have wished, especially in the earlier chapters. But I may say that, on the whole, the theologians with whom I have been most in controversy are those whose contributions matter most to me, not to speak of their friendship. It will occur to readers that I sometimes appear to be addressing myself to the Christian theologian and at other times to the typical modern man and particularly the outsider. That is perfectly true. But the discerning reader will perceive that at many points the person with whom I am arguing is myself, and I am far from thinking that I have completed that great argument and answered all my questions. I can only hope that I may have clarified some issues, and that some lines of thought which have helped me may help others also.

I have used certain parts of the material of this book in giving the Forwood Lectures in the Philosophy of Religion at the University of Liverpool, and in lecturing to the Summer School of Theology at St. Andrews, this year; and students whom I have taught in St. Mary's College will find some of the chapters to be not unfamiliar. The concluding chapter is largely based on an article which I contributed to *The Coracle* in 1942, and for permission to use it I am indebted to Dr. George Macleod, Leader of the Iona Community. The book has profited greatly from criticisms and suggestions made by my brother Professor John Baillie, of Edinburgh University, who read the whole in manuscript, and Professor J. Y. Campbell, of Westminster College, Cambridge, who read the proofs, verified references, and even hunted out some references which I could not supply myself (including the elusive Heine reference on page 172). For these services I wish to express my warmest thanks.

DONALD BAILLIE

St. Andrews, *July, 1947.*

Chapter 1

CHRISTOLOGY AT THE CROSS-ROADS

About half a century ago a distinguished British theologian spoke of the recovery of the historical Christ as the most distinctive and determinative element in modern theology, and went on to speak of the rejuvenescence of theology which was the result. That was by no means a peculiar or merely individual judgment, but may be taken as fairly representative of its age, and every student of theology to-day understands exactly what was meant. But every wide-awake student knows also that the theological scene has changed again in the most unexpected way; so that if a theologian of the 'nineties or the early nineteen-hundreds were to play Rip van Winkle and come alive again to-day, he would rub his eyes in bewilderment at the new orientation of the problem of Christology. Theological thought has largely left behind the movement which we may symbolize by the phrase 'the Jesus of history'; and it is highly important for us to understand the ways in which that has been done, if we are to grasp the Christological problem of to-day.

At first sight it may seem that what has happened has been simply a reaction, a return to what went before, with a jettisoning of all that the movement in question represented. But that would be a superficial judgment. The present situation in Christology is one which could not have emerged before the 'Jesus of history' movement, but only after it. Indeed, some of the tendencies of that movement are carried farther than ever to-day in the very quarters where there has been the most powerful reaction against others of its tendencies. If the historico-critical movement, with its rediscovery of the historical Jesus, laid a new and sometimes startling emphasis on our Lord's humanity, and took it more seriously than it had ever been taken by theologians before in their interpretation of the Gospel story, the present tendency is not to shrink back again from that interpretation, but to carry it farther still, to go all the way with it. And not as a matter of unwelcome historical necessity, but as a matter of faith, of theological truth, of orthodox dogma taken seriously. No more Docetism, no more Monophysite explaining away of the human character of the life that Jesus lived, but a full and unreserved recognition of His human nature as 'homo-ousios' with our own, which means 'essentially the same as ours': that lesson of the historical movement has been well learnt on all hands, and it is common ground to-day.

But at the same time, and even in the same circles, there has emerged another tendency which may seem to point in an opposite direction, and which certainly carries us far away from what I have called the 'Jesus of history' movement: the tendency to lose interest in the reconstruction of the historical human figure of Jesus. This tendency may be found both in the historical criticism and in the dogmatic theology of the present time, and the two are closely connected. In the historico-critical realm the determinative fact is the emergence of the relatively new method which is called *Formgeschichte*, Form Criticism; and its application to the Gospels is a movement of immense significance, raising some old theological problems in a new and acuter form, and presenting to Christology a challenge which has not yet been fully faced. It does all this because it constantly seems to be questioning whether, and how far, the Gospels can be, or ought to be, used as means of recapturing the historical Jesus. By shaking confidence in the possibility, Form Criticism tends to shift the interest. In this way it plays into the hands of the contemporary movement in dogmatic theology which subordinates the Jesus of history to the Christ of dogma, and whose voice would say not only 'No more docetism', but also 'No more historicism'. It is indeed a new variety of historical scepticism about the Gospels as sources for a 'life of Jesus' or a reconstruction of His personality. This is the second of the two factors that go to make the Christological situation and problem of to-day.

The rest of this chapter must be devoted to the illustration of these two factors, with a view to setting the problem of Christology in as clear a light as possible.

I

The End of Docetism

It may safely be said that practically all schools of theological thought to-day take the full humanity of our Lord more seriously than has ever been done before by Christian theologians. It has always, indeed, been of the essence of Christian orthodoxy to make Jesus wholly human as well as wholly divine, and in the story of the controversies which issued in the decisions of the first four General Councils it is impressive to see the Church contending as resolutely for His full humanity as for His full deity. But the Church was building better than it knew, and its ecumenical decisions were wiser than its individual theologians in this matter. Or should we rather say that it did not fully realize the implications of declaring that in respect of His human nature Christ is consubstantial with ourselves? At any rate it was continually haunted by a docetism which made His human nature very different from ours and indeed largely explained it away as a matter of simulation or 'seeming' rather than reality. Theologians shrank from admitting human growth, human ignorance, human mutability, human struggle and temptation, into their conception of the Incarnate Life, and treated it as simply a divine life lived in a human body (and sometimes even this was conceived as essentially different from our bodies) rather than a truly human life lived under the psychical conditions of humanity. The cruder forms of docetism were fairly soon left behind, but in its more subtle forms the danger continued in varying degrees to dog the steps of theology right through the ages until modern times.

But now the belief in the full humanity of Christ has come into its own, and if this new realization was part of 'the rediscovery of the Jesus of history', it has not passed away with the passing of that particular movement, but lives on in the work of those 'catholic' and 'dialectical' schools to which the theology of that m⸱vement is most uncongenial. The theologians who take catholic Christological dogma most in earnest, repudiating every kind of minimizing modernism, and insisting on the deity of Jesus Christ, do not mean that a limit must be set to the humanizing of His mental processes, or that His psychical constitution was different from that of other men, so that His divinity could be detected by a process of psychological analysis. They may indeed wish to repudiate as hopelessly inadequate the account of Jesus given by the 'liberal Protestants' or the 'modernists' of a generation ago, and may even complain that these missed the truth by reason of their prejudice against admitting the 'supernatural'. But they do not mean that these made Jesus too human, for they are eager themselves to go the whole way in acknowledging that our Lord's experience in the days of His flesh was limited by the conditions of human life and human nature in this world.

It seems worth while to illustrate this in some further detail.

(a) *The human limits of our Lord's knowledge.* Right through the Patristic and medieval periods there was a shrinking from the idea that Jesus' *knowledge* was limited by human conditions, and often even a docetic explaining away of such passages in the Gospels as seemed to deny His omniscience.[1] It is a long time now since theology, not only 'rationalistic' but 'catholic', began to recover from this weakness and to learn that Jesus' knowledge was essentially the limited knowledge of a man. I need only refer to Charles Gore's celebrated essay on 'The Consciousness of our Lord in His Mortal Life',[2] in which the Bishop found it necessary deliberately to part company with Patristic and Scholastic views of this matter and to return to the impression gained from the New Testament that Jesus' knowledge was limited by human conditions. This line of thought is carried much farther in Professor Leonard Hodgson's book, *And Was Made Man*, where it is boldly, yet most reverently, maintained that even our Lord's knowledge of His unique relationship to God came to Him empirically as He moved about among men, and it is suggested that, e.g., His knowledge of the past history of the woman of Samaria in John iv, 17, 18, if we are to credit such

---

[1] Doubtless this was partly due to the strong tendency in the Greek Patristic period to identify the sin and evil of humanity with its ignorance, its finite limited knowledge. On this latter, see Reinhold Niebuhr, *Human Nature*, p. 172.

[2] In *Dissertations on Subjects connected with the Incarnation*, first published in 1895.

a detail at all, may be rendered credible not by the ascription to Jesus of omniscience or superhuman ways of knowledge, but by the fact that Orientals do seem even to-day to have sometimes a mysterious gift of insight into what is going on in other people's minds. 'His knowledge was limited to that which could find a channel into His human mind.'[1] It would be easy, but it is unnecessary, to multiply illustrations of how theology has come to acknowledge unreservedly the human limitation of our Lord's knowledge.[2] As long ago as 1912 so careful a theologian as H. R. Mackintosh referred to the subject as one on which controversy was already over.[3]

(*b*) *The human character of our Lord's miracles.* If there is one particularly fruitful insight that has been gained in the modern world in the interpretation of the Gospel story, it is this: that the problem of the 'mighty works' can be disposed of neither by denying them out of hand as unhistorical, nor by accepting them as sheerly supernatural portents because a divine Christ can do anything, but is to be met only by regarding them as works of faith, wrought by the power of God in response to human faith for which all things are possible. There was a time when the miracles were regularly used by Christian apologetics as 'signs and wonders' to prove the divinity of Christ. But there has been a growing awareness that this interpretation is quite at variance with the mind of our Lord Himself. He condemned the desire to have 'signs and wonders' as a basis for faith, and He plainly thought of His works of healing as manifestations of God's love and power which are at the disposal of all men if only they will believe. They were works of God's power, but they were also works of human faith. 'Your faith has cured you.'[4] The apostolic preaching, as reflected in the New Testament, looking back, did indeed treat these miracles as 'signs' of the new age. They were the works of the Messiah. But

---

[1] L. Hodgson, *And Was Made Man* (1928), pp. 40f., 50–6, 159, 192f.

[2] It may be worth while to quote Father Sergius Bulgakov, of the Russian Orthodox Church, who in a frank and impressive paragraph about the human limits of Christ's earthly life and experience writes: 'He Himself claimed to be the Son of God. Yet even this apprehension of His own Personality remained subject to the conditions of human growth.' *The Wisdom of God*, p. 136.

[3] *The Doctrine of the Person of Jesus Christ*, p. 397.

[4] Mark v, 34; x, 52; Luke xvii, 19.

they were also the works of the Kingdom, of the Messianic Age, in which the 'powers of the world to come' were at the disposal of *all* who would believe. God had given such power *to men*. In that sense they were human works. Bishop Gore maintained that this view was definitely taken in the Patristic age by Gregory of Nyssa, and he fully accepted it himself. Speaking of our Lord, he wrote: 'His powerful works, no less than His humiliations, are in the Gospels attributed to His manhood.'[1] He quotes Westcott as taking the same view. 'As far as it is revealed to us, His greatest works during His earthly life are wrought by the help of the Father through the energy of a humanity enabled to do all things in fellowship with God.'[2] The fullest elaboration of this view of the miracles is to be found in Dr. D. S. Cairns's brilliant and original book, *The Faith that Rebels*.[3] Many other illustrations might be quoted.[4] It need hardly be said that this interpretation has been worked out, not with any *minimizing* intention, but rather with a view to doing justice to the witness of the New Testament and to the reality of the Incarnation. Thus the miracles of our Lord are regarded as 'signs' of the Kingdom because they were works of human faith in God, through which 'the powers of the world to come' are brought right into the conditions of human life on earth.

(*c*) *The human character of our Lord's moral and religious life*. This follows from what has just been said. Our Lord's life on earth was a life of faith, and His victory was the victory of faith. His temptations were real temptations, which it was difficult and painful for Him to resist. His fight against them was not a sham fight, but a real struggle. When we say *non potuit peccare*, we do not mean that He was completely raised above the struggle against sin, as we conceive the life of the redeemed to be in heaven, *in patria*. In the days of His flesh our Lord was *viator*. And when we say that He was

---

[1] Gore, op. cit., pp. 140f, 165.

[2] Westcott, *Ep. to the Hebrews*, p. 66.

[3] First edition in 1928.

[4] I may quote further from Prof. L. Hodgson: 'We must . . . think of the powers exercised by Christ as being powers open to manhood where manhood is found in its perfection.' 'The miracles of Christ are worked through faith.' *And Was Made Man*, pp. 133, 140. There is a very interesting paragraph which seems to take the same view in a book from a very different school, already cited, Father Sergius Bulgakov's *The Wisdom of God*, pp. 135f.

incapable of sinning, we mean that He was the supreme case of
what we can say with limited and relative truth about many a
good man. 'He is incapable of doing a mean or underhand thing',
we say about a man whom we know to be honourable; and so we
say in a more universal and absolute way about Jesus: *Non potuit
peccare*, without in any way reducing the reality of His conflict with
His temptations. 'He overcame them exactly as every man who
does so has overcome temptation—by the constancy of the will.'[1]
Christians might have learnt this lesson about our Lord from the
Epistle to the Hebrews from the start, but it is only in the modern
world that it has been fully realized.

The same thing is even truer when we come to what we may call
our Lord's own personal religion. H. R. Mackintosh wrote in 1912:
'Attention has recently been drawn, in a special manner, to the
perfectly human quality of our Lord's religious life,'[2] and he went
on to develop this sympathetically, dwelling especially upon Jesus'
habit of prayer to God. To our forefathers of earlier ages the phrase
'our Lord's religious life' would have sounded quite incongruous.
'The personal religion of Jesus!' How could God incarnate have a
religious life, a personal religion? To speak of Jesus as a religious
man would have astonished them. Yet Jesus was a religious man,
and we should now say that this is implied in the reality of the
Incarnation, that if His life was really a divine *incarnation*, it *must*
have been a life of human religious experience, human faith in
God. Hardly any school of Christian thought would now deny this,
though some would maintain, as we shall see, that the significance
of Jesus for us as the Word made flesh has nothing to do with His
'religious experience'.

In this connection it is worth noting that even among theologians
who profess to accept the full catholic doctrine of the hypostatic
union there is now a manifest unwillingness to distinguish Christ's
manhood from that of other men by speaking of His 'impersonal
humanity'. That is a time-honoured phrase, supposed to be orthodox, and Newman interpreted it fearlessly by saying somewhere:
'Though Man, He is not, strictly speaking, *a* Man.' But most
divines of to-day, whether 'Catholic' or 'Dialectical-Protestant' in

---

[1] William Temple, *Christus Veritas*, p. 147.
[2] *Doctrine of the Person of Jesus Christ*, p. 399.

their orthodoxy, and even while professing to accept in some sense the *anhypostasia* of Ephesus and Chalcedon, would shrink from such a statement, and would quite naturally and without embarrassment speak of Jesus Christ as a man, just as the New Testament writers surely do. 'Whatever else He may be, He is a man', wrote Hoskyns and Davey.[1] And according to the late Archbishop of Canterbury, the humanity of Christ is impersonal only in the sense in which 'the humanity of every one of us is impersonal, and the greater the man, the less merely personal is his humanity'.[2]

All of this becomes more striking than ever when we come to those theologians who are most explicitly in revolt against theological 'liberalism' and the 'Jesus of history' movement: I am thinking of the leaders of the 'dialectical' theology, the 'theology of the Word' or the 'theology of crisis'. Karl Barth is quite clear that the Word became not merely Man, but *a* Man, and insists that the *anhypostasia*, the 'impersonality', never meant that the humanity of Christ had no 'personality' in the modern sense (for which the Latin word would be *individualitas*), but that it had no independent existence.[3] But still more notable is the answer that Barth gives to the question whether it was fallen or unfallen human nature that Christ assumed in the Incarnation. He knows very well that the orthodox tradition, whether Catholic or Protestant, has always most explicitly answered: 'Unfallen human nature.' But Barth himself quite boldly answers: 'Fallen human nature', and maintains that this is what is meant by the Word becoming not only *man* but *flesh*.[4] This is not altogether a new answer. A similar position was taken by the Spanish Adoptionists of the eighth century, and in the early nineteenth century by Gottfried Menken of Bremen, and by the Scottish Edward Irving, whose preaching caused such a stir in London, and who is regarded as the founder of the Catholic Apostolic sect.[5] To say that Christ assumed our fallen human nature may, indeed, mean only that He was subject to pain and death as other men are in this 'fallen' state, but might also be taken to mean

[1] *The Riddle of the New Testament*, p. 209.
[2] W. Temple, *Christus Veritas*, pp. 151f.
[3] Karl Barth, *Kirchliche Dogmatik*, I, ii, 180.
[4] Ibid., I, ii, pp. 167ff.
[5] For the earlier exponents of this view, see A. B. Bruce, *The Humiliation of Christ*, pp. 264ff.

that He inherited original sin as other men do, though He was never guilty of committing actual sin. The latter meaning seems to have been definitely intended by the Adoptionists, and also by Menken, though not by Irving, who was astonished and greatly distressed by the accusation of heresy which ultimately resulted in his deposition from the ministry of the Church of Scotland.[1] Barth is quite conscious that he is adopting a position that has always been regarded as heretical. He maintains, of course, the sinlessness of Jesus, and there is no definite indication that this refers only to 'actual' and not to 'original' sin, so that it is difficult to say what he really means, though it is plain that he is moved (as Irving certainly was) by the conviction that a completely human experience like our own must be ascribed to Christ. It is possible that the difficulty can only be met by the recognition that 'assumption of human nature' is not a wholly satisfactory phrase or concept as applied to the Incarnation, as indeed it hardly belongs to the world of the New Testament. But Barth's Christology employs it, and he does not shrink from saying 'fallen human nature', because that is the only human nature that we know in ourselves.

Apart, however, from what might seem to be an unnecessary and unreal theological dilemma, Barth elsewhere also goes the whole way in recognizing that from the historical point of view Jesus was a man, living His life wholly within the conditions and limitations of humanity. It may indeed be said that he goes more than the whole way, for he seems to hold that, historically regarded, Jesus does not appear as even a very remarkable man. 'Jesus Christ, in fact, is also the Rabbi of Nazareth, historically so difficult to get information about, and when it is obtained, one who is so apt to impress us as a little commonplace alongside more than one other founder of a religion and even alongside many later representatives of His own religion.'[2] Barth seems to hold that there was nothing very distinctive or impressive, nothing very God-revealing, in either the teaching or the personality of this man Jesus. His human life was not a revelation, but a concealment, of God.

---

[1] See Mrs. Oliphant's *Life of Edward Irving*, chaps. xiii and xiv.

[2] Karl Barth, *The Doctrine of the Word of God* (Prof. G. T. Thomson's translation of the first half-volume of the *Kirchliche Dogmatik*), p. 188. I have slightly altered the translation.

This is where the doctrine of the '*divine incognito*', of the 'veiled' nature of the revelation—so characteristic of Barth's thought—reaches its extreme. Barth goes so far as to suggest that, far from having any superhuman kind or source of knowledge in the days of His flesh, Jesus did not, as He faced His passion, even succeed in seeing 'a frontier, a meaning, a future, in what He had to suffer'.[1] It is a good illustration of how much more 'radical' this school can be in its historical approach to the gospels and the human figure of Jesus than were the 'liberal' schools against which it is in such conscious revolt.

It may be worth while to call as witness another outstanding contemporary theologian of the same general tendency, Professor Emil Brunner of Zürich. Brunner accepts the whole Chalcedonian Christology, and takes especial pains to defend and interpret the catholic doctrine that there is no human *person* in Christ, but only the Divine Person who assumes human nature. But he can say quite frankly: 'The life of Jesus is not a blend of natural and super-natural elements. So far as the historical and visible side of His life is concerned, it is quite natural and historical.'[2] It is true, Brunner contends, that from the historical point of view a coherent picture of Jesus is impossible, because the Divine Person is the only key to the hidden unity of His life.[3] And with this we need not quarrel. But immediately thereafter Brunner tells us that the Pauline phrases 'born of a woman', 'born of the seed of David according to the flesh', not only seem to imply that the idea of a Virgin Birth of Christ meant nothing to the apostle, but imply also 'the per-fectly natural character of His human development'. 'He was a "weak" human being like ourselves, who had to eat and drink, who got tired, so also He was a man who had to submit to the will of God, and who had to struggle, "in all points tempted like as we

---

[1] Karl Barth, *Credo* (Eng. trans.), pp. 76–8.

[2] Emil Brunner, *The Mediator* (Eng. trans.), p. 137. See also the important footnote on p. 343.

[3] Emil Brunner, *The Mediator* (Eng. trans.), pp. 359f. But it is important to remember that in every man there is, according to Brunner, not only the historical personality, with an individual character perceptible to the historian or biographer, but also the hidden mystery of the person which lies behind all historical and psychological perception, even behind all self-perception. Ibid., p. 318.

are", a man whom we see asking God, listening to God, praying to God, thanking God, one who was neither omnipotent nor omniscient. He could tremble and faint, and plead with God to remove from Him the bitter cup of suffering. He was a man who lived as a Jew in the late period of the ancient world; who shared the views of His time, and expressed Himself in the language of His people.'[1] It is true that Brunner would not by any means agree with Barth's idea that there is nothing very remarkable about Jesus as an historical human personality, though he brands as grossly unscientific the attempts that used to be so frequent in the 'liberal' schools to trace psychologically the development of the mind of our Lord, especially the dawning of His 'messianic self-consciousness'. This kind of attempt, however, is regarded by Brunner as scientifically absurd and impossible not because there was not a purely natural human development, but 'just as it is impossible to determine the moment when a child first becomes conscious of its own existence as a self'.[2] It is plain how this theologian, whose main interest is to reject every minimizing kind of liberalism or modernism and to establish a full and high Chalcedonian Christology, refuses to secure this by any limitation of the completely human character of our Lord's experience and development in the days of His flesh.

It would be vain to pretend that all the writers whom I have called in evidence would agree with each other or with myself in the matter of Christology or even in what they meant by the humanity of Christ. But it seems fair to infer from the material I have presented that while there is still plenty of controversy on the subject of the Incarnation between Catholic and Protestant schools, between 'incarnational' theologies and 'dialectical' theologies, between the school of 'the Jesus of history' and the school of 'the Word', between 'liberals' and 'neo-confessionals', the issue is not upon the once familiar lines as to whether the life and experience of Jesus is to be conceived in terms of human psychology or in terms of what we may call a superhuman or supernaturalistic psychology. Schools may differ as to whether psychological study of the central figure of the Gospel story is of much value or rele-

---

[1] Ibid., pp. 361, 363 f.
[2] Ibid., pp. 362f.

vance to the Christian faith, but practically all would agree that if we are to psychologize at all, it must be by a human psychology. Psychological studies of Jesus have often in the past been deplorably inadequate and feeble, because they have been blind to the immense gulf between the quality of His spiritual life and that of our own at its highest and best—a gulf so great that in our attempts to understand Him we can only follow afar off with a sense of mystery. But the gulf is not a gulf between human minds and a mind that was not human, for He was made in all things like unto His brethren, His psychical constitution was the same as ours.

Therefore Christology cannot solve its problem by turning into psychology. And the real problem for all schools which take Christology seriously at all is: In what sense do we believe that this human life of Jesus of Nazareth was at the same time—not in some 'psychological' way, but on a deeper level, in a more ultimate analysis, in a transcendent 'dimension'—the very life of God Himself?[1] And what is the relation of that transcendent belief or affirmation to the historical approach that we make to 'the Jesus of history' when we study the Gospel story? That is how the issues seem to have cleared. And they have thus cleared because all serious theological thought has finished with the docetist, Eutychean, Monophysite errors which explained away the humanity of our Lord and thus the reality of the Incarnation. No more docetism! Eutyches, we may say, is dead, and he is not likely to be as fortunate as Eutychus in finding an apostle to revive him!

That is the first factor in the distinctive situation of Christology to-day.

II

A New Historical Radicalism

The second factor in producing a changed situation for Christology is the new radicalism in the historical study of the Gospels

---

[1] Cf. Sir Edwyn Hoskyns: 'Nor is the glory of this sonship something episodic or psychological; it cannot be observed by an historian or analysed by a psychologist. It is accessible only to those who believe. . . .' *The Fourth Gospel*, vol. i, p. 91.

which has come to be associated with the phrase *Formgeschichte* or Form Criticism. Here we are dealing with something much more controversial and questionable, not a piece of ground gained and consolidated once for all, but a battleground where fighting still goes on confusedly and without any certain issue. Moreover, what we have here is not merely a new method or a new set of results in Gospel criticism, but a relatively fresh approach to the whole historical problem of the Gospels. The new method is partly a matter of asking different questions of the Gospels, and the new set of results is closely connected with a shifting of the interest of theologians. Form Criticism is a movement which studies the Gospels historically, not by analysing them into their various source-documents in the way with which we have become so familiar, but by distinguishing the various 'forms', the various types of anecdote, parable, apophthegm, wonder-story, homiletic reminiscence, that were used in the preaching of the early Church about Jesus and grew into the Gospel tradition, in order to assess the age and significance of the individual fragments that make up our Gospels. In this process Form Criticism often seems to throw more light on the question, 'What was the early Christian preaching and message (the *kerygma*) like?' than on the question, 'What did Jesus actually say and do and mean?' And if the results appear somewhat negative and doubtful as regards our knowledge of the life of our Lord, it is often suggested that the Gospels neither can nor should be used by Christian theology in an endeavour to get behind and beyond the 'apostolic witness', the primitive Christian '*kerygma*', to the historical Jesus.

If this produces a new situation in Christology, it is because we have here the relatively new phenomenon of a very radical, sometimes even sceptical, Gospel criticism coming right into the citadel of positive theological thought. Hitherto, on the whole, the very radical critics of the Gospel story had been far from the centre of orthodox theology. They had been very unorthodox, very left-wing, in their theology. With their radical criticism there went hand in hand, as a rule, either a Hegelian or a liberal-humanitarian type of Christology. The more radical they were in their treatment of the Gospel story, the more un-catholic, unconciliar, unconfessional was their theology. Thus the defenders of orthodox Christology, in joining battle with those left-wing theologians, usually made a frontal attack on their critical positions, endeavouring to show that the Gospels are much more trustworthy sources for the life and teaching of Jesus than the critics had allowed, far less infected with legend, far more credible and authentic as history, and therefore far more conducive to the catholic dogma of the Incarnation. But the leaders of the new radical criticism, of the *formgeschichtliche Schule*, are not Hegelians or liberals or modernists in their theological outlook. Theirs is a new kind of radicalism, which is often strongly 'confessional' and even biblicist in its outlook, in reaction against everything that could be branded as 'liberalism' in theology. The two outstanding German leaders of Form Criticism, Rudolf Bultmann and Martin Dibelius, are agreed in holding that our Lord never regarded Himself as the Messiah at all (which is the kind of position which, when taken by Wrede a generation ago, became to Schweitzer the symbol of 'thoroughgoing scepticism'), but they rank themselves with the neo-confessional and biblicist movement in theology. Bultmann definitely expresses the opinion that 'we can now know almost nothing concerning the life and personality of Jesus', because the documents are so fragmentary and often legendary,[1] and so he has been called 'the Strauss of the twentieth century'. Yet in the realm of dogmatic theology, Bultmann would range himself with the 'dialectical' school of Karl Barth; and just as it has been sometimes said that Barth in his celebrated commentary on Romans has read his own theology into St. Paul, so it has been said that Bultmann in his book on *Jesus* (which is quite appropriately rendered into English under the title of *Jesus and the Word*) has read the Barthian theology into the Gospels. That is the novelty in this new radical criticism, so far as concerns its bearing on theology and Christology: it is pursued to its somewhat negative conclusions not by enemies of Christianity, not by 'liberals' or modernists, but by representatives of a new biblicist and confessional orthodoxy, who are glad to use it as a weapon for the destruction of the 'liberalism' of the 'Jesus of history' movement.

As regards the dogmatic theologians themselves, it cannot in-

---

[1] Bultmann, *Jesus and the Word* (Eng. trans.), p. 8.

deed be said that Barth and his followers would give their blessing to the radical criticism of a Bultmann, but they seem to find the movement of Form Criticism, and its whole approach to the interpretation of the Gospels, far more congenial than the work of the 'liberals' who used the gospels simply as 'sources for the life of Jesus' and pursued their criticism with a view to getting behind the apostolic witness and rediscovering the actual historical Jesus.

It is largely on the Continent of Europe that this new and surprising development has taken place, the criticism of the Gospels tending to be more 'radical' than it was a quarter of a century ago, and the dogmatic theology tending to be more credal, confessional and biblicist than it has been for generations. Thus a typical Protestant Continental theologian of the present time, if he came to this country and made a study of contemporary British theology in its most live manifestations, would probably be shocked by the 'conservatism' of its positions in historical criticism and by the unbiblical modernism of much of its doctrinal theology. He would find us too uncritical in our historical approach to the Gospels, and too 'liberal' in our essays at Christological restatement. In his own theology there would seem to us to be a curious synthesis of dogmatism and scepticism. In his use of radical criticism to attack the constructions of 'liberal' theologians in the interests of a more positive and orthodox Christology, he would seem to us to be attempting to 'gather apologetic figs from sceptical thistles', as Harnack once said to the young Friedrich Loofs about the latter's somewhat analogous endeavours in theology,[1] and as a French Protestant once said to me about the tendencies of Karl Barth.

Doubtless this strange situation, while it is new in modern theology, is not quite unprecedented. When in 1902 the Abbé Loisy replied to the liberal Protestantism of Harnack's *What is Christianity?* by writing his brilliant little book, *The Gospel and the Church*, he used radical criticism to rehabilitate catholic Christianity. On the whole his criticism was far more radical than Harnack's. His views on the Gospels shocked many persons to whom Harnack had been a Christian apologist. But this was his method of re-

---

[1] See Loofs, *What is the Truth about Jesus Christ?* p. 122.

butting Harnack's 'liberal' attack on the developments by which Catholic Christianity seemed to have transformed the original simple Gospel into a system of Christological dogma. It was a method of pricking the bubble of 'liberal Protestantism', with its cult of 'the Jesus of history', and of defending the catholic Christian tradition, though not by calling a halt in the march of radical criticism, but by carrying it still farther in a sceptical direction. It must, however, be remembered that though Loisy thus assumed the rôle of *defensor fidei*, he was not accepted in that rôle by the authorities of the Church he was defending, but was naturally regarded as a dangerous Modernist. His book was promptly condemned by the Cardinal Archbishop of Paris, and was subsequently, along with his radical commentaries on the Gospels, placed on the Index by Pope Pius X; while Loisy himself continued to move in a leftward direction.

In some ways a somewhat similar part was played by Albert Schweitzer's epoch-making book, *The Quest of the Historical Jesus*, which first appeared (under the title, *Von Reimarus zu Wrede*) in 1906. Certainly it was one of the powerful influences in the reaction against what I have called the 'Jesus of history' movement, and indeed it was intended as a kind of *reductio ad absurdum* of the long enterprise of writing 'lives of Jesus' and of the 'liberal' reading of Christianity based thereon. And here again the method was not to call a halt to free historical criticism of the Gospels, but to pursue that criticism to a point which startled even 'liberal Protestants', ending in the dilemma between the 'thorough-going scepticism' of William Wrede and Schweitzer's own 'thorough-going eschatologism' in his interpretation of the mind of Jesus. The effect of Schweitzer's own interpretation, as he saw plainly, was to produce a portrait of the historic Jesus so grotesquely 'eschatological' in outlook as to make Him a complete stranger to our time, so remote, mysterious and even unintelligible to us that it seemed to bring to an impasse the whole attempt to make the historic Jesus real as a basis for the Christianity of the modern world. At the same time the book closed on a note of deep Christian devotion in those famous and mysterious sentences which left the world guessing as to what Schweitzer's own Christological position was, but which left no doubt as to his Christian discipleship—a discipleship which has since found such heroic expression in tropical Africa. And yet Schweitzer has never been anything but a 'liberal' in his theology, as both its friends and its foes will agree; and many would say that in his subsequent theologico-philosophical work he 'out-liberals the liberals' from an angle of his own.

In the year following the first publication of Schweitzer's book there appeared in Germany a book which in a much more distinctive way became 'sceptical' and 'modern' for a positive and apologetic purpose, as against the 'Jesus of history' movement. It was entitled: *Ist das liberale Jesusbild modern?* and its author was R. H. Grützmacher, who became known as the leader of the 'Modern-Positive' school of theologians in Germany. The school professed to be more truly 'modern' than the 'liberals', and at the same time more positive in theological outlook. It claimed that a really fearless and thorough historical criticism of the Gospels yields us not the picture of Jesus on which the liberals based their theology, but the faith-portrait which was the basis of the Christianity of the early Church and must be the basis of our Christianity too. In 1910 Heinrich Weinel replied to this and other criticisms in a little book entitled *Ist das 'liberale' Jesusbild widerlegt?* Weinel found it strange that his 'positive' opponents like Grützmacher appeared to be joining in chorus with his completely sceptical opponents like Drews and Kalthoff. Apparently they were virtually united in the contention that the attempts of historical criticism to get back beyond the faith and Christology of the early Church to a 'historical Jesus' had failed and must fail; that it is impossible for us to-day to have any such knowledge of a 'Jesus of history', and that if we could it would be of no use to us in the modern world; and that the essence of Christianity is not a 'Jesus of history', but the Church's doctrine of the God-Man, which is what we really get in the New Testament.[1] Yet, of course, Grützmacher himself would never have admitted that he was thus 'unequally yoked together with unbelievers'. He was ploughing a very different furrow, not only in the realm of dogma but in the realm of historical criticism. Whether he was 'modern' or not, he certainly was not 'modernist', and his critical positions would look quite 'positive' and conserva-

---

[1] H. Weinel, *Ist das 'liberale' Jesusbild widerlegt?* pp. 1ff., 34. I have been unable to see Grützmacher's book, and know it only through Weinel's.

tive alongside those of his liberal opponents, not to speak of the positions of Form Criticism to-day.

Thus, in spite of apparent or real anticipations, it can truly be said that the appearance of Form Criticism has presented us with a new situation, because it marks the entry of a very radical criticism of the Gospels into the citadels of positive and orthodox theology. Here is a new radicalism which commends itself in unexpected quarters by making short work of the 'liberal' reconstruction. A generation ago those who adhered to orthodox Christology were often able to ignore the extremes of negative criticism of the Gospel narrative because the critics seemed to be controlled by certain false assumptions—either Hegelian assumptions, that the Absolute could never really appear to the full at one point in history, or 'liberal' assumptions which ruled out the miraculous. But the Form Critics are not so easily ignored. They are neither Hegelians nor 'liberals', and if they leave it doubtful whether it is possible from the sources at our disposal to gain any substantial knowledge of the career and personality of Jesus, they assure us that it is because the Gospels were not written for any such biographical or historical interest, but in the interests of Christian faith, which has nothing to do with the modern desire to 'reconstruct' the Jesus of history. Such a school may even claim that it can afford to be far more thorough-going and honest in its criticism than its predecessors, since it regards the material in the Gospels as an equally valuable witness to the Word-made-Flesh—which is its true and original virtue—even if it is historically doubtful. We may be disposed to wonder whether this is a case of making a virtue of necessity and cutting the pattern of Christology according to the shrunken cloth of historical material which is all that an impartial Form Criticism leaves, or whether on the other hand it is merely another example of a professedly impartial criticism being controlled by certain theological prejudices; or whether perhaps both of these forces, being inseparable, are acting and reacting on each other. These questions will come up at a later point: meanwhile I am merely pointing out that there is a new situation. In the pre-critical period theologians believed all the material in the Gospels to be historically true. When historical criticism appeared, this was questioned in a wholesale way, but even the 'liberals' assumed (and, as the Form Critics would say, assumed far too naïvely, having got the historico-critical lesson all wrong!) that at least it was possible from the evidence of the Gospels to reconstruct the life of Jesus and recapture His personality, and indeed that modern criticism had made this more possible than ever. But now this is just what the Form Critics regard as a wild-goose chase. 'It seems, then,' says Professor R. H. Lightfoot, one of the leading British Form Critics, 'that the form of the earthly no less than of the heavenly Christ is for the most part hidden from us.'

If there is any weight at all in such an opinion, it presents a challenge to Christological thought which has hardly yet been met. It brings to a head, in a way that cannot be ignored, a question which has never perhaps been quite absent since the critical movement began: How much can we really know about what happened in Palestine nineteen centuries ago, by way of making it a basis for our faith? Occasionally that question has broken out in quite extreme forms, suggesting the answer that Jesus may never have existed at all as an historical person. But now, apart from such absurd freaks of scholarship, we are confronted in a new way with the question whether we can know enough about Jesus to enable us to build a Christology upon Him. It is by challenging us with that question—not by giving us an assured result—that Form Criticism has become a momentous factor in creating the situation which exists for Christological thought to-day. It will make a great difference to the problem of Christology whether we accept or reject the claims of this new historical radicalism.

III

The Cross-Roads for Christology

I have tried to indicate the two factors that go to the making of the peculiar situation which presents itself in Christology to-day: the general agreement that there must be 'no more docetism' explaining away the full humanity of our Lord; and the controversy roused by the new approach to the Gospel story in the school of Form Criticism. We must now endeavour to view these two together and to understand the situation that results.

On the one hand, to many people—those who fully accept the new approach of Form Criticism—it will seem plain that theology must now repudiate what I have called the 'Jesus of history' movement with all its works and ways, and retrace its steps from that false trail opened up during the last century, and look in a quite different direction for a Christology that can be satisfying to-day. It cannot be a case of merely going back to the stand-point of a pre-critical age, as if the 'Jesus of history' movement had never taken place or had left no permanent legacy. It cannot even be a case of returning to the Hegelian type of Christology, which accepted the whole of catholic dogma, but 'with a differ-ence', sublimating it into a symbol of eternal truths of reason with-out the 'scandal of particularity' in a historical Incarnation. Those who repudiate 'historicism' to-day do not mean anything like that, but are most forward to accept 'the scandal of particularity' and to insist on the *Einmaligkeit,* the once-for-all-ness, of the incursion of the Divine Word into history in Christ, even if they utterly refuse the help of anything that could be called the recovery of the his-torical Jesus, which they regard as either impossible or useless or both, as the extremer Form Critics would have it. If these are right, then surely Christology stands where it never stood before.

I am going to argue that they are not right, that there is no stability in a position which accepts to the full the humanity of Christ but has no interest in its actual concrete manifestation and doubts whether it can be recaptured at all; which insists on the 'once-for-all-ness' of this divine incursion into history, but re-nounces all desire or claim to know what it was really like. I am going to try to show that, however defective theologically the 'Jesus of history' movement may have been, however unscientific and over-imaginative its confident reconstructions of the historic portrait, and however one-sided its attempt to make a religion out of such a reconstruction alone, the reaction against it has been equally one-sided and gives up something that we cannot give up if Christianity is a 'historical' religion at all. Therefore my next chapter must be: Why the Jesus of history?

But as soon as we have advanced so far, and given an answer to those who would lead us down one side-road, we shall find our-selves confronted with those who would lead us down another on the other side, asking us whether the Jesus of history is not enough, without any of the mystifications of a 'Christology'. And if it is not theologians who will ask us this question—if to theologians it seems an absurdly naïve and outmoded question—it is none the less important for us to come to terms with it afresh in our own time. For I am convinced that a great many thoughtful people who feel themselves drawn to the Gospel in these days are completely mystified by the doctrine of the Incarnation—far more than we theologians usually realize. And their mystification is made all the greater by the fact that we regard Jesus as being in the fullest sense a man living a wholly human life within the limits of human experience in this world. They might ask whether this very chapter has not exhibited the *reductio ad absurdum* of the attempt to work out a 'Christology' in the traditional sense. They might ask: Why not frankly give up all the theological mystification which, in spite of the rediscovery of the human Jesus, has again in our time begun to obscure the features of that historical figure and even to dull the challenge of His teaching? In view of such questionings, my third chapter must be: Why a Christology?

Thus if Christology to-day stands at the parting of the ways, the fork is not double but triple. And if we refuse to be led down either of the side roads, because each of them represents a false simplification of the problem, we shall then have to rethink the old problems of the Person and work of Christ as they present themselves to theology in this twentieth century; which we shall attempt to do in the fourth and subsequent chapters of this book.

Chapter II

WHY THE JESUS OF HISTORY?

In this chapter we must try to understand both the 'Jesus of history' movement which was so dominant in theology at the beginning of this century and the strong reaction against it which is so unmistakable a feature of theology to-day; and we must try to see what the issues really are and where the truth lies. That is an indispensable preliminary to the attempt to work out a Christology, for the controversial issue which separates these two movements largely determines not only the answer to be given to the Christological problem, but also the very meaning of the problem and the questions that have to be asked.

I

The Return to the Historical Jesus

It need hardly be said that the very phrases 'the Jesus of history' and 'the historical Jesus' are distinctively modern, and would have been unintelligible to earlier generations. They owe their existence to the rise of the modern historical sense and its applications to the literature of Christian origins. They are the natural product of a more 'critical' approach to the New Testament, a new consciousness that it might be possible to get behind creed and tradition and gospel, to penetrate the mists of ecclesiastical dogma, and to find the simple historical truth about Jesus of Nazareth. This whole critical movement carried with it sometimes an appearance of doubt and denial which was intimidating to Christian people and upsetting to those whose faith was not yet stable. But beside the bane grew the antidote. There can be no question that in an age when Christian faith had become for many reasons difficult, and when many earnest souls seemed to feel the ground giving way beneath their feet, an age in which 'religious doubt' was a very widespread and painful experience, the rediscovery of the Jesus of history came like a new revelation. The Christ of the Creeds might be a baffling and mysterious figure, but, after all, the Christological statements in the Creeds professed to refer to an actual historical person, who lived in Palestine at a particular time and 'suffered under Pontius Pilate'. Therefore it must be possible to approach the figure of Jesus by historical methods, and thus at least make a beginning in the understanding of His significance and therefore of the dogmas about Him. Moreover, when this was attempted, it appeared to be marvellously successful. The figure of Jesus seemed to stand out as it had never done before. The mists were penetrated, and there appeared the winning and commanding personality of the Man of Nazareth—'Jesus, divinest when Thou most art man'. It seemed to be a rediscovery of the right starting-point for an understanding of the Christian faith, which had become so obscured; for it was like beginning where the original disciples began.

Moreover, it was not merely a movement in theological circles: it came to play an immensely important part in the plain man's quest of faith in an age of doubt. To many a soul perplexed about the truth of Christianity the movement came with a new prescription and a new promise. 'Put aside for the moment,' it ventured to say, 'your perplexities about dogma, and begin with the historical Jesus. There at least is something plain—plainer than ever in the modern world because of the new historical sense and the work of historical criticism. And that must be a safe starting-point. If the original disciples came to regard Jesus as Messiah and Lord and Son of God, it must have been primarily because His human life and personality had made such an impression on them. That at least is where they began. And you can make the same beginning if you will humbly and honestly study the Gospel story with the help of modern criticism. You also will "see Jesus" as He really was in the days of His flesh on earth, and you will be constrained to follow Him. And as you do, you will begin to understand the dogmas about Him. You will regain your faith, with a better understanding of what Christian faith really is, through the rediscovery of the Jesus of history.' That is how the message ran, and it made an immensely wide appeal, which became widest in a popular sense after the movement had spent its main force in theological circles. During the first generation of the present century there was an extraordinary stream of popular books from the Press on the subject of that historical figure as a rediscovery: books by theological scholars, by literary men, by journalists, by poets, by novelists; by Roman Catholics, by Protestants, by Jews, by seekers, by sceptics; books about the Galilean, the Nazarene, the Original Jesus, the Lord of All Good Life, the Spiritual Pilgrimage of Jesus, the Man Nobody Knows, Jesus as they saw Him, the Jesus of History. What a fascination there was about the rediscovery! How it seemed to open up a new and truly Christian line of popular apologetic!

For our present purpose it is even more important to note the immense impact made by this movement on pure theology. It made theology more Christocentric, and it may almost be said to have transformed Christology by opening up a new approach to Christological dogma. Without the influence of this movement, the modern Kenotic theories of the Person of Christ could never have come into existence. Nor could the 'incarnational' type of theology that has been so characteristic of the Anglican Communion in the modern world. Nor could the Ritschlian theology, which has been so influential far beyond the bounds of its particular school. It might indeed be said that, so far as theological circles are concerned, the movement reached its most characteristic expression and its climax in those two famous Ritschlian books which appeared about the turn of the century, Harnack's *What is Christianity?* and Herrmann's *The Communion of the Christian with God.* The Ritschlian school generally was deeply suspicious of the intrusion of metaphysics into Christian theology, and this was closely connected with its emphasis on the historical Jesus as distinct from the Christ of dogma. To Harnack, the church historian of the school, the history of the early Christian centuries was a story of the gradual adulteration of the original Galilean gospel through the infiltration of Greek philosophy, and thus the true hope of Christian theology must be in a movement back to the Jesus of history from the metaphysical dogmas about His Person. Similarly, to Herrmann, the greatest pure theologian of the school, the starting-point of Christian faith, and therefore of Christian theology, must never be in ready-made metaphysical dogmas about Christ, but in the historical Jesus with whom we are confronted in the Gospel story, and whose inner life becomes to the honest seeker the very revelation of God. There can be no doubt that in its own day and generation Herrmann's book saved the Christian faith of many questioners and gave to many students of theology a new illumination which the younger generation of to-day would find it difficult to understand if they read the book. Yet Harnack and Herrmann belong to one particular school, which was naturally more influential on the Continent than in Britain. And the movement 'back to the Jesus of history' belonged to almost all schools and made a difference to almost all theology. A great British nonconformist theologian, writing shortly before the turn of the century, having headed the Introduction to his book with the phrase, 'The Return to Christ', said: 'We feel Him more in our theology because we know Him better in history. His historical reality and significance have broken upon us with something of the surprise of a discovery. It is certainly not too much to say: He is to-day more studied and better known as He was and as He lived than at any period between now and the first age of the Church.' He went on to speak of 'this recovery of the historical Christ'. Again: 'If a Christian theology means a theology of Christ, at once concerning Him and derived from Him, then to construct one ought, because of our greater knowledge of Him and His history, to be more possible to-day than at any previous moment.'[1] In 1922 a great Anglican bishop wrote: 'Medieval theology allowed itself, by the misuse of dogmatic authority, to obscure the real meaning of our Lord's humanity. The truth came to us in such a book as *Ecce Homo*, and from countless other teachers, with a fresh thrill of delight. The Gospels and the New Testament have come to live again. One of the most vital districts of Christian truth has been

---

[1] Principal A. M. Fairbairn, *Christ in Modern Theology*, pp. 3ff., 297. It is from the same book that I have quoted in the first sentence of the present work.

restored to us.'[1] In 1928 a distinguished Scottish theologian (in a passage directed against an unduly simplified modernism) spoke of 'the extraordinary value of the recovery of the Jesus of history', and described it as 'one of the greatest spiritual events in the story of Christianity'.[2] These are strong testimonies to the theological importance of the movement I have been describing, and it is unnecessary to illustrate it further in this place.

II

The Swing of the Pendulum

Now we are witnessing a really remarkable reaction. In various theological quarters there are insistent voices telling us that the advice given to seekers to begin with the Jesus of history was bad advice; that this is not the light that saves, but an *ignis fatuus*; that the whole movement associated with 'the rediscovery of the historical Jesus' is on a false trail and cannot fulfil its promise; that it is based on a wrong way of using the Gospels, and indeed on a misunderstanding of the Christian religion. Thus in many quarters the very phrase, 'the Jesus of history', has become suspect and uncongenial. I have already, in the preceding chapter, said something about the anticipations, beginnings and growth of this reaction. I will now give some striking examples from contemporary theology, without any attempt to be exhaustive.

The reaction is most unmistakable in certain schools of Protestant theology on the Continent of Europe, especially in the circles indicated by such phrases as 'the Dialectical Theology', 'the Theology of the Word', 'the Theology of Crisis'. The fullest treatment which Christology has received in those circles is in Professor Emil Brunner's massive and impressive book, *The Mediator*.[3] To Brunner the very heart of Christianity undoubtedly is the conviction that the Word was made flesh, that God became Man, in an actual historical human life on earth, the life of Jesus of

---

[1] Charles Gore, *Catholicism and Roman Catholicism*, p. 35.

[2] Principal D. S. Cairns, *The Faith that Rebels*, p. 200.

[3] *Der Mittler*, 1st ed. in 1927. It has been translated into English by Miss Olive Wyon.

Nazareth. Yet it is impossible to read his book without getting the impression that Brunner is not vitally interested in the life and personality of the Jesus of history, but only in the dogmas about Him. It is not that he rejects the modern movement of historical criticism of the gospels from a conservative point of view. He is 'an adherent of a rather radical school of Biblical criticism, which, for example, does not accept the Gospel of John as an historical source, and which finds legends in many parts of the Synoptic Gospels'.[1] And he makes it plain that he does not accept the doctrine of the Virgin Birth.[2] But his Christology is unrelated to all this. 'In faith we are not concerned with the Jesus of history as historical science sees Him, but with the Jesus Christ of personal testimony, who is the real Christ, and whom John shows just as plainly as (I could even say with Luther, still more plainly than) the Synoptists.'[3] Again: 'If once the conviction is regained that the Christian faith does not arise out of the picture of the historical Jesus, but out of the testimony to Christ, as such—this includes the witness of the prophets as well as that of the Apostles—and that it is based on this testimony, then inevitably the preference for the Synoptic Gospels and for the actual words of Jesus, which was the usual position of the last generation, will disappear. This view springs from a conception of Jesus, and of our relation to Him, which cannot really be combined with the Christian faith in Christ.'[4] 'Interpreted as a living picture, it is beyond doubt that the Synoptic picture is far nearer to objective reality, that is, to what we usually call the historical element, much nearer than John. But both pictures have this in common: both mean something quite different from what the modern historical picture sets out to do. If this has once been understood, then it will be much easier to face the question: which is the historical "photograph" of the life of Jesus? The historical picture is possibly still more "human" than the picture given to us by the Synoptists. And why not?'[5] 'Faith presupposes, as a matter of course, *a priori*, that the Jesus of history is not the same as the Christ of faith.'[6] There could hardly be a more radical rejection of the Jesus of history than that.

---

[1] *The Theology of Crisis*, p. 41.
[2] *The Mediator*. (Miss Wyon's trans. of *Der Mittler*), pp. 322ff.
[3] Ibid., p. 159 note.   [4] Ibid., p. 172.   [5] Ibid., p. 185f.   [6] Ibid., p. 184.

Yet the reaction is even more violent in the theology of Professor Karl Barth. The whole of that remarkable enterprise of modern theological scholarship, the attempt to write the life of Jesus and to reconstruct His personality, is in Barth's view quite irrelevant to Christian faith.[1] The idea that faith is in any sense based on the impression made by the personality of Jesus is completely mistaken. The New Testament has no interest in the 'personality' of Jesus, nor in any 'personality', for that very word indicates an attitude and outlook that are alien to Christianity.[2] This approach, Barth holds, can only lead to a kind of 'Jesus-cult' which, even if its beginnings can be found in Zinzendorf, and even if it is akin to the 'veneration of the Heart of Jesus', found in a certain Roman Catholic tradition, is really an apotheosis of a religious hero, and is but a substitute for Christian faith.[3] As we saw in the preceding chapter, Barth actually suggests that, so far as we can get back to the historical Jesus, there is nothing remarkable to be found in His life and character and teaching. The human life of Jesus is not a revelation of God but a concealment of God. 'Even in that function that is most surely His own, the teaching of the people, the training of His disciples, He does not achieve any aims, indeed He does not appear to have so much as striven after any definite aims. . . . Even in personality He does not appear to have had anything like so convincing and winning an effect as an amiable Christian journalism and rhetoric have in recent days delighted to represent.' In all this there is no revelation of God. It is only in the Resurrection and the forty days that followed before the Ascension that there is any revelation of God in Jesus, except that there were during His ministry occasional anticipations of the Resurrection glory in the miracles and the Transfiguration. It is only the eye of faith that can find any revelation of God in the human life and passion of Jesus, and this faith is based upon the miracles, the Resurrection, and the forty days. Does Barth mean

---

[1] *Die kirchliche Dogmatik, Erster Band: Die Lehre vom Wort Gottes, Zweiter Halbband*, 71. Here Barth refers with strong approval to Martin Kähler's *Der sogenannte historische Jesus und der geschichtliche biblische Christus*, published as far back as 1892.

[2] *The Doctrine of the Word of God* (Eng. trans. of *Erster Halbband* of the above), pp. 126, 463.

[3] *Die kirchliche Dogmatik*, I, ii, 150f.

that any faith which the disciples had in Jesus during His ministry was based simply on the miracles, including the Transfiguration, and that this was quite sound and normative? That seems strangely at variance with our Lord's own teaching about the relation of faith to signs and mighty works; which is perhaps an illustration of Barth's curious lack of interest in the *teaching* of our Lord.[1]

In any case, Barth has no sympathy with the notion so prominent in modern theology, that the nature and character and purpose of God were reflected, and thus revealed, in the human life and passion of Jesus. With a complete repudiation of the favourite modern idea of an advancing revelation, Barth holds that the New Testament witness adds nothing to the Old Testament except the fact that now the redeeming act of God has actually taken place in a man called Jesus, so that instead of being viewed from beforehand, by expectation, as by the Old Testament prophets, it is now viewed from after the event, by remembrance, and thus with factual detail. If it should be asked whether we, through the Gospel story of the life and character and teaching of Jesus, know more of the nature of God than could those who lived before the Christian era, Barth's answer would clearly be in the negative. And if he thus entirely repudiates the light which the 'Jesus of history' movement professed to have rediscovered, it appears to be for two reasons, both curiously negative: because it is impossible from the study of the Gospels (which were never meant for such a purpose) to discover what Jesus was like as a human personality; and because, even if we could discover it, the result would be disappointing to those who expected to find a revelation there, since only a 'divine *incognito*', a *veiling* of God, was present in the human life of Jesus.[2]

The impression which we here receive of a curious combination of theological dogmatism with historical scepticism becomes even stronger when we consider the position of Professor Rudolf Bultmann. 'Interest in the personality of Jesus is excluded', he writes, 'and not merely because, in the absence of information, I am making a virtue of necessity. I do indeed think that we can now

---

[1] See *Credo* (Eng. trans.), chaps. viii and x *passim*.
[2] For all this, see *Kirchliche Dogmatik*, I, ii, 77–113. See especially pp. 102, 111, 115ff., 125, 131f., and chaps. viii and x of *Credo*.

know almost nothing concerning the life and personality of Jesus, since the early Christian sources show no interest in either, and are, moreover, fragmentary and often legendary, and other sources about Jesus do not exist. . . . I am personally of the opinion that Jesus did not believe Himself to be the Messiah, but I do not imagine that this opinion gives me a clearer picture of His personality. I have in this book not dealt with the question at all—not so much because nothing can be said about it with certainty as because I consider it of secondary importance.'[1] Speaking of the uncertainty as to how far the Gospels preserve an objectively true picture of Jesus and His message, he says: 'For those whose interest is in the personality of Jesus this situation is depressing or destructive; for our purpose it has no particular significance.'[2] It is not of the Christ of faith and dogma that he thus speaks (since his own theological tendency is in the direction of Barth's dogmatism), but of the Jesus of history, as a figure of which he has hardly any knowledge and in which he has hardly any interest.

The reaction against the 'Jesus of history' movement is not confined to a set of Continental theologians, though the swing of the pendulum in both directions has gone farther, as it usually does, in Continental than in British theology. Even apart from the direct influence of Barth and Brunner upon theology in Britain, there is a more native British reaction, revealing itself in various ways, and not least notably in a type of commentary on the Gospels which is now being written, often more concerned with reconstructing the *kerygma* of the early Church than with reconstructing the historical figure of Jesus. The distinguished Anglican scholar, Dr. Edwyn Bevan, has a striking passage in criticism of the type of theology which attempts to build Christianity upon a perception of the heroic goodness and beauty of the historical Jesus as a human personality without any transcendent dogmas about His divine nature and origin; and in his criticism he appears to go to the other extreme of suggesting that, if we do not assume the dogmas, it is difficult to find in that historical personality anything supremely good and great on which the dogmas could be based. 'As a figure calculated to inspire men to heroic acts of self-sacrifice, it may be

---

[1] *Jesus and the Word* (Eng. trans.), pp. 8f.
[2] Ibid., pp. 13f.

doubted whether the figure of Jesus, if detached from what Christians have believed about Him, is adequate. There are sayings which bid men give up everything for the Kingdom of Heaven's sake, but His own life, unless what Christians have believed is true, does not offer any signal example of self-sacrifice. . . . There is the Cross. Yes, but apart from the belief of the Church, it must be exceedingly doubtful whether Jesus incurred the suffering of the Cross voluntarily, with prevision of the destiny to which His action was leading.'[1] Dr. Bevan's point is that the only outstanding self-sacrifice to be found in the story of Jesus consists not in anything in his earthly career, but in his having come down from heavenly glory and bliss to endure humiliation and death for our salvation. What he is maintaining is not that an honest and discerning contemplation of that historical human life will lead us to the position of the Christological dogmas, but that unless we begin with the dogmas, we cannot see anything particularly notable or divine in that life and personality at all. If there was anything at all in the 'rediscovery of the Jesus of history' as an aid to Christian faith, Dr. Bevan seems here to throw it overboard.

Another Anglican scholar, Professor R. H. Lightfoot, who is perhaps the most notable and certainly the most radical of the British representatives of Form Criticism, closes one of his books with some remarkable sentences which we may take as one more illustration of the same contemporary reaction. 'It seems, then, that the form of the earthly no less than of the heavenly Christ is for the most part hidden from us. . . . And perhaps the more we ponder the matter, the more clearly we shall understand the reason for it, and therefore shall not wish it otherwise. For probably we are as little prepared for the one as for the other.'[2]

III

Truth and Error in the Reaction

What are we to make of this reaction against the 'rediscovery of

---

[1] Edwyn Bevan, *Christianity*, pp. 239f.
[2] *History and Interpretation in the Gospels*, *ad fin.*

the Jesus of history'? How far can we approve and welcome it? And how far are we to deplore and resist it? These are complex questions, for this reaction embraces not one meaning alone, but many. Let us see whether we can distinguish between the true and the false.

(a) In some quarters the reaction may mean simply that none of the modern reconstructions of the historical Jesus does justice to His spiritual magnitude; that He was in reality a much greater figure than modern historical criticism has made Him; in short, that not one of the 'lives of Jesus' is anything like good enough. Doubtless that is true, and may indeed be very much an understatement. But that in itself would merely mean that, while we do need the Jesus of history, these books are not very good history. One thinks of Father Tyrrell's brilliant and famous sentence in criticism of the 'Liberal Protestant' reconstruction of the figure of Jesus freed at last from catholic dogma. 'The Christ that Harnack sees, looking back through nineteen centuries of Catholic darkness, is only the reflection of a Liberal Protestant face, seen at the bottom of a deep well.'[1] Yet Tyrrell, however dissatisfied he was with Harnack's reconstruction, belonged himself to the 'Jesus of history' movement in its more catholic form. And if we agree that all the 'lives of Jesus' have been inadequate reconstructions of that historical personality and career, this may mean that we are looking forward to better ones, which will do more justice to what He was.

But clearly the reaction that I have been illustrating signifies much more than that. Indeed, it sometimes means the very opposite. It sometimes appears to mean, not that we should look forward hopefully to better biographies of Jesus, but that those already written are too hopeful, too naïvely confident, too ready to accept, with an uncritical imagination, whatever details of the Gospel narrative may be made to subserve the modern biographical interest. Doubtless such strictures also contain some truth, and we have all learnt the lesson that the attempt to write 'biographies' of Jesus in the proper sense is delusive. But the contemporary reaction means much more than all these things.

(b) It may mean that the Jesus of history is not enough. And

---

[1] George Tyrrell, *Christianity at the Cross-roads*, p. 44.

such a protest is both sound and necessary. The rediscovery of the historical Jesus was such an illumination to many perplexed souls that they sometimes tried to make a religion out of that alone— out of the practice of gazing back into ancient Galilee and picturing Jesus as their Master in a very human and even sentimental way. Thus religion became an eager and loyal, if sometimes sentimental, following of the Man of Nazareth, as a substitute for Christianity. That has been a real danger, and we cannot wonder or deplore that there has been a reaction against it in various quarters. It could not last very long. For one thing, it soon becomes a weary business to keep straining one's eyes into the distant past for a heroic figure which we have to try to imagine as vividly as possible, when what we need is the living God here and now. And it would hardly be unfair to say that this sentimental Jesus-worship has sometimes tended to leave out God, so that it was virtually a substitution of Jesus for the eternal God. This fashion of thought is what Baron von Hügel once deprecatingly called 'a kind of Christism'. In Germany, a generation ago, it was attacked as a 'Jesus-cult', and even labelled 'Jesuanism' by some of the earliest leaders of the revolt that we have been considering;[1] and the term has been used as a reproach by the Roman Catholic Professor Karl Adam in our own time.[2] We have seen how Professor Barth takes a similar attitude, but even more uncompromisingly, and connects this modern hero-worship of Jesus with two much older phenomena: on the one hand the preoccupation with the human sufferings of Jesus that we find in the Protestant and Pietistic Zinzendorf, and on the other hand the Roman Catholic Veneration of the Sacred Heart of Jesus, which goes back to a contemporary of Zinzendorf's, Margaret Mary Alacoque.[3] It is a far cry from these movements to the modern 'Jesus-cult', but it may be that they all share the tendency to make the human figure of the Galilean, somewhat sentimentally regarded, not a revelation or incarnation of God, but a kind of substitute. 'They seem', wrote Baron von Hügel, 'to have got hold of a kind of Christism now, not

---

[1] See H. Weinel, *Ist das 'liberale' Jesusbild widerlegt?* p. 71. The German word, of course, is *Jesuanismus*.

[2] Karl Adam, *The Son of God* (Eng. trans.), pp. 6ff.

[3] Karl Barth, *Kirchliche Dogmatik*, I, ii, 150f.

God. God is too difficult, Christ is easy (is He easy?). They must have everything easy. We hardly need God if we have Christ. How different this is to our Lord Himself! Did He not come to show us the Father?'[1] Equally relevant is what Sir Edwyn Hoskyns said about the Fourth Gospel: 'Throughout his work the writer is careful to emphasize that Christianity is not an independent cult of Jesus, but the revelation of the Father and the worship of God.'[2]

But here again we must understand that the mistake was not (as Baron von Hügel's words make plain) the emphasizing of the Jesus of history, but rather the failure to be true to the real Jesus of history. The Jesus of history Himself can tell us that the Jesus of history is not enough. For Jesus continually pointed men beyond Himself to God the Father, and the following of Jesus without that constant intercourse with the Father would be a contradiction. As soon as it became a following of the real Jesus, it would pass beyond itself.[3]

So the Jesus of history alone is not enough. But the reaction with which we are dealing means much more than that.

(c) It may mean that we cannot do without a Christology. I believe it is true that we cannot, even if it is not immediately obvious. And I believe that this is partly what accounts for the reaction against the 'Jesus of history' movement. That movement was sometimes impatient of all Christological thought, regarding it even as needless mystification, substituting for it the historical reconstruction, and thus laying itself open to the charge that its theology contained nothing that could fairly be called a Christology. And that is not merely a hiatus in a Christian theology: it is a defect which amounts to a perversion of the whole. It is not merely a question of who Jesus was: It is a question of the whole Christian doctrine of God. Nothing can be plainer than that the great Christological controversies of the early centuries were fundamentally concerned with the question of the nature and purpose of God. And I believe it to be true that if we have no

---

[1] Friedrich von Hügel, *Letters to a Niece*, xxxvi.

[2] Sir Edwyn Hoskyns, *The Fourth Gospel*, vol. ii, p. 546.

[3] I do not at this point take up the question of the relation of the Jesus of history to the 'exalted Christ' in Christian faith, as I shall touch on that at a later stage.

Christology, we cannot have a good theology either, or even, with all our 'historical reconstruction', a good understanding of the nature and meaning of history. I will not develop that argument here, because it will be the main subject of the next chapter.

But while it is true that we cannot do without a Christology, the reaction which we are considering goes much farther still.

(*d*) It may mean that the modern interest in the historical personality of Jesus is something quite alien to the true meaning of the Christian religion. This is undoubtedly one strain of thought with which we have to reckon. From this point of view it is maintained that the genuine Christian interest in the Person of Christ has never had anything in common with the modern humanistic and biographical interest in the 'personality' of Jesus. The latter is said to belong to a different world, the world in which human personality is regarded as the supremely interesting thing, with the sort of interest which gives popularity to-day to intimate personal diaries, volumes of 'confessions', character studies, and all the talk about self-expression and development of personality—all of which is quite alien to the world of the Bible, whether Old or New Testament. Plutarch's *Lives* could not possibly have been written on Hebraic or on Christian soil. Even St. Augustine's *Confessions* could not have been engendered in the world of the New Testament, but only in a Graeco-Roman culture which was interested in human personality as such. In the Biblical world of thought man is not expected to be centred upon his own personality, but on God. It was not (the argument runs) in the human personality of Jesus that the disciples were interested, and still less had St. Paul any such interest, which would have been 'knowing Christ after the flesh'.[1] When we in the modern world discover in the Gospel story a remarkable personality, a heroic character, a 'religious genius',[2] we are reading into the story something which is not there, something in which the evangelists, or their sources, or the tradition they used, or their readers, had not the faintest interest. Their interest was in a divine drama, not in a human personality; in supernatural hap-

---

[1] 2 Cor. v, 16.
[2] Even Baron von Hügel, with all his reaction against sentimental 'Christism', could speak of Jesus as a 'religious genius'. *Selected Letters*, p. 159.

penings, not in the charm of a gracious Galilean.[1] A century ago
Sören Kierkegaard, who anticipated so much of what is being said
to-day, characterized as nonsense all the current talk about 'the
impression made by the personality of the Jesus of history'.[2]
Professor Barth, who has been so strongly influenced by Kierkegaard, speaks of 'personality' as the awkward starting-point of
Ebionite thought, just as he calls 'the idea' the awkward starting-
point of Docetic thought; while he maintains that the starting-
points of both Synoptic and Johannine thought are quite different
from either.[3] From this it would seem to be a natural corollary
that it is illegitimate to use the Gospels, and impossible to use them
successfully, as sources for the historical reconstruction of the
'personality' of Jesus.

There is undoubtedly a certain amount of truth in the considerations indicated in the above paragraph. There is a certain kind of
interest in human 'personality' which is not only absent from the
New Testament but alien to the Christian religion and to any true
Christian ethic, and which belongs rather to modern humanism
and individualism. To a true Christian ethic the 'chief end of man'
is not the cultivation of his personality, or even the formation of
his character on ideal lines, or anything so self-centred and in-
troverted as that, but faith and love towards God as He comes to
us through our relationships with our fellow-creatures—in short,
'to glorify God and to enjoy him for ever'. Concentration on the
development of personality or the cultivation of character does not
really produce a soundly integrated personality, and certainly does
not produce the Christian character. The good man, in the Christian sense, is not centred upon himself, but on God. All of that is
very true and very important. But surely it does not exclude all
contemplation of the Christian character as an ideal, or all interest
in human personalities. It excludes the 'humanistic' and 'Pelagian'
attitude to human personality, but not the attitude in which we
look through and beyond the will of man to the grace of God. And

---

[1] For such ideas, see Bultmann, *Jesus and the Word*, pp. 8, 72ff., 79, 84ff.,
215f.; Martin Dibelius, *Gospel Criticism and Christology*, pp. 16, 54, 61ff., 101; and
many passages in Barth's and Brunner's writings.

[2] Kierkegaard, *Philosophical Fragments*, p. 51.

[3] Barth, *The Doctrine of the Word of God*, p. 463.

as regards the historical personality of Jesus, those considerations do indeed exclude the approach that leads to a mere 'Jesus-cult' (which, as we saw, would be so untrue to the real Jesus), but not the approach by which, as St. Augustine said, *per hominem Christum tendis ad deum Christum.*

As regards the New Testament, it is absurd to suggest that it knows nothing of *that* sort of interest in human character and personality, and, in particular, in the character and personality of Jesus Christ. Otherwise, what is the meaning of that important strain of New Testament teaching which sets Jesus before us as the prototype of the Christian character, as the *example* of how human life ought to be lived? It is idle to maintain that St. Paul had no interest in the human character of Jesus, and to base this judgment on his having written: 'Even though we have known Christ after the flesh, yet now we know him so no more.'[1] For the passage probably means, not that St. Paul had now given up an interest in the human Jesus which he had cherished at an earlier stage of his Christian career, but that in becoming a Christian he had given up his former conception of the Messiah. Professor Dibelius, asserting with truth that the early Christians were not interested in history or biography as such, admits that St. Luke does show an interest in the human qualities of Jesus, but maintains that this is explained by St. Luke's own literary and biographical interest and is not Christian in its origin.[2] Yet it is as truly part of the New Testament as anything else! Professor H. G. Wood goes so far as to say that the figure of Jesus appealed to the ancient world as 'a heroic figure'.[3] Hero worship may, as an attitude to human personality, be alien to the Christian spirit. But can it be doubted that in the Epistle to the Hebrews we find a deep interest in the human character and indeed the moral struggle of Jesus, which leads us to something beyond the human and which is very near the heart of the Gospel?

It is true that the Church has passed through periods when, doing false honour to Christ through unconscious Docetism and

---

[1] 2 Cor. v, 16.
[2] M. Dibelius, op. cit., pp. 16, 54.
[3] H. G. Wood, *Christianity and the Nature of History,* p. 96. Cf. Karl Adam, *Christ our Brother,* pp. 97, 105.

Monophysitism, it almost lost the human figure altogether. But, according to the late Professor Burkitt, 'the dawn of a new era comes with St. Francis of Assisi . . . and it is hardly too much to say that he rediscovered the human Jesus who had wandered of old through the streets and the fields of the Holy Land'. 'From the time of St. Francis onwards the figure of the human Jesus has never lost its charm.'[1] That may be an overstatement, for the rediscovery had to be made more than once, and most notably, as we have seen, in the nineteenth century, when the development of modern historical criticism had opened up such new possibilities. But it is false to suggest that the interest in the historical Jesus is a mere product of the modern historical-critical movement, or that in some sense it is a merely 'historical' and not a truly religious or Christian interest. It may much more reasonably be maintained that Christianity, through its persistent and inevitable interest in the historical episode which it calls the Incarnation, gave birth to a new historical outlook, and thus in due course to the whole movement of modern historical research.[2] It is common in certain theological circles to-day, partly through the influence of Form Criticism, to maintain that it is illegitimate to use the Gospels as historical 'sources' for the reconstruction of the Jesus of history, since they were never meant to serve the purpose of historical evidence, but that of Christian witness. Yet in those very circles (one cannot help noticing) the Gospels are used precisely as his-

---

[1] F. C. Burkitt, *Jesus Christ: an Historical Outline*, pp. 81f.

[2] It is interesting to find Hoskyns and Davey, who belong in a sense to the reaction against the 'Jesus of history', and whose work is somewhat akin to Form Criticism, writing as follows: 'The recognition of the paramount importance of a particular history and of the necessity of a critical reconstruction of it is not new in the life of the Church. What is new is the emergence during the past two centuries of a precise method of handling historical evidence and an unshakeable confidence in the adequacy of the new method.' 'It is commonly supposed that the modern method of historical investigation has been perfected outside the field of Biblical studies, and that it has then been applied to the Bible. The opposite is, however, nearer to the truth. The method emerged from the heart of Biblical study. . . . Nor is this fortuitous. Christian theology has been creative in the field of historical investigation, because the theologian has been compelled to a delicate sense for the importance of history by a faith which is grounded upon a particular event.' *The Riddle of the New Testament*, pp. 10f.

torical 'sources', not indeed for the reconstruction of the figure of Jesus, but for the reconstruction of the *kerygma* and the attitude of the early Church—though the early Church itself, in producing the Gospels, was supremely interested in the figure of Jesus!

It seems to me that a good deal of confusion would be averted if we reminded ourselves that the phrase, 'the Jesus of history', means simply and precisely: 'Jesus as He really was in His life on earth', which includes of course what He did and said, what He intended and what He taught. The phrase does usually imply that in certain respects we must give a different account of this from what was given in the pre-critical period, but that will be pretty generally recognized. The phrase may doubtless be used with a false preconception of what 'history' is, and that is not an altogether simple question, as we shall see in the next chapter. When we speak of 'Jesus as He really was', we must not mean 'Jesus as a figure which can be described and authenticated by a cold and detached criticism'. For that would not be real history at all. I am sure that this is a fertile source of confusion in the whole matter: the habit of setting 'history' and 'faith' too sharply against each other, with the assumption, which Brunner actually seems to make, that a really historical study of Jesus could not give us the kind of figure that would be of any use to faith! By a historical picture Brunner means the 'photographic' kind of portrait which would of necessity leave the deepest things out: he actually speaks of the historical 'photograph', as if it were axiomatic that a camera could exhaust the possibilities of portraiture and do better work for the science of history than could the portraiture of a great artist.[1] But that is a poor sense of the word 'historical', and would give a quite arbitrary limitation of meaning to the phrase, 'the Jesus of history'. It is true in a sense that the science of history cannot directly introduce the supramundane and the divine into its nexus of causes and effects, cannot penetrate into a suprahistorical 'dimension'. In that sense the 'historical' is the 'human'; the sphere of history is the life of man, the dimension of humanity. But even then, are we to forget that the *humanity* of our Lord is vital to Christian faith? And can even His humanity be worthily studied without the sympathy and

---

[1] See Brunner, op. cit., 185f.

insight of faith? Without this, surely the historical study of such a subject would be vain. It would not be soundly historical. The result would be bad history. It would not give us Jesus as He really was. It would not give us the Jesus of history.[1] When we have understood this, we have disposed of the argument that the interest in the historical personality of Jesus is a kind of interest which is alien to the world of the New Testament and to the world of Christian faith.

IV

Can We Dispense with the Jesus of History?

We have now reached a point where we can grapple with the fundamental question whether Christian faith needs 'the Jesus of history'. Ought we to go the whole way with the reaction against the 'rediscovery of the historical Jesus', or is there here something vital to our faith? The question is not whether we should be content to cut the cable altogether and free Christianity from all connection with an historical episode: I am not concerned with those who are prepared to transform the whole story of the Incarnation into a symbolical myth, but with those who, while soundly insisting on the actual historical reality of the episode of the Incarnation, wish to dissociate this entirely from all historical attempts to reconstruct the central figure. Accepting and embracing the dogma that God became man, they are not interested, as men of faith, in trying to ascertain what kind of man He became, in the sense in which that would be observed by contemporary eye-witnesses. From this point of view Kierkegaard characteristically maintained that there was no advantage at all in being a contemporary of Jesus and thus directly witnessing the Word made Flesh, since from the truly spiritual point of view it is believers, not con-

---

[1] I am glad to find Professor Barth, against whom I have been arguing so much in this connection, saying something very like this. See *The Knowledge of God and the Service of God* (Gifford Lectures), pp. 66f. And Brunner himself writes: 'Faith alone is able to know rightly the historical reality of Jesus Christ,' op. cit., p. 162.

temporaneous eyewitnesses, that are His real 'contemporaries'. There is a sense in which that is profoundly true, though it is equally true that believers in later ages are dependent on the testimony of the actual eye-witnesses and on the impression of the figure of Jesus which these are able to convey through the Gospel story. But according to Kierkegaard: 'If the contemporary generation had left behind them nothing but the words, "we have believed that in such and such a year God appeared among us in the humble figure of a servant, that He lived and taught in our community, and finally died", it would be more than enough.'[1]

Would it really be enough and more than enough? There is the whole question in a nutshell. And one is disposed to reply: If no more than that was necessary, why was even that necessary? What would it avail us to be able to say so much, if we could say no more? If no revelation of the nature of God were to be found in the incarnate life, what would be the gain of believing that God therein became man? If the 'divine incognito' remains in this extreme form, what saving virtue is there in the dogma of the Incarnation? If there is no revelation, no 'unveiling', of God in the human personality and career of Jesus, but only a 'veiling'; if God in Christ is as much as ever a *deus absconditus*, not a *deus revelatus*; what are we the better of the coming of God in Christ? Where is the light that saves us, the knowledge that sets us free? Someone may reply that Christianity, being different from Gnosticism, has never believed in salvation by illumination, by *gnosis*, and that God became man not to give us knowledge but to give us life and power, not to tell us something new, but to *do* something, once for all, for our redemption. But there will be grave danger of our giving a sub-Christian and magical account of this salvation unless we remember that God saves us by *revealing* Himself to us, enlightening our minds with the knowledge of Himself, not in a 'Gnostic' sense, but by that method which was so intolerable and incredible to the Gnostics, the way of Incarnation in a real human life. And while the revelation of God to us men on earth must always continue to be in some sense and measure a 'veiled' revelation, surely to Christian faith it is *less* veiled at that point, of the Incarnation,

---

[1] Kierkegaard, op. cit., pp. 51ff. and 87.

than anywhere else; which is precisely what we mean when we speak of that as God's supreme 'unveiling' or revelation.

Moreover, we cannot be content to say that the revelation is simply in the fact or dogma of God becoming man, not in any impression of the human personality of Jesus. We have seen how according to the teaching of Karl Barth the episode of the Incarnation did not convey any fresh revelation of the nature and activity of God, and thus the New Testament says nothing more than the old, though it says it differently by looking back to the fulfilment instead of looking forward to it as the Old Testament had to do. Thus the New Testament, like the Old, is a witness to the revelation of the *hidden* God. If there was any unveiling, it was not (according to Barth) in the life and teaching and character and passion of Jesus, but in the resurrection and the forty days that followed, with occasional anticipations in the Transfiguration and the miracles. But if that were the whole truth, it would be very difficult to answer the question: On what is *our* Christian faith based? If we cannot validly find any revelation of God in the portrait of Jesus as an historical person, how are we ever to reach and accept the dogmas about Him? If we cannot get so far as to know what He was like, or if that has nothing to do with the real meaning of the story, then how can we go so much farther and know that God was incarnate in Him? In short, the question of the relevance of 'the Jesus of history' raises ultimately the whole problem of the basis and rationale of our Christian belief in the Incarnation.

Now, it hardly needs to be said that the rediscovered 'Jesus of history' cannot be used as a kind of ready-made *proof* of the Incarnation, the kind of proof which would proceed directly, with compelling necessity, from the authentic historical portrait to the transcendent dogmas; for, after all, the majority of those who were actual eyewitnesses of the incarnate life were never led to any such faith at all. It is equally plain that our belief in the Incarnation cannot be based simply on 'signs and wonders', on miracles and Resurrection, in the sense that these can first be proved historically and then be taken as certifying the dogmas. It would be strangely out of keeping with the New Testament, especially the teaching of our Lord, to base the faith of the original disciples simply on such 'signs and wonders' regarded as ocular demonstrations; and no one will maintain that we to-day, having no ocular demonstration, can proceed by first proving these occurrences on sheer historical evidence and then using the results to bear the weight of our Christian faith. To each Christian to-day, as to Simon Peter of old, in response to the confession, 'Thou art the Christ, the Son of the living God', there come with unabated truth the words: 'Flesh and blood hath not revealed it unto thee, but my Father which is in heaven.' It is neither ocular nor historical proof, but divine revelation, the *testimonium Spiritus Sancti internum*. And yet it remains true that the revelation came to Peter as an inward witness to the Jesus whom he knew in the flesh, and it comes to us as a witness to the Jesus whom we know as an historical personality through the Gospel story.

The pity is that the 'Jesus of history' movement partly falsified this truth by dwelling too exclusively on the impression made by the historical personality on the individual soul. It was a false isolation both of the 'personality' of Jesus and of the seeking soul, and it is no wonder that it caused a reaction. The classical example is to be found in Herrmann's great book: *The Communion of the Christian with God*. This book gave illumination to many seeking souls a generation ago, but, looking back to-day, one cannot help being astonished at the narrow and elusive basis which it proposed for Christian faith: the impression made upon the individual soul by 'the inner life of Jesus' as it is encountered in the Gospel story. It was characteristic of that age (the age of the 'rediscovery') to speak so confidently of our knowledge of 'the inner life of Jesus' and to stake everything upon that. It was equally characteristic of the age to isolate the individual so excessively in this matter of faith, basing so much on his solitary experience of confrontation with the historical Jesus, and largely forgetting his dependence on the witness and authority of the Church.[1] All of that is very one-sided. It is not the mere picture of the Jesus of history, constructed by historical science, that lays hold of us for our salvation, but the whole Christian story, with both its historical and its supra-historical elements, which was the substance of the original

---

[1] But see Chap. ii, § 30, of Herrmann's book (4th ed.) where he deals with 'The mediation of true communion with God by means of the Christian community.'

kerygma: the story of how the Son of God became man in Christ for
our salvation, suffered and died on the Cross for our sins, arose
from the dead, ascended into heaven, intercedes for us there continually, and gives Himself to us through the Holy Spirit. And how
does that story authenticate itself to us, so that we become sure of
its truth? Not by any mere historical argument (of 'flesh and
blood'), but by the work of the Holy Spirit in our hearts through
the witness of the Apostles and of the whole 'catholic and apostolic
Church'. When the story is told us, as worked out in the Church,
and with the testimony of the Church, the Holy Spirit applies it
to our hearts, it opens our eyes, and we know that it is true. All of
this is indispensable to a sound Christian theology, though it has
often been forgotten.

But equally indispensable, surely, is the actual portrait of the
historical Jesus, connecting these claims firmly with historical
reality. Apart from that, we do not know why we should say these
things *about a particular historical figure*, Jesus the carpenter of
Nazareth. In short, we do not know who it is about whom we say
these marvellous things, and therefore cannot know why we say
them. We should be professing to believe we know not what, and it
would be a new kind of *fides implicita!* Nor can we justify this on the
ground of the witness and authority of the Church; for apart from
all authentic knowledge of the personality of the Jesus of history
it is difficult to see how the Church itself could continue to be
justified in saying these things about a particular historical figure.
If it is true that 'no man can say, Jesus is Lord, except in the
Holy Spirit', it is equally true that no man can say it, in the truly
Christian sense, except through a knowledge of what Jesus actually
was, as a human personality, in the days of His flesh. In the ages
of authority Christians may indeed have largely dispensed with
this, and Christian faith, however impoverished, managed to live
without it. But in the modern age of criticism and questioning,
the rediscovery of the human historical personality came as a new
realization of the historical content of the dogmas: men found in
the Gospel story a real human personality which constrained them
to say, with the Church and in the Holy Spirit, 'Jesus is Lord',
and 'God was in Christ', and 'The Word was made flesh'. And I
cannot believe that this rediscovery, coming in the time of need as

a veritable revelation with a rejuvenating power, was from the Christian point of view a delusion, or was anything less than a recovery of something which is vital to Christian faith.

It is because the school of Karl Barth repudiates all these things that it has incurred the charge of not having a truly incarnational theology. One almost ventures to say that it does not take the Incarnation quite seriously. It builds indeed upon the Word of God; but does it build upon the Word made flesh? In his *Kirchliche Dogmatik* Barth tells us that the central text of the New Testament is John i, 14, 'The Word became flesh and dwelt among us'; but confesses also that in his early commentary on *Romans*, which so took the theological world by storm, he had failed to do justice to this central truth.[1] One cannot help asking whether his theology has yet done justice to it.[2] He has reacted so violently against the 'Jesus of history' movement that he does not seem interested in the historical Jesus at all. His theology has become so austerely a theology of the Word that (if one may venture with the greatest respect to say so) it is hardly a theology of the Word-made-Flesh. If the adherents of the 'Jesus of history' movement were in danger of becoming the new Ebionites, the Dialectical theologians, in spite of their insistence on the full humanity of Christ, are so little interested in it in their Christology that they might seem to be in danger of becoming the new Monophysites. But really their position is quite a new one, belonging to the twentieth century, and it might be given the new title of Logotheism, because it is so strictly a theology of the Word of God rather than of the Incarnation of the Son of God, the Word made flesh. With all its emphasis on the incursion of the Divine into human life once for all in Jesus Christ, it has no interest in studying the resultant life as an historical phenomenon; and this is not because it would put back the

---

[1] *Kirchliche Dogmatik, Zweiter Halbband,* pp. 56, 135.
[2] This criticism has repeatedly been passed upon Barth's theology, even by friendly and sympathetic critics. Nicolas Arseniev made this criticism at least of the earlier phase of Barth's theology (*We Beheld His Glory*, pp. 40–6, 65f). Otto Piper remarks that neither Tillich nor Barth 'takes seriously enough the fact that God became flesh and dwelt with man in a certain limited historical time and space' (*Recent Developments in German Protestantism,* p. 144). Martin Dibelius remarks that 'the Dialectical Theology, while very Pauline, neglects the Gospels' (*Gospel Criticism and Christology,* pp. 12–16, 103f).

hands of the clock by rejecting modern historical criticism (far from it!) but because 'the Jesus of history is not the same as the Christ of faith' (Brunner). I do not believe that this can be a stable position for theology. It would ultimately stultify the whole doctrine of the Incarnation. 'If righteousness is by the Law', said St. Paul to the first Christian generation, 'then Christ died for nothing'; and we might now say, in this twentieth century: If revelation is by the Word alone, then Christ *lived* for nothing, and the Word was made flesh in vain. That is the ultimate answer to our question as to whether we can dispense with the Jesus of history.

V

Can We Know the Jesus of History?

But the question remains: Can we really claim to know Jesus historically? I cannot resist the impression that at least one main cause of the theological reaction we have been considering is the suspicion, fostered by Form Criticism, that in this twentieth century the historical Jesus is beyond recapture; that, whether we like the situation or not, we do not possess the material evidence for a portrait of Jesus of Nazareth; that it is really impossible now to know what He was like, 'what manner of man' He was. It is highly important for us to get this issue clear. To say that the cry of 'Back to Jesus' is a vain and foolish cry may mean two very different things. It may mean that the cry was a cry of unbelief, and that it is impossible to go behind the apostolic and evangelic witness and find a *different* Jesus, a pre-Christological Jesus, since the real historical Jesus was just such as He appears in the testimony of the New Testament. But it may also mean something very different and much more negative: that the New Testament documents, which have been too confidently used as 'sources' for the life of Jesus, are not adequate to that end, since the tradition was shaped for quite a different (a missionary and homiletic) purpose, and therefore it is impossible to get back to the actual figure of Jesus and know what He was. These two positions are constantly confused with each other. In a sense they both rest upon the perception that the Gospels and the other New Testament writings were never intended to be used as sources for an historical reconstruction. But on the one hand this perception is used in the interests of faith (it may be even a too conservative faith), while on the other hand it conduces to a somewhat sceptical treatment of the Gospel story, with the suggestion that the real historical Jesus is beyond recapture. It is with this latter that we are now concerned, and it is closely connected with Form Criticism. It is true that Form Criticism is in intention but a new method of investigating the actual facts of the Gospel story, but it frequently gives the impression of using the Gospels as sources only for the historical reconstruction of the life and message of the Apostolic Age, with the implication that that is as far as we can go and that we cannot know the historical Jesus.

Can we know the historical Jesus? That is the question that has been sharpened in our time by the emergence of Form Criticism and that we must face for a moment before we close this chapter.

It is obvious that, even if I had the capacity, I could not in this place attempt an examination of the whole movement of Form Criticism, but can only make some comments relevant to our present problem. As regards our question whether we can know the real Jesus of history, it seems plain that we have here something which in the nature of the case cannot be *proved* except by the actual exhibition of a self-authenticating portrait on a full scale, and this is not the place for drawing such a portrait. But the tendency of some Form Critics, in reaction against source criticism, to suggest a negative answer and thus largely to give up the quest of the historical Jesus, seems to me to be unconsciously based on a 'defeatist' approach to the problem which cannot be objectively justified.

Form Criticism tends to tell the enthusiastic student of the historical Jesus that a good deal of what the latter finds in the Gospels proceeds really from his own imagination, perhaps from modern sentimentalism, perhaps from a subjective reading of his own views and interests into the ancient documents. For this subjective and unscientific procedure the Form Critic professes to substitute a more objective and scientific method of interpretation, a new way of determining what the Gospel material means and how much of it is original and primitive, by thinking oneself back into the situation and interests of the early Church which produced it. But however useful this method may be as a supplement to the older methods of source criticism, one may be pardoned for wondering whether it guarantees any greater objectivity. Indeed, one sometimes receives from the work of the Form Critics a precisely contrary impression. It has, for example, been remarked that Bultmann in his reconstruction of the teaching of Jesus simply reads his own dialectical theology into the Gospels; so that, as Tyrrell said that Harnack's Jesus was but the reflection of a Liberal-Protestant face, we might say that Bultmann's Jesus is but the reflection of a Barthian face. [1] Whether that would be quite fair or not, Form Criticism seems at many points to be even more at the mercy of subjectivity than were the older methods: more dependent upon the individual critic's 'sense' of the situation of a saying or an incident. Moreover, the Form Critics often seem, tacitly and even unconsciously, to make a number of initial assumptions, which are far-reaching but far from self-evident, such as the following: (a) that all the Gospel material is in one or other of the recognized 'forms', and that these are easily identified and distinguished; (b) that those who shaped and transmitted and wrote down the tradition had no 'biographical' or 'historical' interest, but a purely homiletical and Christological interest (surely an exaggerated antithesis); (c) that at the time when the tradition was taking shape there were in the Christian Church none surviving of those who had been eye-witnesses of our Lord's ministry;[2] (d) that the 'situation' (*Sitz im Leben*) of any saying or incident must be a situation in the primitive Church, not in the actual life of our Lord. Thus the Form Critic often tantalizes us by stopping short with the question: *What did the primitive community mean by this story?* He stops short (why?) of the much more important question (to which the other may well be ancillary): *What did our Lord mean when he said or did this thing?* Indeed, when the Form Critics

---

[1] It is true that Bultmann renounces all attempt to reconstruct the *personality* of Jesus, and is content to interpret His teaching—though I do not know how these two can be kept quite separate.

[2] This point is well made in a book to which I owe more than this, E. Basil Redlich's *Form Criticism*.

set out to classify the Gospel sayings and incidents under the various 'forms' of the primitive *kerygma*, and to understand why the tradition tells this, what the purpose and interest of the primitive community was in shaping this or that story and embodying it in the tradition, it seems seldom to occur to them that the story may have been handed on simply or primarily *because it was true*, because the incident had actually taken place in the ministry of Jesus, and was therefore of great interest to His followers, even if they sometimes failed to understand it.

Yet surely we should expect those men, believing what they did about Jesus, to be immensely interested in recalling anything that He had said or done, simply because He had said or done it, however remote they might be from the modern 'biographical' interest. This is of course no safeguard against the accretion of legend, nor does it mean that the exigencies of the preaching had no influence in the formation of the tradition. There was always a strong selective influence, amid the great wealth of material: otherwise 'the world itself could not contain the books that should be written'. The tradition would continually select what was most directly relevant to the *kerygma*. And yet it seems clear that it faithfully passed on a number of details which it was at a loss to interpret. For example, it seems highly doubtful whether the makers of the Gospel tradition understood what was meant by the phrase 'the Son of Man' on the lips of Jesus. Yet they faithfully passed it on, sometimes in passages where in the Greek it hardly makes sense and may even be a mis-translation from the Aramaic. They passed it on because Jesus had used it. And many a story which they had to tell must have included bits of characteristic detail that were not directly relevant to the homiletic need. These were included, not with any conscious 'biographical' interest, in the modern sense, but simply because they were part of a true story. Such details may even be specially significant because they were not inserted with any conscious and special purpose. They simply mean that the personality of Jesus 'could not be hid' when His followers were testifying of Him to the world.

There is a deeply interesting passage in Professor C. H. Dodd's *History and the Gospel* which shows how the methods of Form Criticism itself may be used to throw light on the personality and habits of Jesus in a way that is above all suspicion of subjectivity. He sets side by side nine separate passages from the Gospels, thoroughly diverse in respect of their 'forms' and the immediate motives of their inclusion in the tradition. A more diverse selection could hardly be made. 'But all of them in their different ways exhibit Jesus as an historical personality distinguished from other religious personalities of His time by His friendly attitude to the outcasts of society.'[1] The fact that the makers of the Gospel tradition had no conscious purpose of emphasizing this characteristic in passing on all those nine reminiscences makes the actual convergence far more significant; and it is in such ways (Professor Dodd gives a number of similar examples) that the historical personality of Jesus comes to stand out unmistakably. Thus I cannot believe that there is any good reason for the defeatism of those who give up all hope of penetrating the tradition and reaching an assured knowledge of the historical personality of Jesus. Surely such defeatism is a transient nightmare of Gospel criticism, from which we are now awaking to a more sober confidence in our quest of the Jesus of history.

---

[1] C. H. Dodd, *History and the Gospel*, pp. 90–101. The passages are: Mark ii, 14; Mark ii, 15–17; Luke xix, 2–10; Luke vii, 36–48; John vii, 53–viii, 11; Luke xv, 4–7 = Matt. xviii, 12–13; Luke xviii, 10–14; Matt. xi, 16–19 = Luke vii, 31–5; Matt. xxi, 32.

Chapter III

WHY A CHRISTOLOGY?

In contending for a true understanding of the doctrine of the Incarnation at the present time, a writer has the double responsibility that has always to be borne by a belligerent occupying a central geographical position: he has to fight on two fronts. Thus, having in the foregoing chapter faced those who wish to sacrifice the Jesus of history to a high Christology, I must now turn my eyes in another direction and face those who wish to sacrifice Christology to the Jesus of history. Having rediscovered the Jesus of history, they say: Is not that enough? Why be burdened with the mysteries of a Christology? Those who thus question are not indeed in the present theological fashion. To theologians the question may seem so naïve and so outmoded as to be hardly worthy of attention in a theological book. But theologians are apt to be deaf to the questionings of the outside world. And in that outside world at the present time I am persuaded that there is a very large number of thinking people who, while deeply impressed and even captivated by the human figure of the historical Jesus, are completely mystified by the doctrine of the Incarnation and by what may be called 'the return to Christology' among theologians. Surely it is important for theology to become quite clear as to what it has to say to such questioners, and not only for their sake, but also for its own, because this is a matter of understanding, in full view of all ancient and modern misunderstandings, what Christology really is and what it is about.

I

Christ without Christology

It will be well for us to begin by doing full justice to this position and stating it in its full strength. Historically it goes back to the discovery that in the actual development of Christianity Christology is a later appearance than the original 'Galilean gospel'. It is important to distinguish truth from error in this discovery. It does not mean that even the earliest of the four Gospels is free from Christology, or that we can get back to any stage, however early, in the formation of the Gospel tradition, when it was a plain tale without Christology. The days are past when the line could be drawn as easily as that, and we can see now that the telling of the story of Jesus was Christological through and through from the start. The advance of Biblical criticism has itself made this clear, especially perhaps the work of the Form Critics. But this must not be taken to settle the question whether there was anything that can be called Christology in the actual 'Galilean gospel' preached by Jesus Himself. Some leading Form Critics go so far as to deny that Jesus ever regarded or spoke of Himself as the Messiah. Half a century ago Harnack, with his Ritschlian bias against ecclesiastical dogma in anything like a metaphysical sense, remarked with satisfaction that the original Gospel message in the teaching of Jesus was not about the Son but about the Father. The whole Ritschlian reading of early Church history tended to regard the system of Christological dogma as an intrusion of Greek metaphysics into the pure original Gospel of Jesus. In view of all this, it became natural to suspect Christology of actually obscuring the authentic Christian message. Weinel protested against that obsession with Christology which pushed into the background the actual content of Jesus' teaching; and pointed out, following Reitzenstein, that in that age of Christian beginnings there were plenty of religions whose founders were claimed as divine wonder-workers, plenty of beautiful myths and cosmogonies, while the really unique thing in Christianity, which kept it from being absorbed into that maelstrom, was the content of the teaching of Jesus, especially His teaching about human sin and divine forgiveness. It was this, Weinel maintained, more than any Christology, that distinguished Christianity.[1] That may well seem to some to be a salutary reminder to-day, in face of those schools of theological thought which make a great deal of Christology, but make very little of our Lord's own teaching, though He spent so much of His time upon it in the days of His flesh. And so there are many who feel themselves to be nearer to the original Gospel when they go to the other extreme, taking Jesus as their supreme teacher and guide, without any Christological mysteries concerning His 'Person'.

But those who thus wish to have Christ without Christology do not usually intend to reduce His rôle to that of teacher alone. The Gospel means to them much more than a body of timeless teaching about God; and if they are merely mystified by the Christ of Christology, they hold fast to the Jesus of history, and not merely as teacher, but as leader and guide, as pioneer of faith and supreme revealer of God. If the history of mankind may under one aspect be conceived as an agelong quest of the Divine, an upward struggle, a perennial seeking after God, with slow and gradual success, through many wanderings, then Jesus may be conceived as the climax of the enterprise, the supreme seeker and finder of God, the great discoverer in the realm of the Divine, 'the greatest and best Believer that ever lived', as one of the Puritans called Him;[2] mankind's supreme pathfinder, who can lead us to God because He found the way Himself. Jesus may be all this to those who wish to dispense with the mysteries of Christology. And even more: they will say that He is not only the pathfinder, but is Himself the path, the living Way, through whom alone we can surely come to the Father. They will ascribe all this to the Jesus of history.

But, they will ask, is not that enough? Why introduce mystification again by calling Him divine? 'In order to give us authentic tidings of the character of God, Jesus did not require actually to *be* God.'[3] And if we do call Him God, do we not thereby destroy again at a stroke the picture so marvellously built up by modern

---

[1] H. Weinel, *Ist das 'liberale' Jesusbild widerlegt?* p. 41.

[2] Quoted by D. S. Cairns, *The Faith that Rebels*, p. 117.

[3] A. S. Pringle-Pattison, *Studies in the Philosophy of Religion*, p. 252.

historical criticism, the picture of the Jesus of history as the Man who can lead us men to God? Once again, as in the theology of Cyril of Alexandria, a high Christology will take away the human Jesus and give us a docetic Christ. Once again for the warm living human portrait which so greatly helps our faith there will be substituted a 'Byzantine' image, or a 'heraldic' Christ, who cannot be for us men the Way to God, because He is not human. Or if the high Christology of orthodox dogma does make Him fully human, and if we are to take that quite seriously, as theologians do in the modern world, then what does it *mean* to say that He is God? Does it mean anything? Is it not mere needless mystification? Should we not be content with the Jesus of history, as the way to God? The eternal God, and the historical Jesus—is not this enough? These are the familiar but persistent and impatient questions that we now have to face.

What does Christian theology to-day say in reply? It will certainly not reply by denying all that the objector has been urging. It will agree with many of his pleas, so far as they go. It will grant that Christology has sometimes damaged Christianity, obscured the humanity of Christ, and sold the Gospel to Docetism— and all through an over-simplification of the issues. It may also point out that these are 'old unhappy far-off things, and battles long ago', long since settled, so far as theology is concerned. And then it will try to carry the objector further by asking him some searching questions, lest he in his turn should be guilty of over-simplification. In short, when the perplexed objector speaks of the eternal God and the historical Jesus, and asks whether this is not enough, the living theology of to-day will take him on to new ground by asking him two questions in return: Are you sure that you know what you mean by 'God'? And are you sure that you know what you mean by 'history'?

A consideration of these two questions may be the best remedy for that over-simplification of the issues which makes people content to do without a Christology; and it will certainly give us the opportunity of bringing into perspective certain thoughts that have emerged in a new way in our time, as to what Christology really means.

II

Christology and the Nature of God

It is vitally important to learn, as the whole development of modern theology has been helping us to learn, that the real Christological question is not simply a psychological or an historical question about Jesus, as to His psychical constitution, as to how His mind worked, as to His 'self-consciousness', and what claims He made; but is fundamentally a question about the nature and activity of God.

It is perfectly true from the historical point of view that in mankind's agelong enterprise of the quest of God, Jesus is the climax. He is the greatest of all believers, 'the pioneer and the perfection of faith', the supreme spiritual pathfinder, mankind's supreme discoverer of God. He is all these things, and if He were not, He could not be more. But is that the whole truth? If Jesus was the supreme discoverer of God, I should wish to carry the high argument yet further by asking: What kind of God did He discover? And there need be no hesitation about the answer, for we have His own report. What kind of God, then, do we find in His teaching? Is it a God who would wait to be discovered? No, indeed. It is a God who takes the initiative, a God who is always beforehand with men, a 'prevenient' God who seeks His creatures before they seek Him. Nowhere does this appear more unmistakably than in that very element of His teaching which we found Weinel exalting at the expense of Christology—His message about human sin and the divine forgiveness. It is well known how the Jewish scholar Claude Montefiore, when he set himself to see whether there was anything quite new in Jesus' teaching, anything which no Jewish prophet or rabbi had ever said before Him, singled out this one thing as quite distinctive: the picture of the Divine Shepherd going out into the wilderness to seek a lost sheep, the picture of God as not merely receiving those who turn to Him, but as taking the initiative in seeking those who have not turned to Him. That, he says, is 'a new figure' and 'one of the new excellences of the Gospel'. So that is the kind of God whom Jesus 'discovered': a seeking God, whose very nature it is to go the whole way into the wilderness in quest of man.

Now that does not consort well with a theology which speaks only of the human quest of the Divine, and which will say no more even about the climax of the quest than that it is the supreme discovery by the supreme human pathfinder. Such language makes one wish to ask: What was God doing during the long ages when man was seeking Him? Did He leave man to do all the seeking? That would be like the scene on Mount Carmel when the priests of Baal could not get an answer from their God and Elijah kept baiting them with satirical suggestions, telling them to call a little louder, because their God might be absent-minded or possibly even asleep. [1] The point of such excellent satire was that the living and true God is not like that. And even if to those who are weary of waiting God sometimes seems to be a *deus absconditus*, yet the God whom we find in the Bible is a God who 'does things', [2] a prevenient God, who reveals Himself, and calls men, and visits them. There is a good deal in the Bible about men seeking God, but there is much more about God seeking men, and coming upon them unawares when they were not seeking Him, and even when they were disposed to flee from Him. [3] The whole story in the Bible suggests not so much phrases like 'human quest' as phrases like 'divine revelation', 'divine vocation', 'divine visitation'. And if that long story represents reality, and if Jesus truly was the climax of it, leaving nothing more to be desired or waited for, then there must be something further to be said about Jesus than that He was the supreme discoverer of God. If Jesus was right in what He reported, if God is really such as Jesus said, then we are involved in saying something more about Jesus Himself and His relation to God, and we must pass beyond words like 'discovery' and even 'revelation' to words like 'incarnation'. 'In order to give us authentic tidings of the character of God', I quoted from a philosopher, 'Jesus did not require actually to *be* God.' Is that, then, all that Jesus did—to

---

[1] 1 Kings xviii, 27.

[2] J. A. Froude said to the aged Carlyle that he could only believe in a God who *does* something. With a cry of pain the old man replied: 'He does nothing.'

[3] Cf. the stories of the calls of Moses, Gideon, Samuel, David, Elisha, Amos, Isaiah, Jeremiah, Jonah, Paul.

bring us authentic tidings, as from a distant realm, of a God who takes no initiative Himself to seek us out? If God is like that, then Jesus was wrong about Him, the tidings He brought were not authentic, and He was not even a true discoverer. But if He was right, then there is something more to be said, something Christological; and if we leave it out, we are leaving out not only something vital about Jesus, but something vital about God. That is to say, if we have not a sound Christology, we cannot have a sound theology either.

It is a commonplace to say that most of the great heresies arose from an undue desire for simplification, an undue impatience with mystery and paradox, and an endeavour after a common-sense theology. And it is plain that the theology which repudiates all high Christology suffers from precisely these weaknesses. God our Father and Christ our Teacher: that sounds easy. It has an attractive simplicity—which is wholly illusory. It is as if, in contrast with the mysteries of Christology, the idea of God were quite easy, free from all paradox. It is as if the idea of God were a kind of counter, or a coin of fixed value in some universal system of currency, which could be handed out to all comers in the name of Jesus the Teacher, and accepted by everybody without difficulty. It is as if, while the idea of Incarnation presents great difficulty, it were a much easier matter to believe in God our Father. But is it easy to believe in God? In the kind of God that Jesus gives us? Not a 'deistic' God, or even a 'theistic' God (for Christianity is not theism plus Christology), waiting for men to discover His existence and then pass round the idea with its proofs; but the God whom we find in the New Testament? Is it easy to believe in such a God? Is it easier than to believe in the Incarnation? Surely the Incarnation is not an added difficulty, but is rather the sole way in which the Christian conception of God becomes credible or even expressible. It is only an extreme theological naïveté that can be blind to the mystery and paradox of the word 'God' in the Christian sense; and we shall never do justice to the height of that paradox—we shall never do justice to the love of God—if we leave out the supreme paradox of the Incarnation.[1] Such an omission would fatally im-

---

[1] This line of thought will be taken up again when we come to the very heart of our argument in chap. v.

poverish and compromise our faith in God. That is why it is necessary to retort: Are you sure that you know what you mean by 'God'? 'Whosoever denieth the Son, the same hath not the Father: he that confesseth the Son hath the Father also.'[1] That is as true against modern as it was against ancient Gnosticism. For the whole Christological question is a question about God.

For a whole generation now theology has been coming to a clearer understanding of this. We may think of William Temple's bold statement in an early essay (1912): 'The wise question is not "Is Christ Divine?" but "What is God like?"'[2] That may indeed be understood in a sense which would falsify the issue again by another over-simplification, and this has sometimes happened, with the suggestion that Christology can be exhausted in sayings such as 'God is like Jesus', 'Jesus reflects the character of God', 'Christianity gives us a Christlike God'. These sayings are doubtless true so far as they go, but they cannot stand by themselves. Dean Inge once wrote: 'The controversy about the Divinity of Christ has been habitually conducted on wrong lines. We assume that we know what the attributes of God are, and we collect them from any source rather than the revelation of God in Christ. . . . But surely Christ came to earth to reveal to us not that He was like God, but that God was like Himself.'[3] That was well said in its time, but to take it as the whole truth would be to fall into a common-sense simplification such as makes for heresy—in this case perhaps the Semi-Arian heresy which substituted *homoiousios* for *homoousios*! 'Like Christ' prompts the question, '*How* like?' and may lead either to an 'Ebionite' Christology or to the quite pagan (and Arian) conception of a demigod, an intermediate being who is neither God nor man. There is a sense in which it may truly be said that God cannot be like anyone else and that no one can be quite like God except God Himself. A true Christology will tell us not simply that God is *like* Christ, but that God was *in* Christ. Thus it will tell us not only about the *nature* of God, but about His *activity*, about what He has done, coming the whole way for our salvation in Jesus

---

[1] 1 John ii, 23.
[2] In *Foundations*, p. 259.
[3] W. R. Inge, *Outspoken Essays* (Second Series) (1922), p. 49.

Christ; and there is no other way in which the Christian truth about God can be expressed.

The Dialectical theologians of our age are most impressive in their assertion of this principle, that Christology is not a subsidiary study, or a limited department of Christian theology, but is at the very centre, and indeed is all-inclusive, because it is fundamentally concerned with our doctrine of God. Emil Brunner writes: 'The question, "What think ye of Christ?" is in no sense a deflection of interest from the main body of Christian truth. From the beginning this has always been the central question within the Christian Church, and from the outset the Christian answer to this question has always been the same: It is "the power of God unto salvation", as Paul defines the Christian faith. The question, "Who is He?" means the same as the other question, "What has God to say to us in Him?" The one cannot be answered without the other. . . . Unless you know who He is, you cannot know what God has to say to you. . . . For the question, "Who is He?" is the same one which says, "What part does God take in this whole process? What happens?" '[1] Karl Barth writes: 'An ecclesiastical dogmatic must indeed, as a whole and in all its parts, be Christologically determined, as surely as the revealed Word of God, attested by Holy Scripture and proclaimed by the Church, is its one and only criterion, and as surely as this revealed word is identical with Jesus Christ. If dogmatics does not in principle understand itself as Christology, and succeed in making itself intelligible as such, it has certainly succumbed to some alien domination, and has come very near to losing its character as ecclesiastical dogmatics.'[2]

It is quite plain that this is the kind of Christological interest that we find in the New Testament. We never find there anything that could be called a Jesus-cult, or a Christology interested simply in the question of who or what Jesus was, apart from the action of God the Father. Whatever Jesus was or did, in His life, in His teaching, in His cross and passion, in His resurrection and ascension and exaltation, it is really God that did it in Jesus: that is how the New Testament speaks. It becomes most striking of all

---

[1] Emil Brunner, *The Mediator* (Eng. trans.), p. 234. Cf. pp. 400ff.
[2] I have translated these sentences from Barth's *Kirchliche Dogmatik, Erster Band, Zweiter Halbband*, p. 135.

in connection with the reconciling death of Jesus. When His early followers spoke of His death on the cross as a supreme expression of love for men, it was not so much of the love of Jesus that they spoke as of the love of God who sent Him. In the New Testament we find no Prometheus as the suffering friend and helper of men, set over against a jealous High God. In the New Testament, as we shall see more fully in a later chapter, it is the love of God Himself that is seen in the sufferings of Christ. In the New Testament the love of Christ and the love of God are the same thing: the two phrases can be used interchangeably.[1] 'God was in Christ, reconciling the world unto Himself', and 'it is all of God'.[2]

It is true that in certain parts of the New Testament, not only in the early Petrine speeches in the Acts but in some of the Epistles, we seem to find the elements of a Christology which makes Christ a superhuman being and yet not quite a divine being: a being quite distinct from God and subordinate to Him. The same thing may be said of certain of the early Fathers after the ApostolicAge. This led the philosopher Locke to remark that 'the Fathers before the Council of Nicaea speak rather like Arians than orthodox'.[3] And it is curious to remember that the English Arians of the seventeenth century professed to base their position purely upon the direct study of the New Testament, taken as absolutely inerrant, and understood in the most naïvely literal way.[4] But it is easy for us to see how unhistorical and unfair this treatment of the New Testament material was. It was based upon the assumption that the function of the New Testament is to provide a complete, ready-made and final theology, which only needs to be pieced together by the student and then reproduced; whereas, in truth, if we use the New Testament in that way we shall merely falsify its real witness. Its function is not to provide us with a ready-made theology of the Christian faith (for the task of theology has to be done over again in age after age, and is never finished), but rather to witness to the faith. It comes from an age when Christian

---

[1] See Rom. vii, 35, 38f.
[2] 2 Cor. v, 18f.
[3] See King, *Life and Letters of John Locke* (1843), p. 297.
[4] See the interesting passage in John Dickie's *The Organism of Christian Truth*, pp. 219ff.

theology, as yet in its infancy, was but beginning to tackle the problems which have occupied theologians ever since; and to interpret and assess its theological beginnings in the light of later controversies would be an historical and theological blunder. The New Testament gives us not the final theology but the supreme and classical testimony to Christ.[1] And no one can maintain that this testimony, as a witness of faith and devotion, as an expression of the actual Christian attitude to Christ, falls short of the highest or savours of anything 'heretical'. There is nothing lacking in the *practical* Christology of the New Testament. In its conception of the coming and the work of Christ, 'everything is of God', and the love of Jesus is the love of God in a sense which makes nonsense of Arianism. So its whole theology is Christological, and its whole Christology is a witness to God as 'the Father of our Lord Jesus Christ'.

The same thing is essentially true of Patristic thought. The questionings of the Patristic writers about Jesus were questionings about His relation to the Father, and therefore were questionings about God. What kind of God could they be sure of? How far and in what way was God involved in the phenomenon of Jesus? That is the real significance of the Logos-Christology of the second, third, and fourth centuries, with its endless discussions, repeated and developed by one writer after another, about the nature of the Logos and the relation between the Logos and God. Sometimes these discussions appear to have little to do with Jesus. They have, in fact, everything to do with Him. For the belief that Jesus was the incarnation of the Logos was what gave these discussions such a burning interest for Christians. If Jesus was the incarnation of the Logos, then the vital question was that of the relation of the Logos to God, because on that hung the whole question of the character of God and His attitude to men. Was it the very God Himself that was manifested in Jesus?

To the earlier Logos-theologians the Logos was hardly a 'personal' being, but was the Wisdom or Glory or Reason or Word of God; or, more definitely, God's creative and condescending and redemptive purpose which leads Him out of His eternal self-

---

[1] Cf. Dorner's saying that the first age of the Church was that of the ἐκκλησία μαρτυροῦσα in contrast with the later ἐκκλησία θεολογοῦσα.

hood into the life of mankind. Thus when Justin, Irenaeus, Tertullian, Clement and Origen set themselves to grapple with the question as to whether the Logos was of the very being of God Himself from all eternity, the discussion was not on some remote point of ancient metaphysics. The question was: Is the redeeming purpose which we find in Jesus part of the very being and essence of God? Is that what God is? Is it His very nature to create, and to reveal Himself, and to redeem His creation? Is it therefore not some subordinate or intermediate being, but the Eternal God Himself, that reveals Himself to us and became incarnate in Jesus for our salvation?[1] When we come to the Arian controversy, the same issue becomes still plainer. It was not a matter of theological hairsplitting, or a dispute about a diphthong. It was not an argument as to whether there was in Jesus a supernatural incarnation of the heavenly pre-existent Logos or Son of God, for the Arians themselves believed that the Logos or Son of God, who had existed from before all ages in glory as a heavenly being above all angels, had come to earth through a virgin birth, lived a supernatural life in a human body, was crucified, rose from the dead, and ascended to heaven, to be worshipped with divine honours. They believed all that. But what availed all that, when they did not believe that this Logos was of one essence with God the Father? To the Arians God was remote, inaccessible, incapable of directly approaching the created world. And thus it is not the eternal God Himself that comes to us in Christ for our salvation, but an intermediate being, distinct from God, while God Himself is left out, uncondescending, unredemptive. That is what Athanasius and the Council of Nicaea would not be content with. They could not accept such a Christology because it involved a hopelessly unsatisfying theology, a sub-Christian view of God. 'Arius never speaks of the love of God.'[2] The Arian Christology was far simpler, far easier to state, far more readily popularized, than the paradoxical doctrine maintained by Athanasius and the Church. But it was again a case of the oversimplification which loses half the truth. And the more difficult

---

[1] It is important to remember that in the Philonic tradition the Logos, so far as hypostatized at all, was conceived as an intermediate being, between God and man.

[2] So Gwatkin.

Christology of Athanasius and the Church (however much it may have needed, and will need, restatement in successive ages) genuinely enshrined the truth of the Gospel, not only because of what it tells us about Jesus, but because of what it tells us about God.[1]

Dr. H. G. Wood, referring to Cicero's complaint that the gods of Epicurus *do* nothing, asserts that what appealed to the ancient world in Christianity was *God's action* in sending Christ.[2] It gave them a new view of God, which nothing else could do, and which could not be fully expressed except by the doctrine of divine Incarnation. In the beginning was the Word, and the Word was with God, and the Word was God. . . . And the Word became flesh, and dwelt among us . . . full of grace and truth.' Thus Christology is bound up with the whole Christian apprehension of God, and to leave it out would be to sink, perhaps unawares, to a sub-Christian theology. 'The saying of John', says Calvin, 'was always true: Whosoever denieth the Son hath not the Father. For though in old time there were many who boasted that they worshipped the Supreme Deity, the Maker of heaven and earth, yet as they had no Mediator, it was impossible for them truly to enjoy the mercy of God, so as to feel persuaded that He was their Father.'[8]

That is why those who wish to have God and the Jesus of history without Christology must be answered with the question: Are you sure that you know what you mean by God?

III

Christology and the Meaning of History

The other question that must be put is: Are you sure that you know what you mean by *history*? This brings us to another way in

---

[1] Bethune-Baker pointed out that in the Confession presented by Arius and his sympathizers to his Bishop about A.D. 321, the word 'Father', as applied to God, is actually avoided! See an article on 'Arius and Arianism', in *Expos. Times*, 1934.

[2] *Christianity and the Nature of History*, pp. 89, 93.

[8] Calvin, *Institutes* (tr. Beveridge), Book ii, chap. vi, §4. It is important to understand the difference between a 'Mediator' and an 'intermediate being'.

which in recent years the significance of Christology has been interpreted, especially in Protestant theology on the Continent; and this range of ideas seems worth considering at the present point of our study. I mean the ideas that Christology is essentially concerned with 'the meaning of history' and that its essential content is 'Christ as the centre or middle-point of history'. This is associated particularly with the name of Paul Tillich, to whom the Christological problem, far from being outworn and superannuated, is 'the most immediate problem of our present existence', because it is the question of the interpretation of history. This line of thought has been taken up to a greater or less degree by thinkers as diverse as Barth, Gogarten, Otto Piper, Hans-Dietrich Wendland, and there is something akin to it in the writings of C. H. Dodd and H. G. Wood in England and Reinhold Niebuhr in America.[1]

This is something new as compared with the discussions that have been going on among theologians for generations about the relation of Christian faith to history. Even in the early days of Christianity the problem of the relation of faith to events of mundane history was present in the struggle against Gnosticism and Neo-Platonism. With the rise of modern historical criticism the problem arose in a new form, when the historical elements in Christian belief came to be questioned from an historical point of view, and this has gone on ever since. Since the Christian creed contains statements about ancient events, it is at the mercy of historical criticism, and thus seems at the best to forfeit its certainty. How can we be quite sure about any alleged event in the ancient world, especially if the actual historical evidence is meagre? And how can Christian faith afford to be bound up with historical statements that are questionable? These questions have never been far from the minds of theologians since the time of the Enlightenment in the eighteenth century, and they were brought to a sharp point, which they have never quite lost, by the absurd controversy which flared up about the year 1910, under the influence of the completely negative conclusions of Arthur Drews, William Benja-

---

[1] As long ago as 1866, Westcott wrote: 'The Resurrection is the central point of history, primarily of religious history, and then of civil history, of which that is the soul.' *Gospel of the Resurrection*, p. 6. (Quoted A. M. Ramsey, *The Resurrection of Christ*, p. 79.)

min Smith and Paul Jensen, as to whether Jesus as an historical figure ever existed at all.

Under pressure of such problems, as well as of certain new political ideologies spreading in Europe, theological thought has in recent decades raised in a quite novel way the question as to what history itself is; and the very words 'history' and 'historical', which used to seem so clear, have become ambiguous and difficult and even mysterious.[1] The new thing is the idea that instead of history sitting in judgment on Christian faith, intimidating it, or putting it on the defensive, we should rather think of Christian faith sitting in judgment on our conceptions of history, or at least setting history in a new light and compelling us to reinterpret it. This is somewhat analogous to the process described in the earlier part of the present chapter (Section II), as regards the relation of Jesus to God—our rediscovery of the fact that Christology should be understood as telling us not merely what Jesus is but what God is, because only in Christ is God made plain to us. Similarly in regard to history, which we thought was a plain tale without any intrinsic mystery (even if it sometimes had perplexing problems of evidence), we are now being taught the lesson that we do not know what history is, or how to interpret it, until we get an absolute point of vantage from which to view it,[2] and that the very meaning of Christology is to show us that this point of vantage is to be found in Christ. Thus theological thought in our time has been concerning itself in a new way with 'the interpretation of history', 'the meaning of history', 'the clue to history'. It is not only that history remains a vast and undifferentiated chaos of non-significant detail unless we approach it with some principle of selection, some

---

[1] I find this especially in the most stimulating works of Reinhold Niebuhr. I think the difficulty is partly due to the fact that the English word 'history' may mean either the process of events or the *story* of that process, and sometimes means both together. In Niebuhr's usage the word seems most commonly to mean 'human existence on earth'—as it were, the human side of geography. But I do not think the difficulty exists only in English. I am not clear as to the relation between the German words, *Geschichte* and *Historie*; but it is worth noting that Martin Kähler, writing a book in defence of the real Christ as against 'the Jesus of history', called it *Der sogenannte historische Jesus und der geschichtliche biblische Christus* (1892).

[2] I need hardly mention that something similar has been said by philosophers like Croce in Italy and Collingwood in this country.

interest, some *questions to ask*, and therefore some 'values' to dictate the questions. There is also the further perception that history has no ultimate meaning, no pattern or direction—that indeed the human race on earth has no history in the true sense at all—unless some temporal point or points in it can be found to possess an absolute significance in the 'prophetic' or 'eschatological' sense; unless an absolute time-scheme, a *Heilsgeschichte*, a 'sacred history' can be perceived in it by faith. And according to Tillich the very meaning of Christology is the finding of the determinative point in Jesus Christ, the 'centre of history'. In the case of spatial measurements the beginning and the end of a track determine the location of its middle point; but in the case of history in the true sense the historical point which reveals the meaning of the whole process must be called the centre, because it alone gives a meaning to 'beginning' and 'end'. And for Christian faith that point is Christ.

'My Christology and Dogmatics', says Tillich, 'were determined by the interpretation of the cross of Christ as the event of history in which this divine judgment over the world became concrete and manifest.'[1] 'It is self-deception when profane interpretation of history, of the progressive or revolutionary, conservative or organic type, considers itself capable of treating history without regarding the Christological question.'[2] 'The old Christological struggle has been transformed into a struggle about a Christian or a semi-Pagan interpretation of history. . . . These questions replace the old question as to the relationship of the two natures in Christ.'[3]

There is an obvious kinship between Tillich's conception and the time-scheme that Karl Barth works out, in which the death and resurrection of Christ and the forty days that followed make an end in principle of the old sinful time of this world, 'the time of Pontius Pilate', and inaugurate the new time of Christ, in which His people live by faith, though they also have to live on in this world, subject

---

[1] Tillich, *The Interpretation of History*, p. 32. This is the title given to the volume containing the English translation of several short works by Tillich (*Scribners*, 1936). In citing sentences I have made some slight alterations in the translation.

[2] Ibid., p. 243.

[3] Ibid., p. 261 note. Tillich writes this with direct reference to the conflict of ideologies in Germany in the years between the two world wars.

to the conditions of the old time, for the 'interim' period which must elapse before Christ finally makes an end of history.[1] H.-D. Wendland uses in a similar way the idea of Christ as the centre of history.[2] Otto Piper criticizes Barth's and Tillich's use of the phrase, 'centre of history' with reference to Christ, saying that it implies a cyclic view of history which is incompatible with the biblical view.[3] But he himself uses the phrase as a description of the Church, and he treats the life and death of Christ as the turning-point of history even in a more positive (less 'dialectical') way than either Barth or Tillich. This was the end of the Old Aeon, in which satanic powers were at large. They are now fettered by Christ, and it is He that now determines the course of history, not they. This was literally a new start in history, by which the balance of power in this world was fundamentally changed, though even the New Aeon has a paradoxical character, and we still have to wait for the final consummation.[4] Somewhat similar to this is the 'realized eschatology' which Prof. C. H. Dodd works out on a basis of New Testament exegesis. In his view the New Testament *kerygma* is that the 'end of history', which gives a meaning to history, has actually entered the historical process in Christ, and yet not made an end of it in the temporal sense. It still goes on; but now its meaning is revealed, and believers can live in the new world revealed, the new creation.[5] Dr. H. G. Wood makes Christ a turning-point in history in a still more empirical and observable sense. He quotes Dr. A. D. Lindsay's dictum that the death of Socrates stopped the moral rot of Greece, and takes this as an analogy of how the death of Christ changed the human situation, so that 'life can never be the same again'.[6] This seems to me to be something quite different from what is meant by Barth and Tillich when they speak of Christ as the centre of history. They do not mean (though perhaps Piper does)

---

[1] For Barth's working out of this, see especially his *Credo*, and his *Kirchliche Dogmatik*, I, ii.

[2] See his essay in *The Kingdom of God and History*. ("Church, Community and State" Series, Vol.iii.)

[3] Otto Piper, *God in History*, p. 19 note.

[4] Ibid., pp. 19 note, 51f., 71, 116ff.

[5] C. H. Dodd, *The Apostolic Preaching*, *History and the Gospel* and an essay in *The Kingdom of God and History*.

[6] H. G. Wood, *Christianity and History*, pp. 10–32.

that the world is observably different since Christ came, in a way that can be traced empirically by an historian. (Only the 'Jesus of history' could be epochmaking in that sense!) They mean something much more 'dialectical'. And for the dialectical theologians generally Christian faith has no interest in Jesus as the 'Founder' of a religion whose achievements can be traced upon the page of history in an empirical account of 'the difference Christ has made' or of the *gesta Christi* through the ages.[1]

It is impossible in this place to discuss all these ideas and their relation to each other. But in the context of this present chapter it is important to clear our minds as to Tillich's view, that the reason why we must have a Christology is because the question of Christology is identical with the question of the meaning of history, and that the answer to this question is that Christ is the centre of history.

There is deep truth, it seems to me, in the idea that Christology stands for the Christian interpretation of history as against other interpretations. It is not only that the Christian belief about Christ gave a new meaning to history by transcending the ancient cyclic theory, though that is important enough. It is probably impossible for us to realize how meaningless the course of history was to the ancients, to whom it was an endless series of cycles, leading to nothing but unlimited repetition. There was indeed the Platonic and mystical method of escape from the shadows of the visible scene to the timeless realities of the realm of Forms; and there was the purely apocalyptic refuge of expecting an imminent divine intervention which would annihilate the whole process and provide something better. But each of these was really an escape. Neither of them gave history a positive meaning. It was Christianity that did this, by producing a real eschatology, a concrete time-scheme, a sacred story, which was firmly connected with history by the conviction that at its central point the Divine had actually come right into history. From that central point faith could look backwards and forwards, and everything fell into its place in a sacred story whose centre was the Christ who had come in the Flesh: Creation, Fall, Promise and Prophecy, the coming of Christ in the

---

[1] Cf. Emil Brunner, *The Mediator* (Eng. trans.), pp. 80 ff.

fulness of the time, His life and death and resurrection and ascension, the coming of the Holy Spirit, the Church and the spreading of the Gospel, the Second Coming and the final consummation. That is the story that overcame the cyclic view of history, and it all depends on the Christology at the heart of it.

But for us it is much more important to see how Christology is necessary as against *modern* misinterpretations of history, particularly the purely humanistic, evolutionary and 'progressive' view. We have been dealing in this chapter with the imaginary objector who wishes to have Christ without Christology, and I have suggested that such an attitude is really bound up with a sub-Christian conception of God. I now suggest that it is based on a conception of history which is humanistic and evolutionary rather than Christian. Jesus the pathfinder, the supreme seeker and discoverer of God, the crown and flower of humanity in its agelong upward struggle—is not that enough? But is it? If that were taken as the whole truth, as a substitute for the mysteries of Christology, would it not fit into a purely evolutionist philosophy much better than into the Christian view of history? Does it not indeed imply that the questioner is, perhaps unawares, working with such a philosophy of progress, of the 'ascent of man', culminating in Jesus? Even if he speaks of the 'finality' of Jesus, he may still be working with such a philosophy of history. Christian faith throughout the centuries has not spoken of 'finality', because it has not thought in terms of human progress. It has rather told a sacred story, stretching back into the past and on into the future, with Jesus of Nazareth as the determinative point; and it was not a story of human evolution or advance but of divine action from the Creation to the final consummation.

Now it is perfectly true that our theological forefathers made this a very short and simple story, foreshortening both the backward and the forward vista, and reducing the whole history of the world to a few thousand years, in a way that seems to us childishly naïve. We now look back to vast ages of geological time, and we look forward to possible millions of years for man on earth, so that instead of feeling that we are living in 'the end of the age', we may rather feel that (as the late Archbishop of Canterbury said) 'we are the early Christians'. Indeed in our version of 'the sacred

story' we should not regard either the creation or the consummation as events in history at all. Yet the sacred story, with the actual
historical Jesus at its centre, remains the indispensable expression
of the Christian view of history. And it is not simply a story of
human seeking and finding, of spiritual progress and discovery,
with Jesus as the climax. That is a true story from its own point of
view; but the very meaning of Christology is that there is something more to be said, something which sheds a new light on the
whole historical process, so that we can regard it not only as a
human development, but also, from the point of view of Christian
faith, as a story with a 'plot', God's eternal plan which 'was made
flesh' in Jesus Christ. To drop Christology is in effect to drop all
that—both the Christian view of God and the Christian view of
history, which are indeed bound up together.

Not that this answers the whole Christological question, or
exonerates us from the never-ending task of thinking out the
meaning of the Incarnation. It should rather point us to that task
with a new interest and understanding. I cannot think that Tillich
is right when he says that the old Christological battle about the
relationship of the two natures in Christ has been simply transformed into a battle between the Christian and a semi-pagan
interpretation of history, a controversy as to 'what the relation
should be between divine and human activity with respect to the
Kingdom of God'.[1] It is greatly to Tillich's credit as a theologian
that he has succeeded in rescuing the Christological problem from
the region of barren logomachy and in relating it closely to the
contemporary ideological struggle in which he himself has been so
'valiant for the truth upon earth'. But surely his Christology over-
reaches itself when he treats the dogma about the God-Man as
merely a symbol of the true nature of history, without any interest
in the question as to whether what the dogma says is true about an
actual historical Jesus. 'To practise Christology', he writes, 'does
not mean to turn backward to an unknown historical past or to
exert oneself about the applicability of questionable mythical categories to an unknown historical personality.'[2] With all his deep
interest in Christology he regards it as quite independent of the

---

[1] Op. cit., p. 261, with footnote.
[2] Op. cit., pp. 264f.

question whether Jesus ever existed as an historical personality at all.[1]

But if it is—if the idea of the incarnation of God in a man is a purely 'mythical' idea, which could not possibly be actualized in an historical person—then what light does it throw on history? It must surely be a false light. The Christian view of history cannot then be sound. The idea of God becoming man is indeed a marvellous idea, and if the thing happened, in however paradoxical and ineffable a sense, it must be by far the most epoch-making, the most 'historic', of all events, and its implications for the meaning of history are immense. But if it did not and could not actually happen, what then? It can hardly be 'historic' if it is not even historical! And if it *could* not happen, then history is *not* like that, after all! Tillich seems in fact to have 'one foot in sea and one on shore' as regards Christology. With all his insistence on the Christian interpretation of history, 'Christ as the centre of history', he appears to be held fast by the old Hegelian Christology which accepted all the dogmas, but only by dissolving them into symbolic truths (because the Absolute cannot pour its fulness into any one historical moment) and thus remained high and dry above the waves of historical criticism, but at the cost of handing history over to an evolutionary interpretation which falls short of the Christian view of history.

Christology stands for a Christian interpretation of history, but it can stand for that only because it stands for the conviction that God became man in the historical person of Jesus. We must have a Christology in that sense, or we have no Christology at all, and we cannot escape from its traditional problems by turning it into a symbolical philosophy of history.

IV

The Problem of Christology

What, then, is the question with which Christology has to deal?

---

[1] Ibid., p. 33.

I will bring this chapter to a close by endeavouring to set the question in as clear a light as possible, and will even say some quite simple and elementary things which need to be said over and over again in order to clear the ground of misunderstandings.

The Christian doctrine of the Incarnation does not mean that Jesus was not a man but a God. The New Testament writers knew very well that He was a man, and spoke of Him quite unequivocally as such; and few theologians now would make the distinction of saying that He is rather 'Man' than 'a man', though that distinction has sometimes been made in the past. Moreover, Christianity does not teach that Jesus was 'a God'. Indeed if we are using language in a truly Christian way, there is no such entity as 'a God'. There is only one God, and in the Christian sense there could not conceivably be more. Tertullian said: '*Deus, si non unus est, non est.*'[1] And Peter Damiani, the medieval divine, commenting on the words uttered by the serpent in Eden ('Ye shall be as gods', Gen. iii, 5) remarked that the Devil was the first grammarian when he taught men to give a plural to the word 'God'.[2] It should have neither a plural nor the indefinite article. It is a proper name.

Again, Christianity does not teach that Jesus was some kind of intermediate being, neither God nor man in the full sense, but something between. That mythical kind of being is quite familiar in ancient pagan religion, not to speak of Christian angelology; and so far as Christology is concerned, that is very much the conception of Christ that constituted the greatest of the heresies, Arianism. That is something quite different from the Christian doctrine of the Incarnation. When a New Testament writer tells us that 'there is one God and one Mediator between God and men', he does not mean that the Mediator belongs to some intermediate type of being, for he goes on at once to describe the Mediator as 'a man, Christ Jesus'.[3] Jesus was not something between God and Man: He was God *and* Man.

But, again, this does not mean that Jesus was simply God or the eternal Son of God inhabiting a human body for thirty years on

---

[1] Tertullian, *Adv. Marc.*, i, 3 (quoted by Barth).
[2] I owe this to G. G. Coulton, *Studies in Medieval Thought*, p. 87.
[3] 1 Tim. ii, 5.

earth, so that while the living physical organism was human, the mind or spirit was divine. That is another of the great heresies, the Apollinarian.[1] It would mean that Jesus was not truly and perfectly human, but that it was a case of God having a partly human experience, or even taking a temporary human disguise; which is much more like the old pagan stories of divine theophanies than like the Christian idea of Incarnation. It would mean that in the experience of Jesus we could draw a line between the divine and the human element, a boundary where the human ceased and the divine began, so that each was limited by the other. But Christianity teaches that there was no such boundary or limit to either the one or the other. Each covered the whole field on different planes. Jesus is God and Man ἀχωρίστως, without boundary.

But further, it does not mean that Jesus began by being a man, and grew into divinity, became divine. That is another idea that has often emerged in Christological thought but has never satisfied the Church. It is broadly what is known as Adoptionism. Christian theology has indeed sometimes, both in the early Greek Fathers and in the Eastern Orthodox tradition down to the present day, conceived the salvation of each one of us as a sort of deification, by which we are changed into the divine nature. But it has never said this about Jesus Christ. It has taught that what He is by nature we can become by adoption; or even that He became man in order that we might become God. This last expression itself must be suspect, because if taken strictly it would seem to imply either a pantheistic conception or the idea that there can be more gods than one. But even to speak of a man becoming *divine* involves us in manifest errors. It is not an accident that the adjective 'divine' hardly occurs in the New Testament.[2] The word belongs to quite a

---

[1] In maintaining that the σῶμα and the ψυχή of Jesus were human, Apollinaris was surely using ψυχή in the Aristotelian sense of 'life' or the 'vital principle' in a biological reference, so that he made the living body of Jesus to be human, and the mind or spirit (νοῦς, πνεῦμα) to be identical with the eternal Logos.

[2] In Acts xvii, 29, τὸ θεῖον is practically a substantive, meaning 'the Godhead', 'the Deity'. The only other passage is the very late 2 Pet. i, 3, 4, where the adjective appears twice: '. . . seeing that his divine power and virtue hath granted unto us all things that pertain unto life and godliness . . . that ye may become partakers of the divine nature. . . .'

different world.[1] Indeed it seems alien to the New Testament writers, in all the varieties of their Christology, not only to say that Jesus *became* divine, but even to say that He was or is divine. That is not how they would have put it, because in the world of the New Testament, even though it is written in Greek, the word God is a proper name, and no one could be divine except God Himself. Therefore it is more congenial to Christian theology to say that Jesus is God (with the further refinements of meaning provided by the doctrine of the Trinity) than to speak of Him as divine; and certainly it will not say that He *became* divine.

Does Christianity, then, teach that God changed into a Man? Is that the meaning of 'and was made man'? That at a certain point of time God, or the Son of God, was transformed into a human being for a period of about thirty years? It is hardly necessary to say that the Christian doctrine of the Incarnation means nothing like that. Such a conception bristles with errors. God does not change, and it would be grotesque to suggest that the Incarnation has anything in common with the *metamorphoses* of ancient pagan mythology. Moreover, it is highly important to remember that, according to Christian teaching, the deity and the humanity of Christ are not merely successive stages, as if they could not co-exist simultaneously. If no boundary can be drawn between them by way of analysing the constituents of His make-up ($\dot{\alpha}\delta\iota\alpha\iota\rho\acute{\epsilon}\tau\omega\varsigma$, $\dot{\alpha}\chi\omega\rho\acute{\iota}\sigma\tau\omega\varsigma$), neither can temporal boundaries be drawn, as if He had been first God, then Man, and then, after the days of His flesh were past, God again, with manhood left behind. These are all travesties of what Christian faith has to say about the Incarnation.

The misinterpretations that I have been rejecting in the last few pages are so crude and elementary, and the disclaimers are so familiar and obvious, that these pages must seem absurdly superfluous in a theological essay. Yet this rudimentary critique of old heresies has its own uses even to-day, as we may see in the chapters that follow. The total effect of the disclaimers is to repudiate every

---

[1] Cf. F. H. Brabant: 'We cannot but feel that the very wide employment of the adjective "divine" [in the age of Plotinus] was one of the things against which Christianity had to make a stand, in order to secure any real meaning for a "personal God".' Essay on 'Augustine and Plotinus', in the symposium, *Essays on the Trinity and the Incarnation*, p. 311.

possible over-simplification of the doctrine of the Incarnation. But the procedure has been entirely negative, and now we are left with an immense paradox upon our hands, the paradox of the God-Man. Some will maintain that this is as far as theology can ever go, and that it is vain for us to try to penetrate the mystery of *how* Jesus is both God and Man, since we are only men ourselves and not God. But it is impossible to acquiesce in the idea that nothing can be said about the Incarnation except in negatives, or that nothing more can be said than what was said in the great Creeds, which enshrined the mystery without explaining it. What the early Ecumenical Councils have done for us by their doctrinal decisions is the preliminary and negative task of repudiating the various errors, the heresies, which were always of the nature of over-simplifications. The definitions adopted were the right answers to the questions that were then being asked. But language is constantly changing and is always imperfect as a vehicle of meaning, and thus a theological question is never put in a really perfect form or in a form that will last for ever. St. Athanasius spoke of the Nicene Creed as στηλογραφία κατα πασῶν αἱρέσεων, 'a signpost against all heresies'.[1] That is exactly what it was. By rejecting the various errors it protected the mystery. But it does not relieve successive ages of the task of thinking out the meaning of the mystery. That is the perennial task of theology: to think out the meaning of the Christian conviction that God was incarnate in Jesus, that Jesus is God and Man.

God *and* Man: that conjunction 'and' is the crux. It is interesting to find two very different theologians, R. C. Moberly and Karl Barth, dwelling in their own ways on this fateful word 'and', pointing out that in that phrase it is given a very special use. According to Moberly, it is easy to over-emphasize the 'and': he suggests that Christ 'is not so much God *and* man as God in, and through, and as, man'.[2] Barth characteristically suggests on the other hand that in the phrase 'God and Man', and only in this phrase, has the word 'and' its legitimate theological use; and declares that this 'and' is the incomprehensible act by which the

---

[1] See Foakes-Jackson, *History of the Christian Church to A.D. 461.* 4th ed., p. 325.
[2] R. C. Moberly, *Atonement and Personality*, p. 96.

Word 'became' flesh.[1] These things must indeed always be beyond our comprehension, and yet the endeavour to understand them is the endless task of Christology.

---

[1] *Kirchliche Dogmatik*, i, ii, 150 and 176.

Chapter IV

CRITIQUE OF CHRISTOLOGIES

In this chapter I propose to discuss certain lines of Christological thought that have been prominent in modern theology. There seem to me to be three trends of thought that call for examination and criticism in the interests of our present purpose. First, there are the endeavours of various theologians to work out the meaning of the Incarnation on the basis of *Anhypostasia*, the old conception that in Christ there was no distinct human personality, but divine Personality assuming human nature. Second, there are the endeavours to build a Christology on the idea of the divine *Kenosis*—the so-called Kenotic theories. Third, there is the very distinctive Christology of Karl Heim, which works with the ideas of Leadership and Lordship.

I

Anhypostasia

Several modern theologians have taken up and sought to work out in modern terms the ancient doctrine that Christ is not a human person, but a divine Person who assumed human nature without assuming human personality—the doctrine that gave rise to the familiar phrase, 'the impersonal humanity of Christ'. It was in the controversy with Nestorius in the fifth century that this idea was set forth by Cyril of Alexandria (though some writers maintain that it was actually anticipated by the heretical Apollinarius). Nestorius, who refused to call the Virgin Mary 'Theotokos',

'Mother of God', maintaining that she was not the Mother of the eternal Divine Son but of the human Jesus, was accused of dividing Christ into two persons. Against this position Cyril worked out the idea, which passed into Catholic dogma, that there was no man Jesus existing independently of the Divine Logos: the human element in the Incarnation was simply human *nature* assumed by the Second Person of the Trinity. There was no human *hypostasis* or *persona*: the *persona* was the Divine Son, while the human nature was ἀνυπόστατος—'impersonal humanity'. And this may seem *prima facie* to be an answer to the question of how Christ can be God and Man without being two distinct individuals.

Now it is notoriously difficult to determine what precisely this doctrine meant when it was first enunciated and accepted by the Church. Unless we are careful we shall find ourselves understanding it in a sense very difficult to distinguish from the Apollinarianism which had already been condemned, or in a sense very similar to the Monothelite heresy which was subsequently condemned. It is easy to understand its negative bearing, as a repudiation of what was taken to be the Nestorian position. But it is highly doubtful whether the phrase 'impersonal humanity' conveys what was intended, just as it is likely that *hypostasis* and *persona* did not mean just what we mean by either *person* or *personality*. And few theologians now would defend the phrase or would hesitate to speak of Jesus as a man, a human person. H. R. Mackintosh wrote: 'If we are not to trust our intuitive perception that the Christ we read of in the Gospels is an individual man, it is hard to say what perception could be trusted.'[1] R. C. Moberly wrote: 'Human nature which is not personal is not human nature.'[2]

Yet Moberley also wrote the following passage, which seems to me to slip into the false idea that Christ is 'man', but not *a* man: 'If He might have been, yet He certainly was not, a man only, amongst men. His relation to the human race is not that He was another specimen, differing by being another from everyone except Himself. His relation to the human race was not a differentiating but a consummating relation. He was not generically, but in-

---

[1] H. R. Mackintosh, *The Doctrine of the Person of Jesus Christ*, p. 390.
[2] R. C. Moberly , *Atonement and Personality*, p. 92.

clusively, man.'[1] Here is error, surely, mingled with truth. Surely whatever else Jesus was, He was a member of the human race, the human species, a man among men, or one man among others. However true may be the conception of human solidarity, or of the solidarity of Christ with mankind, or of Christ as the 'representative Man' through whom we come to God, it remains true that He was a man among men. Let us remember that, while 'God' is not a common noun but a proper name, the word 'man' is simply and purely a common noun; so that, while to speak of Jesus as 'a God' is nonsense from a Christian point of view, it is equally nonsense to say that He is 'Man' unless we mean that He is a man. 'Man' in any 'inclusive' sense can only mean either the whole human race or human nature, which in itself is an abstraction.[2] And to say that Jesus is either of these would plainly be absurd.

I find it equally difficult to understand Professor Hodgson when, without tying himself to such language as 'the impersonal humanity of Christ' or 'not a man but Man', he declares nevertheless that the doctrine underlying these phrases is 'essential to any adequate Christology'.[3] 'We should ... think of the Incarnation as the entry by One who is divine upon an experience of life under certain conditions, namely, those which are involved in being the subject of experiences mediated through a body in this world of space and time; for to be the subject of such experiences is to be human.'[4] 'What we mean by manhood in its most spiritual essence, its νοῦς (to use Apollinarius's term), is to be the self-conscious subject of experiences mediated through a human body', and 'the Incarnation is to be thought of as the entry upon experience of such a life by the divine Logos'.[5] Professor Hodgson's aim here is,

---

[1] Ibid., p. 86.

[2] Cf. H. R. Mackintosh: 'In the domain of reality there is no such thing existing independently as *humanitas*, or "man in general". ... No one can represent a man who also *is* the nature common to all members of the class "man".' Ibid., p. 389. But Professor Otto Piper takes a different view, asserting as against medieval Nominalism that the essence of a genus is *not* a mere abstraction but has genuine subsistence. *God in History*, pp. 55ff.

[3] Leonard Hodgson, in *Essays on the Trinity and the Incarnation*, edited by Rawlinson, p. 383.

[4] Ibid., p. 379.

[5] Ibid., p. 387.

having replaced the philosophy of 'substance' by a sound modern philosophy of the self as 'subject', to restate the catholic doctrine of the Incarnation in modern terms. But the Christology which he reaches seems to me to be a restatement in modern terms, not of the catholic doctrine, but rather of the Apollinarian heresy. According to this heresy, while the physical and biological element ($\sigma\hat{\omega}\mu\alpha$ and $\psi\upsilon\chi\acute{\eta}$) in Jesus, i.e. His living body, was human, the mind ($\nu o\hat{\upsilon}s$ or $\pi\nu\epsilon\hat{\upsilon}\mu\alpha$) which functioned through it was not a human mind, but was identical with the Divine Logos.[1] Doubtless Apollinarius interpreted the working of this in a much more docetic way than would Professor Hodgson: he assimilated the humanity of the incarnate life to the life of God, whereas Professor Hodgson would give a very human account of it. Yet I would submit, with the greatest respect, that the latter's theory seems very like an unconscious acceptance of the Apollinarianism with which Cyril's doctrine has so often been charged. The only 'mind', he seems to teach, that was in the incarnate Christ was the divine mind of the Second Person of the Trinity, which entered on a human experience by functioning through a human body. Does this mean that the Son of God changed into a man? It is impossible to believe that Professor Hodgson would wish to put it in that way. But if Jesus was not a man at all, but simply the divine Son of God having experience through a human body, so that the only 'subject' of the experience was God the Son, there seems to be no room left for what we surely find in the Gospel story: Jesus as a man having experience of God in faith and prayer, where God is not the 'subject' but the object.[2]

The same difficulty occurs to one immediately on reading Emil

---

[1] If Apollinarius sometimes makes a twofold, sometimes a threefold, division of human nature, it makes no difference at this point. To him the $\sigma\hat{\omega}\mu\alpha$ and the $\psi\upsilon\chi\acute{\eta}$ meant simply the body with its vital principle, in other words the living body; and his doctrine was that while in other men the living body is inhabited by a human mind ($\nu o\hat{\upsilon}s$ or $\pi\nu\epsilon\hat{\upsilon}\mu\alpha$), in Christ it was inhabited by the divine Logos.

[2] I do not question that there may be a sense in which God has experience of God, or God as subject has experience of God as object. That may, as has often been said, be one of the truths enshrined in the doctrine of the Trinity. But surely that was not what was happening in the Incarnation, in those parts of our Lord's experience which we may describe as His faith in God and His praying to God.

Brunner's interpretation of the *anhypostasia*.[1] He makes a distinction between the 'personality' of Jesus, as an observable historical phenomenon, and His 'Person', which is a hidden suprahistorical mystery. The former is purely human, the latter is divine. The former is simply the 'human nature' assumed by the Second Person of the Trinity, taking the place of a human 'person' in Jesus. Brunner means that in every man there is this distinction between the inner mystery of the 'person', the ultimate subject, on the one hand, and on the other hand the historical 'personality'. This seems to be simply the familiar distinction made by psychologists between the 'transcendental ego' and the 'empirical ego'. But then it must be sheer nonsense to maintain that in the case of Jesus the one was divine while the other was human. For the transcendental and the empirical ego are not distinct entities at all, but the two sides of the same entity, the ego observed from without as object and the ego lived from within as subject. Each is a sheer abstraction when separated from the other, for a man is one ego, not two. But apart from that, if the only 'subject' in the experience of Jesus was God the Son, what was happening when Jesus was praying to God (which is such a characteristic feature of the Gospel story)?[2] To explain this away would be sheer docetism, and Brunner would hardly maintain that it was the Second Person of the Trinity praying to the First Person. Was it then the human nature of Jesus praying to God? That is meaningless, for 'human nature' thus separated is an abstraction.

In some passages Brunner seems to teach that it is sin that makes each one of us personally distinct from God, and that sinless humanity, as it exists in Jesus, would have no such personal distinctness from God. Thus instead of the mystery of a human 'person', which is sin, Christ has the mystery of the divine 'Person'. 'To be a human being means to be a sinner',[3] and so it would follow that Jesus was not a human being: His 'Person' was identical with God.

---

[1] Emil Brunner, *The Mediator* (Eng. trans.), pp. 265ff., 318ff., 345–54.

[2] It is strongly emphasized also in Heb. v, 7.

[3] Op. cit., pp. 145, 319ff., 346, 498. I have no idea how this is to be reconciled with another idea, very much sounder, which Brunner uses elsewhere, that 'only in the Word are we personal'. See p. 347, note: but see also Brunner's *The Divine Imperative* (Eng. trans. of *Das Gebot und die Ordnungen*), p. 606, where he rejects 'the Gnostic idea . . . that individuality is the result of sin'.

But is that sound teaching? Fallen mankind is indeed sinful, but it is highly heretical to teach that man is *essentially* sinful.[1] Moreover it is extremely significant that this was precisely the basic error in the thought of Apollinarius, which led him into his great Christological heresy about the humanity of Christ. All this does, as it seems to me, lead straight to Apollinarianism, if it leads anywhere at all.

Some years ago Dr. H. M. Relton wrote a scholarly and suggestive essay in Christology,[2] in which, recognizing that 'impersonal humanity' is a meaningless phrase, he passed from *anhypostasia* to the *enhypostasia* proposed by Leontius of Byzantium and John of Damascus: the idea that the humanity of Christ, while not impersonal, can be described as not having *independent* personality, but being personal in the Logos. The human nature is personalized in the Divine Logos which assumes it, and is thus not impersonal (ἀνυπόστατος) but 'in-personal' (ἐνυπόστατος). Dr. Relton soundly argues that 'without God, human personality is incomplete, and that He alone can supply it with that which alone can help it to its full realization'. From this it is a natural conclusion that the manhood of Christ is not less personal but more fully personal than that of any other man, because of its complete union with God, and certainly Dr. Relton regards Him as not only 'Man' but *a* man in the fullest sense. This is a real contribution, and I find it very congenial and instructive. But I cannot help feeling that it is a pity to express it in terms of *enhypostasia*. It is difficult to see why this term, with all its associations, should be used at all unless it is meant to indicate that, even if the human nature of Christ is 'personalized' in the hypostatic union, the 'subject' is

---

[1] Brunner actually writes the following: 'We are sinners because we are human beings; the idea of a sinless historical human life is from the Christian point of view an impossible idea.' (Ibid., p. 320.) How does Brunner reconcile this with his belief that Jesus lived a sinless life on earth, or even with the belief, which he doubtless holds, that the redeemed in heaven live sinless lives without ceasing to be men? They are not living 'historical' lives, as on earth, but they are still human beings.

[2] H. M. Relton, *A Study in Christology*. Dr. Relton is not the first to develop this idea of *enhypostasia*, as distinct from *anhypostasia*, in Western Christendom. Some of the early Reformed theologians made regular use of the idea. See A. B. Bruce, *The Humiliation of Christ*, App., Sect. iii, note E.

always and exclusively the Second Person of the Trinity; and that would at once bring back all our difficulties as regards Jesus having a human experience of God.

Moreover, there seems to be no sound reason why we should feel constrained to think in terms of either *anhypostasia* or *enhypostasia* in our Christology. If it is the case (as many at least will agree that it is) that the technical term *hypostasis* or *persona* in the statement of Trinitarian doctrine does not mean just what we mean by 'person' in modern speech, the 'hypostatic union' surely cannot be translated *simply* as 'personal identity', and it is difficult to put a clear meaning into the idea of one *hypostasis* or *persona* of the Trinity taking the place of a human centre of consciousness in a human life. If, on the other hand, we maintain that Jesus was in every sense a human person with a human centre of consciousness, while being also the Incarnation of the divine Word, the second *persona* of the Trinity, there is no reason why that should be taken as implying the Nestorian heresy of dividing Christ into two persons—a heresy which may never have existed in that form except in the imagination of its opponents, and which Nestorius himself, whatever may have been his errors, almost certainly never entertained. [1]

I do not know whether Father Thornton's Christology in his difficult book, *The Incarnate Lord*, should be classed among modern re-interpretations of the *anhypostasia*. But so far as I can understand his argument, it seems to me, like other views which I have been criticizing, to exclude the possibility of recognizing the Jesus of the

---

[1] As long ago as 1876 Professor A. B. Bruce had the insight to raise the question: 'Were Nestorius and those who thought with him *Nestorians* in the theological sense?' He concluded that it was only by implication, and not by conscious intention, that they occupied the 'Nestorian' position of dividing Christ into two persons (*The Humiliation of Christ*, 1st ed., pp. 64f.). Since then this has been more than confirmed through the discovery in a Syriac translation of a work of Nestorius himself which had always been known to the Assyrian (Nestorian) Christians, though unknown to the western world. (An edition with English translation was published in 1915 by G. R. Driver and Leonard Hodgson under the title, *The Bazaar of Heracleides*.) The discovery led to the publication of two excellent little monographs on Nestorius: J. F. Bethune-Baker, *Nestorius and His Teaching* (1908) and Friedrich Loofs, *Nestorius and His Place in the History of Christian Doctrine* (1914). Both of these books defend Nestorius against misinterpretation, and it is now pretty generally agreed among theologians that, whether Nestorius was orthodox or not, he was never a 'Nestorian'.

Gospel story as a real man. Father Thornton bases his Christology on the idea that the Incarnation is the final stage in the ascending series of organic unifications which the scientists call evolution; so that apparently the relation of Jesus to humanity is somewhat of the same kind as the relation of humanity to the merely animal world. 'In each new level which appears all the previous levels are representatively taken up and included; so that at the summit of the series man is in some sense a microcosm of the whole, including within himself all levels of the series. The series is thus taken up in man on to the level of spirit. But it does not reach its end in man, because he shares the unfinished character of the series. Now if the Incarnation brings creation to its true end in God, this must mean that the cosmic series is gathered up into the human organism of Jesus Christ. . . . As the series is taken up into the human organism, so in Christ the human organism is taken up on to the "level" of deity.'[1] But on this view it would surely be impossible to regard Jesus as a man among men, a member of the human species: He would belong rather to a further stage, and would be a new species. It is vain to reply that man not only belongs to a higher species than all other animals, but is also himself an animal, taking up into himself all the previous stages. For the 'animal' in man is a different thing from the animal on lower levels, being transformed by the new unification on the level of spirit. The body of a man is different in essential ways from the bodies of other animals; and the mind of a man is very different from the mind of any other animal (even if it is difficult to know precisely where and how to draw the line)—so different that we cannot penetrate far into the latter. So far as we do try to penetrate, we speak of 'animal psychology', realizing that it is a very different thing from human psychology, and that even its instincts are not the same as the corresponding human instincts. Similarly it seems to me that, on Father Thornton's theory, we should need a 'divine psychology' for the interpretation of the mind of Jesus Christ, for His mind would not function as a human mind. Such a Christology would, with the best will in the world, run inevitably into Apollinarianism or Monophysitism or some form of Docetism. The divine and the

---

[1] L. S. Thornton, *The Incarnate Lord*, p. 225.

human are brought together in such a way that the human no longer remains truly human in Christ. His humanity becomes quite different from ours; whereas catholic Christianity has always taught that His humanity is essentially the same as ours, that in respect of His manhood He was of one essence (*homoousioos*) with ourselves. Neither His body nor His mind was *essentially* different from the bodies or minds of other men. He was in every sense a member of the human race.[1]

Thus in spite of the difficulty and complexity of Father Thornton's argument, his theory appears to me to be one more oversimplification of the Christological problem. The relation between the divine and the human in the Incarnation is really much more paradoxical, a much deeper mystery. We have to reckon with a life that was wholly human and wholly divine, neither side limiting the other at all.

As regards the conception of *anhypostasia*, I do not question that in its day and in its environment it played a useful and necessary part, mainly as a bulwark against any kind of Adoptionism which would speak of Jesus as having independently attained such a height of human goodness that God at last stepped in and chose and adopted Him to divine honours. That brings God in at the end. But a true Christology will bring God in at the beginning, realizing that in the life of Jesus from the start there was no independence of God. Jesus lived His life in complete dependence on His Father, as we all ought to live our lives. But such dependence does not destroy human personality. Man is never so truly and fully personal as when he is living in complete dependence on God. That is how human personality comes into its own. This is not 'impersonal humanity', but humanity at its most personal.[2] The only *anhypostasia* in the case is not a denial of personality, but a denial of independence,[3] and it seems to me to be misleading to call it by that name.

---

[1] My criticism of Fr. Thornton's view is, I think, fundamentally the same as the criticism made by Dr. J. K. Mozley in a passage to which I feel myself directly indebted. See Mozley, *The Doctrine of the Incarnation*, pp. 146f.

[2] This point will be elaborated in chap. v.

[3] As Dr. Relton sees.

II

Kenosis

The Kenotic Theory of the Incarnation belongs distinctively to modern times. It takes its title indeed from St. Paul's language in the second chapter of the Epistle to the Philippians, where he says that Christ 'emptied himself' (ἑαυτὸν ἐκένωσεν),[1] and the idea of the divine self-emptying has been widely used in Christian theology. But the Kenotic Theory is something more specific and can hardly claim the direct support of that lyrical Pauline passage or mistake its poetry for theological theory.[2] It is doubtful whether anything corresponding to the theory can be found in ancient Christian thought.[3] The beginnings of it in the modern world are sometimes traced to Zinzendorf, but it was only in the nineteenth century that the idea was taken up and elaborated theologically as a theory of the Incarnation, mainly on the European continent. During the last half century it has played a considerable part in British theology, and has been adopted by a good many prominent divines in this country as a basis for Christology. I do not propose to examine the details of these various essays in Christological thinking which can be regarded as forms of the modern Kenotic Theory, but only to scrutinize the central idea and to ask whether it really meets the problem of the Incarnation.

According to the central idea of the Kenotic Theory, what happened in the Incarnation was that the Son of God, the Second Person of the Trinity, the Divine Logos, laid aside His distinctively

---

[1] Phil. ii, 7.

[2] Some scholars hold that in this passage St. Paul is not using his own language but is quoting an early Christian hymn.

[3] On the question whether support can be found in the Patristic age for the Kenotic Theory, see J. M. Creed, *The Divinity of Jesus Christ*, p. 77, and also Creed's essay in *Mysterium Christi*, p. 133. He quotes Thomasius of Erlangen, the founder of modern Kenoticism, as admitting that very little definite support for the theory can be found in Patristic literature; and he quotes Friedrich Loofs of Halle in a similar sense. 'The nearest approach to it is to be found in the heresiarch Apollinarius', who said, 'Incarnation is self-emptying'.

divine attributes (omnipotence, omniscience, omnipresence) and lived for a period on earth within the limitations of humanity.

It is easy to see why this theory belongs peculiarly to the modern world, and why in the modern world it looks at first sight very promising. It is because it apparently enables us to combine a full faith in the deity of Jesus Christ with a completely frank treatment of His life on earth as a human phenomenon, the life of a man. Thus it tackles the Christological problem in the peculiarly sharp form which it has assumed in modern times. It gets away entirely from the docetism which has so often infected Christology and which explained away the humanity of Jesus by applying to the story of His life a kind of supra-human psychology. It is able to go the whole way in using human categories about Jesus: He lived a man's life, His mind worked as a man's mind, His knowledge was limited to human knowledge, His equipment to human equipment. But then in what sense was He God? How could God be so limited? The Kenotic Theory has a ready answer. Jesus was indeed identical with the eternal Son of God, one in essence with the Father and equal in power and glory. But in becoming incarnate He 'emptied Himself' of those attributes which essentially differentiate God from man; so that the life He lived on earth was a truly human life, without omnipotence or omnipresence or omniscience, a life subject to the conditions and limitations of humanity, as are the lives of all men. Thus we seem to get a real God-Man, and an intelligible meaning for the Incarnation, thoroughly congruous both with the New Testament idea of the divine condescension and self-emptying and with the modern treatment of the Gospel story and the rediscovery of the 'Jesus of history'.

Yet I cannot think that this use of the idea of divine self-emptying will bear examination. To say this is not to deny that the *kenosis* of which St. Paul speaks is a reality to which a place must be given in Christian thought. But I cannot think that its right place is that which has been given to it by the holders of the Kenotic Theory in the specific sense indicated above, as a solution of the problem of Christology, a theological account of what happened in the Incarnation. To this there seem to be insuperable objections, which I will proceed to indicate.

1. I am not aware that a good reply has yet been made to the

simple question asked by the late Archbishop of Canterbury in objection to the Kenotic Theory. 'What was happening', he asked, 'to the rest of the universe during the period of our Lord's earthly life? To say that the Infant Jesus was from His cradle exercising providential care over it all is certainly monstrous; but to deny this, and yet to say that the Creative Word was so self-emptied as to have no being except in the Infant Jesus, is to assert that for a certain period the history of the world was let loose from the control of the Creative Word.'[1] It is vain to reply that the question presupposes a crude and false separation of the Persons of the Trinity from each other, or to quote the sound principle: *opera Trinitatis ad extra sunt indivisa*. For the Kenotic Christology itself presupposes precisely such a separation, and could not even be stated without it. Thus any crudity or naïveté which may seem to characterize the Archbishop's question derives directly from the theory which it is intended to criticize, since his method is that of *reductio ad absurdum*. Is there any answer?

2. Instead of giving us a doctrine of Incarnation in which Jesus Christ is both God and man, the Kenotic Theory appears to me to give us a story of a temporary theophany, in which He who formerly was God changed Himself temporarily into man, or exchanged His divinity for humanity. This is true even if the Kenoticist maintains the *anhypostasia* in the sense of impersonal humanity. For though the Son of God thus keeps His personal identity in becoming the subject of the human attributes which He assumes, He has divested Himself of the *distinctively divine* attributes; which would imply, if language means anything, that in becoming human He ceased to be divine. If, however, the Kenoticist gives up the idea of the *anhypostasia*, impersonal humanity, and regards Jesus as in every sense *a* man, a human person (as do some holders of the Kenotic Theory)[2] then the situation becomes still stranger. The Kenoticist would then be involved in saying that He who before the Incarnation had been a divine Being now turned into a man, with human instead of divine attributes, for the time. He *had been* God, but now He was a man. If taken in all its implications, that seems more like a pagan story of metamorphosis than like the

---

[1] William Temple, *Christus Veritas*, pp. 142f.
[2] E.g. H. R. Mackintosh.

Christian doctrine of Incarnation, which has always found in the life of Jesus on earth God and man in simultaneous union—the Godhead 'veiled in flesh' but not *changed into* humanity. Surely the relation between the divine and the human in the Incarnation is a deeper mystery than this.[1]

3. The difficulties of the Kenotic Theory become still greater when we go on to ask: Was the *kenosis* merely temporary, confined to the period of the Incarnation of the Son of God, the days of His flesh on earth? The holders of the theory would *logically* have to answer: Yes. The presupposition of the theory is that the distinctive divine attributes (of omniscience, etc.) and the distinctive human attributes (of finitude) cannot be united simultaneously in one life: that is why the Incarnation is explained as a *kenosis*. Therefore when the days of His flesh come to an end, Christ resumes His divine attributes, and His *kenosis*, his humanity, comes to an end. His human life is left behind when He ascends to the right hand of the Father. Thus, on the Kenotic theory in that specific sense (which is what we are concerned with) He is God and Man, not simultaneously in a hypostatic union, but *successively* —first divine, then human, then God again. But if that is really what the theory amounts to—and I do not see how it can be otherwise interpreted—it seems to leave no room at all for the traditional catholic doctrine of the *permanence* of the manhood of Christ, 'who, being the eternal Son of God, became man, and so was, *and continueth to be*, God and man in two distinct natures, and one person, *for ever*'.[2] Now it may indeed be exceedingly difficult to interpret this doctrine and to answer all the questions which it raises.[3] But if we state the problem in such terms at all, surely we cannot deny the doctrine altogether and maintain that the human nature of Christ ended when the days of His flesh on earth ended. That would make nonsense of the Incarnation, and indeed would indi-

---

[1] It is interesting to find Father Bulgakov, of the Eastern Orthodox Church, who himself makes large use of the idea of divine *kenosis* in another way, writing as follows: 'It is essential to realize that, contrary to the various kenotic theories of Protestantism, our Lord in His abasement never ceased to be God, the second Person of the Holy Trinity.' Sergius Bulgakov, *The Wisdom of God*, p. 134.

[2] *Westminster Shorter Catechism*, Ans. to Q. 21 (my italics).

[3] On this see chap. vi, sect iv, below.

cate that the theorist did not regard Jesus Christ as a real man at all.[1]

It may occur to the reader to object that the above criticism is made in forgetfulness of the distinction between time and eternity. While we men live in time, and our experience is subject to the limitations of temporality and successiveness, God 'inhabits eternity', and no temporal accounts of His activity can be adequate to the 'eternal' quality of His life. We are compelled to speak of His activity in temporal terms, but unless we keep reminding ourselves of their inadequacy, we shall continually be making difficulties for our thinking. That is quite true. But if it applies to my criticism of the Kenotic Theory, it is because it applies first of all to the theory itself. The Kenotic Theory of the Incarnation depends on a temporal way of describing the divine activity, and if we try to express it in a purely non-temporal way, the theory disappears.

There are other ways in which Christian theology can use the idea of divine *kenosis*. Russian Orthodox thought has made considerable use of the idea, not only in connection with Incarnation and Atonement, but as indicating something which is involved in Creation itself, and even in the Trinity.[2] But that is something quite different from the Kenotic Theory as a Christology, and this last is what I find unacceptable.

III

Leadership and Lordship

Under this heading I propose to examine the Christological theory worked out by Professor Karl Heim of Tübingen in his book

---

[1] Professor Horst Stephan of Marburg, in his well-known *Glaubenslehre* (p. 146), criticized the modern Kenotic Theory as follows. By conceiving the Incarnation as a real self-limitation of the Second Person of the Trinity (instead of a divine *assumptio* of human nature) the theory makes God mutable, and also *either* robs the historical Jesus of the divine element *or* destroys his humanity. Stephan was thinking of the Kenotic Theory in German theology, mainly at Erlangen, in the second half of last century.

[2] See Bulgakov, *The Wisdom of God*, pp. 133ff., and Gorodetzky, *The Humiliated Christ in Modern Russian Thought*, chap. v.

entitled *Jesus der Herr*.[1] It seems worth while to include this in our study, not only because of the great eminence which Heim has rightly enjoyed as a theologian, but also because of the very distinctive and original nature of his Christology.

Heim takes the notion of Leadership (*Führerschaft*) which is so widespread to-day, as his clue to a satisfying Christology. The Hellenistic cults of the ancient world created the new religious category of Kyrios (κύριος) which found its true fulfilment in Christ as Lord, and the category of Leadership has a similar significance for to-day. Thus, according to Heim, we are in a better position to-day than were our forefathers of the Enlightenment or of the Idealistic period for the understanding of the Lordship of Jesus, because instead of concentrating on true *ideas* we know what it is to give unconditional obedience to a Leader (*Führer*). (This would seem to imply that democracy makes against the understanding of New Testament Christianity!) In this fallen world, infected as we are with original sin, it is impossible for us men to rise above the polarity of our earthly experience and to guide our own lives or have any direct knowledge of God. Therefore we need a Leader whom we can unquestioningly follow, and God has given us such a Leader in Jesus. This does not mean that Jesus left behind Him a code to be obeyed. The original apostles seldom quote the words of Jesus for the guidance of themselves or of the Church. Leadership must be something more direct. It must be an I-Thou relationship between the Leader and his followers, giving present guidance at each moment, and the early Christians were conscious of Jesus as a living Lord with whom they were in touch. Can we have the same experience? Yes, we can, and we must, if Jesus is to be our Leader and Lord. We can have it through the Holy Spirit. The Holy Spirit is the encompassing medium or continuum in which we can have direct contact with Jesus, and it is only in that moment-to-moment contact with our Leader that we can have any knowledge of God at all. We cannot say why it is

---

[1] *Jesus der Herr* is the second volume of a tetralogy, the general title of which is *Der evangelische Glaube und das Denken der Gegenwart*. The first volume of the series has been translated into English by Professor E. P. Dickie under the title of *God Transcendent*, but *Jesus der Herr* is not available in English.

precisely at that point that we find the leadership we need. For we do not choose our Leader, but He chooses us, and it is not a case of our taking possession of Him in the sense of accepting His ideas, His programme, His ethic, as our own. That would turn the I-Thou relationship into an I-It relationship. No, we simply follow our Leader, through direct contact with Him. There is no reason why we should not have such a relationship with Jesus who lived on earth nineteen centuries ago; for the I-Thou relationship is independent of space and time, and transcends all temporal and geographical distances. So Jesus becomes our contemporary, and this direct personal relation to Him is the very essence of Christianity. Thus the relation between God and man is permanently changed since Christ came: not in the sense that we have direct access to God or direct knowledge of Him (to claim that would be to anticipate the final consummation) but in the sense that we have Jesus as a living contemporary, to lead us to God. That is the meaning of having Jesus as Leader, and that is Heim's Christology.

I find it is impossible to study this Christology without the uneasy feeling that the 'leader' category, which it uses as its clue, is not being used in its most worthy sense. Leadership is constantly spoken of to-day, in many different quarters, and perhaps too much, as one of the great needs of the age. But surely there is a false and a true, and the true leadership is not that which merely demands blind and unintelligent assent and obedience. The true leader 'gives a lead' to the people by endeavouring to 'carry them with him' in an intelligent perception and acceptance of his objectives. He is indeed ahead of them and can see farther, but he is eager to let them see for themselves as much as possible of what he sees. It seems plain that in the moral and religious realm, and even in social and political life apart from very limited and temporary objectives, this is the only kind of leadership that is of any value at all. The other kind, which demands *blind* obedience, has played havoc with human life in our own time. Yet it is this latter that Heim appears to take as his clue to Christology. His thesis, indeed, is that Christ and Christ alone is called to exercise that absolute leadership which has with disastrous consequences been arrogated to themselves by other leaders. He is the one true Leader and Lord. Thus Heim's thesis may be regarded as a valiant Christian retort to those other claims, and it is in that spirit that it was put forward in an environment which made all Christian protest difficult and perilous. But can the category of leadership, as Heim conceives it, yield a sound Christology?

Let us examine his meaning more closely. What does Heim mean when he asks and answers the question whether and why we need a *Führer* in the life of faith? Is he simply asking the old question whether we need an absolute *external* authority in religion? At some points that appears to be what he means; and if he meant an internal authority, why should he have to take so much trouble to prove our need? What he has to prove is the necessity of an actual historical Leader, to lift us above the polarity of our human experience and to guide us to God. And Heim does treat of the actual Jesus of history among His disciples in the days of His flesh: that was the beginning of His leadership. Moreover, it appears in Heim's description as a leadership which demanded, not understanding, but blind and unquestioning acceptance and obedience. He lays the very strongest emphasis on that aspect of the authority of Jesus. Jesus' commands needed no higher legitimation than His own personal injunction. His disciples were to do this and that, not for any reasons which they could share with Him, but solely and simply for His sake, because He asked it ('for my sake'). His endeavour during His ministry was not primarily to give men a doctrine or a world-view, but to bring them into personal relationship with Himself, as the Leader to whom God had given plenipotentiary power. But is not this an extremely one-sided view of our Lord's earthly ministry? It can hardly be questioned that our Lord spent a large part of His time in teaching, and that a great deal of His teaching was not about Himself or His relation to God or to His disciples, but about God's ways and the nature and demands of His kingdom. And on these matters He spoke with an authority very different from the dictatorial authority of the *Führer* who imposes his will and demands blind and unintelligent obedience. Yes, it must be said that even Jesus, speaking with such immense authority, did not approach men in that way. He spoke with the authority of truth, and on that He relied. His endeavour was to make people see the truth for themselves. He did not ask men to give up thinking, but rather seems to have deliberately awakened their minds by asking penetrating questions. According to Bishop Gore: 'He shrank from making dogmatic statements. Plainly He preferred to stimulate the minds of His disciples to discover the truth (e.g. the truth about Himself) for themselves.'[1] Again: 'No teacher ever showed more belief than our Lord in the capacity of the ordinary man to think rightly, if he be only sincere and open-minded. He did not, except rarely, use the dogmatic method. It would seem as if He feared to stunt men's growth from within thereby.'[2] That may be a one-sided overstatement, but is it not historically truer than Heim's account of the leadership of Jesus in the days of His flesh?

It is, however, when he comes to Christ's leadership of later generations that Heim's use of the 'leadership' category becomes most confused and confusing. It is not, of course, on Heim's view, by an authoritative code of conduct bequeathed to us that Jesus becomes our Leader, but by a direct I-Thou relationship with us in the present, which is possible through the Holy Spirit. Here we seem to move away entirely from the idea of an *external* authority to something very like the *testimonium Spiritus Sancti internum*. And surely such an inward authority is something very different from the kind of leadership that Heim describes. It certainly calls for unconditional obedience, but it is not *blind* obedience. It is by 'enlightening our minds in the knowledge of Christ' that the Holy Spirit calls us to the Christian life. And if Heim describes this as an I-Thou relationship, transcending time and making Jesus our contemporary, it gives us, plainly, not an external authority but an inward guidance. It is not guidance by 'the Jesus of history' in the limited sense, but by Christ present in our hearts through the Holy Spirit. What kinship has this with the kind of *Führerschaft* which Heim adopts as his clue? It is of the essence of the latter to give an absolute external authority, whose guidance has to be unconditionally obeyed by us even if we do not at all understand it; and it is difficult to see how *such* leadership could be exercised except during the lifetime of the leader, since it does not operate through a general code of conduct that could be

---

[1] Charles Gore, *The Philosophy of the Good Life*, p. 198.
[2] Ibid., in *A New Commentary on Holy Scripture*, p. 286.

handed down. As regards *inward* guidance from moment to moment, I do not see that this can be illustrated at all by the *Führerschaft* familiar in the modern world, unless the guidance is conceived in an automatic and unintelligent manner quite unworthy of the traditional Christian language about the Holy Spirit enlightening our minds in the knowledge of Christ.

If we further pursue the Christological question about Jesus' relation to God, it is exceedingly difficult to clarify Heim's answer. Who and what is this Jesus? And why is He our Leader? His leadership, says Heim, is not eternal, but has both a beginning and an end. It began with the Incarnation, when God, for reasons which we cannot penetrate, appointed this Man to be our Leader. It will come to an end in the final consummation, when the Son will hand over all authority to the Father (as in 1 Cor. xv, 24–8). For the period of Jesus' earthly life, His followers had the Leader with them in the flesh. For the period between that and the final consummation, we have the Leader with us through the Holy Spirit. But if we take all this in the sense which Heim's 'leader' category seems to require, it appears to leave us at two removes from God. We cannot have any knowledge of God except through Jesus, from whom we have to take everything absolutely on trust; and we cannot know Jesus (in this interim period) except through the Holy Spirit. On Heim's principles it would seem necessary to go on to ask: How do we know the Holy Spirit? However deeply true it may be in the traditional catholic sense of the words that we know God in Christ through the Holy Spirit, the meaning becomes different and very problematic on the basis of Heim's Christology. Is the Holy Spirit God? If not, are we left at two removes from contact with God? Or if the Holy Spirit is God, how can we men (who in the polarity of our experience cannot know God directly) know God the Holy Spirit? On Heim's principles it would appear that we should need another absolute leader in the flesh, to distinguish the true from the false for us in this realm of the Spirit of God.

Thus I cannot see that Heim's use of the 'leader' category helps him to answer the Christological question. Indeed, he does not seem to me to answer the Christological question at all. He does not succeed in making clear his doctrine of 'Jesus our Contemporary'. Is Jesus the only person in history who can be 'contemporary' with the people of any or every generation? And is it Deity, or Divinity, that enables Him thus to transcend time? So far as I can discover, that is not what Heim means, but rather that the I-Thou relationship even between two men is possible across the centuries, transcending by its very nature all intervals of time. Yet that would seem to make nonsense of his doctrine of the Holy Spirit. But again—apart from the question of contemporariness— Heim never tells us why Jesus is able to do for men what they cannot do for themselves. Man cannot rise above the 'polarity' of our human experience and come to know God for himself. How was Jesus able to do it? And therefore how is He qualified to be our Leader? It is 'personality', according to Heim, that qualifies for leadership. What then of the personality of Jesus Christ? Is it His personality in the human sense, as a phenomenon which can be studied historically, that makes Him Leader? That does not appear to be what Heim means, for He does not make much of 'the Jesus of history' as our guide. Is it then the 'Person' of Christ in a transcendent sense, as defined in catholic dogma? But Heim does not make much use of this either. He gives no answer to the question how this Jesus is related to God, except that God has appointed Him to be our absolute Leader. In this matter he even out-Ritschls the Ritschlian school. The Ritschlians, it might be said, refused to answer the Christological question except on the level of 'value-judgments', for they made little of the Christological definitions of catholic dogma, which seemed to them to contain alien metaphysics with which Christian faith has nothing to do. But then the Ritschlians built upon the Jesus of history, upon the approach that God makes to us through the human personality that we encounter in the Gospel story. That gave some content to the Ritschlian Christology, taking the place of the rejected metaphysical definitions. But Heim's Christology makes as little of the one as of the other, and seems strangely lacking in positive content as regards either the personality of Jesus or the nature of God. The book which contains it has a great many good things to which it is difficult to be fair in such a brief summary and criticism as this. It betrays a highly original and often penetrating study of the New Testament, and it breathes a truly Christian devotion to our Lord.

But all this is much better than its distinctive Christological theory, which has been vitiated by the unhappy choice of the 'Leadership' category as its central principle.

Chapter V

THE PARADOX OF THE INCARNATION

We must now come to grips directly with the central problem of Christology, for which the foregoing chapters have been clearing the ground. What do we mean by saying that God was incarnate in Jesus? In what sense was Jesus both God and Man? How could that one life be both completely human and completely divine?

I

The Paradoxes of Faith

There is a sense in which the *mysterium Christi* must always remain a mystery. The late Archbishop of Canterbury remarked that 'if any man says that he understands the relation of Deity to humanity in Christ, he only makes it clear that he does not understand at all what is meant by an Incarnation'.[1] Yet assuredly Dr. Temple did not mean that nothing at all can be said about the nature of the 'hypostatic union', for that would itself be virtually a confession that we do not know what we mean when we speak of God being incarnate in Jesus. The Incarnation presents us indeed with the supreme paradox, and I do not believe that we can ever eliminate from it the element of paradox without losing the Incarnation itself. But this is not the only point at which we are beset with paradox in our Christian belief: this is rather the point at

---

[1] W. Temple, *Christus Veritas*, p. 139.

which the constant and ubiquitous paradox reaches its peak. And if we try to isolate absolutely the mystery of the Incarnation, failing to connect it with the all-round paradox of our Christian faith and experience, we shall end by having on our hands a mystery which is not a *religious* mystery at all and has no bearing on our actual religious life. The mistake is not to assert paradox in the doctrine of the Incarnation, but to miss the paradox everywhere else. I confess that certain schools of theology in the modern world seem to me to be sometimes in danger of that mistake, especially, perhaps, Anglican theology (of which I would always wish to speak with profound respect and with a sense of heavy debt). Modern Anglican theology has tended to be intolerant of paradox, smoothing out contradictions, sometimes almost turning itself into a common-sense Christian philosophy, semi-Pelagian rather than Augustinian or Calvinistic in its mood (is this the proverbial Semi-Pelagianism of British thought?)—until it comes to the doctrine of the Incarnation. Then it becomes quite different, treating the *mysterium Christi* as a solitary exception, a hard kernel which is never soluble in any howsoever powerful solvent of theological thought. The result is to make the theological system as a whole too 'rational', and by contrast to make the Christological dogma too 'irrational', too little connected with the rest of our theology, too much a sheer mystery, whose meaning we do not know. Paradox may then become a mere *asylum ignorantiae*, a theological mystification, instead of being a truly religious mystery, close to experience and to faith.

It may be worth while at this point to reflect for a moment upon the nature and place of paradox in Christian doctrine. There can be no doubt about the widespread recognition, in our time, of the presence of a paradoxical element in all religious thought and statement, whether it is called paradox, antinomy, dialectical contradiction and tension, or anything else. The thought of Sören Kierkegaard has been described as *par excellence* 'the theology of paradox', and every student knows how deeply Kierkegaard has influenced the philosophical and religious thinking of our age. But there are many other historical sources of this tendency, and it betrays itself in one form or another in very diverse schools of theological thought. Without attempting to trace its sources or to distinguish its various expressions, I must try to indicate the sense in which it seems to me legitimate and sound.

The reason why the element of paradox comes into all religious thought and statement is because God cannot be comprehended in any human words or in any of the categories of our finite thought. God can be known only in a direct personal relationship, an 'I-and-Thou' intercourse, in which He addresses us and we respond to Him. As it has sometimes been put, God cannot legitimately be 'objectified'. This does not mean that religion is thrown back upon the 'subjective', against which we have so often been warned by the wise counsellors who tell us to turn away from our own feelings to the 'objective realities' of our faith. In that sense, in contrast with religious subjectivism, it is wholesome to be reminded that God is an objective reality. Yet we cannot know God by studying Him as an object, of which we can speak in the third person, in an 'I-It' relationship, from a spectator-attitude. He eludes all our words and categories. We cannot objectify or conceptualize Him.[1] When we try, we fall immediately into contradiction. Our thought gets diffracted, broken up into statements which it seems impossible to reconcile with each other. How then can we have any theology, since theology is bound to objectify God, to speak of Him in the third person, with human words and the categories of finite minds? The answer is that we must indeed do these things if we are to have any theology at all, and we must have theology; but we shall have to pay the price—it will always be a theology of paradox. The price is not too great to pay, for we must theologize; and indeed the very act of worship, particularly corporate worship, involves the use of words and thoughts about God, and to think or speak of God at all is to run into antinomy, dialectical contradiction, paradox.[2] Father Bulgakov (who prefers the term 'antinomy' to 'dialectical contradiction', and maintains that they mean quite different things) writes as follows. 'An antinomy simultaneously admits the truth of two contradictory, logically incompatible, but ontologically equally necessary asser-

---

[1] Cf. Martin Buber: 'God is the Being . . . that may properly only be addressed, not expressed.' *I and Thou* (Eng. trans. of *Ich und Du*), pp. 80f.

[2] See John Baillie, *Our Knowledge of God*, pp. 219–27.

tions. An antinomy testifies to the existence of a mystery beyond which the human reason cannot penetrate. This mystery nevertheless is actualized and lived in religious experience. All fundamental dogmatic definitions are of this nature.'[1]

Father Bulgakov goes to the root of the matter when he says that while the mystery cannot be stated in words without contradiction, it is actualized and lived in religious experience, that is, in the direct faith-relationship towards God. The attempt to put our experience of God into theological statements is something like the attempt to draw a map of the world on a flat surface, the page of an atlas. It is impossible to do this without a certain degree of falsification, because the surface of the earth is a spherical surface whose pattern cannot be reproduced accurately upon a plane. And yet the map must be drawn for convenience' sake. Therefore an atlas meets the problem by giving us two different maps of the world which can be compared with each other. The one is contained in two circles representing two hemispheres. The other is contained in an oblong (Mercator's projection). Each is a map of the whole world, and they contradict each other to some extent at every point. Yet they are both needed, and taken together they correct each other. They would be either misleading or mystifying to anyone who did not know that they represent the surface of a sphere. But they can serve their useful purpose for anyone who understands that they are intended simply to represent in handy portable form the pattern covering the surface of this round earth which he knows in actual experience. So it is with the paradoxes of faith. They are inevitable, not because the divine reality is self-contradictory, but because when we 'objectify' it all our judgments are in some measure falsified, and the higher truth which reconciles them cannot be fully expressed in words, though it is experienced and lived in the 'I-and-Thou' relationship of faith towards God. It is only the paradoxes of which this can be said that are justifiable in theology. There is great danger in the habit of falling back too easily upon paradox in our religious thinking, and it would ultimately make all theological argument impossible. There should always be a sense of tension between the two opposite sides of our

---

[1] Sergius Bulgakov, *The Wisdom of God*, p. 116 note.

paradoxes, driving us back to their source in our actual religious experience or faith. That is where we must refine our theological statements, purging them of needless contradictions and testing them 'whether they be of God'. Thus no paradox in theology can be justified unless it can be shown to spring directly from what H. R. Mackintosh called 'the immediate utterances of faith'; for since a paradox is a self-contradictory statement, we simply *do not know what it means or what we mean by it* unless it has that direct connection with the faith which it attempts to express.

Now it seems to me that Christian faith, when thought out, conceptualized, and put into human language, runs into paradox not only in the doctrine of the Incarnation, but at every vital point. We must not imagine that the other doctrines are easy and unparadoxical, and that mystery appears only when we come to the Incarnation. It is indeed the central paradox: how can the same life be explained as a completely human life in the continuum of history and as the life of God Himself? But there is similar paradox whenever in Christian thought we introduce God as the ultimate source of anything in our experience: He comes in, as it were, on the vertical line from the eternal world (*'senkrecht von oben'*) to touch the horizontal line on which we inevitably have another explanation in empirical terms. And the mystery of the Incarnation is the climax of all the Christian paradoxes. They all point to it, they all have an organic connection with it, and indeed they are all revealed by it. For these paradoxes are peculiar to Christian theology, and distinguish it from the various dualisms and pantheisms which beset it on opposite sides. These Christian paradoxes come of thinking out the religion of the Incarnation.

Let me indicate one or two main points where this paradoxical element is found.

(*a*) *The doctrine of Creation.* There is something quite distinctive about the Christian idea of *creatio ex nihilo*. It is not found anywhere else. It is peculiar to the religion of the Incarnation. It is highly paradoxical. It does not compete with anything that science may say about the temporal process by which things have come to be what they are. If it is taken as an answer to the question of world-origins in a scientific sense, it sounds absurd. 'God created all things out of nothing.' Even when taken as answering a more ultimate question, it seems far less satisfactory, far more difficult to state, than the other answers which it is intended to exclude. On the one hand is the dualistic answer which conceives of God as a great artificer taking an already existing raw material and moulding His world out of it. That is quite easy to state. But it is quite a pagan view, and it gives us an unworthy conception of God, a false conception of matter as godless and inherently evil, and therefore ultimately even an inadequate ethic and an inadequate doctrine of immortality. On the other hand is the pantheistic answer, which conceives of God as creating all things out of Himself, out of His own substance. This is not really creation, but emanation. Again it is easily stated, and as it lent itself to the great pantheistic systems, so it has lent itself easily to absolute idealism in the modern world. But it also is quite a pagan view, destroying the true attitude of man both to God and to the world. No, says Christian faith, God did not fashion the world out of a raw material which He found, nor did He generate the world out of His own substance. He created all things out of nothing. This is highly paradoxical. It does not seem to be the kind of position that could ever be reached by a process of inference from the phenomena, or that can even be stated without paradox. In contrast to every theory of temporal origins, it probably involves the idea that time itself is part of creation, and this again is highly paradoxical. Yet these paradoxes are inescapable. Theology is driven to them. Moreover, it is *Christian* theology in particular that is driven to them. It is, we may say, in the endeavour to think out the religion of the Incarnation that the human mind has been led even to the paradoxes of Creation—to the peculiarly Christian and wholly paradoxical doctrine of *creatio ex nihilo*.

(*b*) *The doctrine of Providence*. It seems plain that this doctrine also is inseparable from paradox. Here again we have a paradoxical relation between the horizontal and the vertical plane. The whole texture of our life in this world is a network of causes and effects on the empirical level, and everything that comes to us comes through the continuum of history, with all its determinants, of natural law and human action around us; and on the horizontal plane that is all that is to be said about it by way of explanation. But every Christian believes also that whatever comes to him comes from

God, by God's appointment, God's providence. And not simply in the sense that God works through the natural (including the psychological) laws of His own ordaining; as if, having 'wound up' the universe to run by these laws, He had then left it to run its course. The Christian believes that in some sense everything comes to him *directly* from God, whose working is always individual. And this becomes highly paradoxical when we reflect that in the historical or horizontal network of determinants there are many which are directly contrary to the will of God. The course of my life may be profoundly affected by some injury which has befallen me through the deliberately evil volition of a fellow-man, who seeks to do me harm and is thereby acting directly against God's will. Yet as a Christian I also believe that the thing has come to me from God, who is all-good and all-loving, and who makes all things work together for good to those who love Him. This is highly paradoxical. But it is impossible to escape from the paradox without running either into a dualistic doctrine of a finite or limited God, on the one hand, or into a pantheistic doctrine, which explains away the reality of evil, on the other. And if we take either of these courses, we lose the Christian doctrine of Providence altogether. Moreover, however paradoxical this doctrine may be when we try to think it out theologically, the mystery that lies behind it is grasped by countless unsophisticated Christian men and women in the actual life of faith. Here again the paradox arises out of actual religious experience, and indeed Christian experience. The doctrine of Providence in its fullest and most paradoxical form is peculiar to Christianity. Here again, as in the case of creation, we may say that it is in the endeavour to think out the religion of the Incarnation that the human mind has been driven to the paradox. We can see this happening in the New Testament with special reference to the scandal of the crucifixion of Jesus. Faithful souls in Israel had long been wrestling with the problem of how the belief in God's rule could be compatible with the dreadful things that were allowed to happen among men; and this came to a head when Jesus was condemned and crucified. This was the worst thing that had ever happened through the sin of men. Yet they came to believe that this was also the best thing that had ever happened in the providence of God. We can see it, with all its paradoxical contradictions, in the early chapters of the Acts of the Apostles.[1] The crucifixion of Christ was the supreme instance, driving men to think out afresh the whole problem of divine rule in the world; and the result was the highly paradoxical Christian doctrine of Providence.[2]

Now if it is thus true that the Christian faith, the religion of the Incarnation, runs into paradox at one point after another, may not these secondary paradoxes point us towards an understanding of the supreme paradox of the Incarnation itself? May they not give us some small hint of how it can be true that a phenomenon which emerges in the continuum of temporal and terrestrial history is also, and in a deeper sense, an incursion of the eternal, the Divine? That seems to be especially true of the paradox of Providence which we have just been considering. Indeed, if we could be content with the type of Christology (criticized in Chapter III) which makes Christ the 'centre of history' but has nothing to say about His Person, then the doctrine of Providence would cover the whole, and Christology would be merely a special application of it to the supreme instance. But that is not enough; for though it would give us the incursion of the Word of God into human history, it would not give us the Word made flesh, God incarnate in a particular human life. Therefore it can only be said that the paradox of Providence points us from afar in the direction of the paradox of the Incarnation.

Is there any further paradox in our Christian experience of God which can give us a nearer approach?

Yes, I think there is.

---

[1] 'Him, being delivered up by the determinate counsel and foreknowledge of God, ye by the hand of lawless men did crucify and slay.' Acts ii, 23. 'Of a truth in this city against thy holy Servant Jesus, whom thou didst anoint, both Herod and Pontius Pilate, with the Gentiles and the peoples of Israel, were gathered together, to do whatsoever thy hand and thy counsel fore-ordained to come to pass.' Acts iv, 27f.

[2] May I refer to a fuller elaboration of this argument about the paradoxical nature of the Christian doctrine of Providence in my volume *Faith in God* (1927), chap ix, especially pp. 295–308.

II

The Central Paradox

A far greater and deeper paradox than those which we have been considering lies at the very heart of the Christian life and vitally affects every part of it. It is what we may call the paradox of Grace. Its essence lies in the conviction which a Christian man possesses, that every good thing in him, every good thing he does, is somehow not wrought by himself but by God. This is a highly paradoxical conviction, for in ascribing all to God it does not abrogate human personality nor disclaim personal responsibility. Never is human action more truly and fully personal, never does the agent feel more perfectly free, than in those moments of which he can say as a Christian that whatever good was in them was not his but God's.

This astonishing paradox, so characteristic of Christianity, can be widely illustrated from Christian literature of all ages. We may begin with the familiar words of St. Paul: 'By the grace of God I am what I am: and his grace which was bestowed upon me was not found vain; but I laboured more abundantly than they all: yet not I, but the grace of God which was with me.'[1] We may go on to St. Augustine, who after quoting the above words makes the following comment: 'O mighty teacher, confessor and preacher of grace! What meaneth this: "I laboured more, Yet not I"? Where the will exalted itself ever so little, there piety was instantly on the watch, and humility trembled, because infirmity confessed all the truth.' Again: 'Therefore, blessed Paul, thou great teacher of grace, I will say it without fear of any man. . . . : Thy merits are recompensed with their own crown of reward; but thy merits are the gifts of God.'[2] Again: 'Even if men do good things which pertain to God's service, it is He Himself that brings it about that they do what He commanded.'[3] This extraordinary doctrine of a God who not only

---

[1] 1 Cor. xv, 10.
[2] *De gest. Pelag.* cc. 35 *seq.*
[3] *De praedest. sanctorum,* c. 19.

demands obedience of us but supplies it Himself is summed up in St. Augustine's famous prayer: 'Give what Thou commandest, and command what Thou wilt.'[1] Or take this from St. Anselm of Canterbury in the eleventh century: 'What a man has, not from himself but from God, he ought to regard as not so much his own as God's. For no one has from himself the truth which he teaches, or a righteous will, but from God.'[2] To which we may add this from a prayer attributed to St. Anselm: 'Whatsoever our heart rightly willeth, it is of Thy gift.' Or take what Thomas à Kempis in the fifteenth century hears Christ say about His saints: 'They glory not of their own merits, for they ascribe no goodness to themselves, but all to me.'[3] Or take this from the Westminster Confession in the seventeenth century, concerning the good works of believers: 'Their ability to do good works is not at all of themselves, but wholly from the Spirit of Christ. And that they may be enabled thereunto, besides the graces they have already received, there is required an actual influence of the same Holy Spirit to work in them to will and to do of his good pleasure.'[4] Or take the familiar words of a nineteenth-century hymn:

> *And every virtue we possess,*
> *And every victory won,*
> *And every thought of holiness*
> *Are His alone.*[5]

We can never ponder enough upon the meaning of this paradoxical conviction which lies at the very heart of the Christian life and is the unique secret of the Christian character. It is this that makes so wide a gulf between the Christian way of life and any 'mere morality', so that in a sense Christianity transcends morality altogether and there is no such thing as a Christian ethic. The question is often asked whether the impossible ethic of the Sermon on the Mount has any relevance to our life in this world, as a code to be practised or an ideal on which to mould our characters.

---

[1] *Conf.* x, 29.
[2] *Cur Deus homo*, Book i, chap. ix.
[3] *De imit. Chr.*, iv, 58.
[4] *Westminster Confession of Faith*, XVI, iii.
[5] By Harriet Auber.

But the truth is that in the last analysis a Christian does not live by practising any ethic or moulding himself on any ideal, but by a faith in God which finally ascribes all good to Him. To detach the ethic from the whole context of the Christian secret is to make it irrelevant because it is impossible. The main function of the impossible ethic is to drive us away from ourselves to God: and then there grows that peculiar kind of goodness which can never be achieved by mere moral endeavour, the Christian kind, which is all unconscious of itself and gives all the glory to God.

Thus the paradoxical Christian secret, while it transcends the moralistic attitude by ascribing all to God, does not make us morally irresponsible. That is part of the paradox. No one knows better than the Christian that he is free to choose and that in a sense everything depends upon his choice. Pelagius was quite right to insist upon that, if he thought it was being compromised by the extreme statements of the zealous Augustine. My actions are my very own, expressions of my own will, my own choice. No one else can choose for me or relieve me of the responsibility. When I make the wrong choice, I am entirely responsible, and my conscience condemns me. And yet (here is the paradox) when I make the right choice, my conscience does not applaud or congratulate me. I do not feel meritorious or glow with self-esteem—if and in so far as I am a Christian. Instead of that I say: 'Not I, but the grace of God.' Thus while there is a human side to every good action, so that it is genuinely the free choice of a person with a will, yet somehow the Christian feels that the other side of it, the divine side, is logically prior. The grace of God is prevenient. The good was His before it was ours. That comes first, and in a sense that even covers the whole. It is not as if we could divide the honours between God and ourselves, God doing His part, and we doing ours. It cannot even be adequately expressed in terms of divine initiative and human co-operation. It is false to this paradox to think of the area of God's action and the area of our action being delimited, each by the other, and distinguished from each other by a boundary, so that the more of God's grace there is in an action, the less is it my own personal action. That is precisely the mistake that misled the morally ardent Pelagius. From the historical and psychological standpoint the good actions of a Christian are purely his own actions. And even from the religious and Christian point of view that aspect is indispensable. Without it the other side would lose its true meaning, and the good man would be simply a perfect marionette, or an automaton, as Huxley wished he could be. We are not marionettes, but responsible persons, and never more truly and fully personal in our actions than in those moments when we are most dependent on God and He lives and acts in us. And yet the divine side is somehow prior to the human. Whatever good there is in our lives and actions (and it is but fragmentary) is 'all of God', and it was His before it was ours, was divine grace before it was human achievement, is indeed a matter of God taking up our poor human nature into union with His own divine life, making us more truly personal, yet also more disposed to ascribe it all to Him.

This is the deepest paradox of our whole Christian experience, and it runs right through it, woven into its very texture. It is, moreover, virtually peculiar to Christianity. More than all the other paradoxes, it is a distinctive product of the religion of the Incarnation.

What I wish to suggest is that this paradox of grace points the way more clearly and makes a better approach than anything else in our experience to the mystery of the Incarnation itself; that this paradox in its fragmentary form in our own Christian lives is a reflection of that perfect union of God and man in the Incarnation on which our whole Christian life depends, and may therefore be our best clue to the understanding of it. In the New Testament we see the man in whom God was incarnate surpassing all other men in refusing to claim anything for Himself independently and ascribing all the goodness to God. We see Him also desiring to take up other men into His own close union with God, that they might be as He was. And if these men, entering in some small measure through Him into that union, experience the paradox of grace for themselves in fragmentary ways, and are constrained to say, 'It was not I but God', may not this be a clue to the understanding of that perfect life in which the paradox is complete and absolute, that life of Jesus which, being the perfection of humanity, is also, and even in a deeper and prior sense, the very life of God Himself? If the paradox is a reality in our poor imperfect lives at all, so far as there is any good in them, does not the same or a similar paradox, taken at the perfect and absolute pitch, appear as the mystery of the Incarnation?

St. Augustine is not afraid to connect the one mystery with the other. 'The Saviour, the Man Christ Jesus, is Himself the brightest illustration of predestination and grace.' 'Every man, from the commencement of his faith, becomes a Christian by the same grace by which *that* Man from His formation became Christ.'[1] And Calvin, commenting on this, can say: 'Therefore when we treat of the merit of Christ, we do not place the beginning in Him, but we ascend to the ordination of God as the primary cause.'[2] St. Anselm, after writing the sentences I have quoted earlier, goes on to make the same connection. 'What a man has, not from himself but from God, he ought to regard as not so much his own as God's. For no one has from himself the truth which he teaches, or a righteous will, but from God. Christ therefore came not to do His own will, but the Father's, because the righteous will which He had was not from His human but from His divine nature.'[3] It might almost be said that in that passage at least St. Anselm treats the divine-human Christ as the supreme instance of the familiar Christian paradox.

III

The God who was Incarnate

Let us leave the above argument for a moment and make another beginning from a different point—it will come to the same thing in the end.

Let us ask: With what conception of God have we embarked on our Christological quest? What do we understand by the word 'God'? When endeavouring to confront, in an earlier chapter, those persons who are willing to believe in God but not in the

---

[1] Augustine, *De praedest. sanct.*, I, xv.

[2] Calvin, *Inst.*, II, xvii, i. It is only fair to add that Calvin in the context is arguing, against objectors, that there is no incompatibility between the idea of God's grace freely redeeming us and Christ's merit earning redemption for us, since Christ's merit itself derives from the grace of God.

[3] Anselm, *Cur Deus Homo*, Book I, chap. ix. Cf. chap. x.

Incarnation, I was constrained to ask: Are you sure that you know what you mean by 'God'? And now I must pursue the question further. It is astonishing how lightly many people assume that they know what the word 'God' means. But it is still more astonishing that even when we profess Christian belief and set out to try to understand the mystery of God becoming man, we are apt to start with some conception of God, picked up we know not where, an idol of the cave or of the market-place, which is different from the Christian conception; and then to attempt the impossible task of understanding how such a God could be incarnate in Jesus. If the Incarnation has supremely revealed God, shown Him to us in a new and illuminating light, put a fresh meaning into the very word that is His name, *that* is the meaning that we must use in facing the problem of the Incarnation, because that is what God really is. It is only as Christians that we can hope to understand the Incarnation. Why then should we as theologians work with any other conception of God than that which as Christians we believe to be true?

What then do we mean when we speak of 'God'? We mean something unique, something that cannot be fully conceptualized. Thus if we rightly understand the word 'God', if we give it the only meaning it ought to have, we cannot possibly speak of 'Gods' of even strictly of '*a* God'. The word 'God', rightly understood, is (as I have said repeatedly) not a common noun but a proper name. That is why Brunner makes the idea of 'the name of God' so important in his theology, and conceives of revelation as 'God telling us His name', on the basis of the story of Moses and the burning bush, and many other biblical passages. [1] And yet this is not like any other proper name. It does not indicate particularity, one instance of a class, for God is not in any class.[2] Common names, say the logicians, possess connotation, but proper names possess only denotation. May it not be said, however, that 'God' is the one proper name that does possess connotation? And yet it is a connotation that cannot be fully conceptualized. Its meaning cannot be expressed without paradox. What then does it mean? With what

[1] Emil Brunner, *The Mediator* (Eng. trans.), pp. 219, 231, 270, 280. See also Karl Barth, *The Doctrine of the Word of God*, pp. 364f.

[2] Cf. Thomas Aquinas: *Deus non est in aliquo genere, Summa theol.*, I, iii, 5.

meaning shall we use the word, as we try to understand how God could be incarnate?

Does it mean, fundamentally, the Maker of all things? No, that is not enough, nor is it a true starting-point; for however truly that phrase may be used in its place, it does not, when taken by itself, give us the meaning of 'God' at all. If we could say no more than that about God, we could not even say that, in its true sense. For if we could say no more than that, then it could only have been by such logical processes as the argument from design or the cosmological proof that we reached that conception. And by such routes we could only reach a pantheistic *deus sive natura*, or a *prima causa* in the natural sense at the beginning of a causal chain, or a supreme artificer, like Paley's invisible watchmaker inferred from the watch found lying on the ground. But none of these conceptions is what is meant by God. When Augustine questioned earth and sea and sky about God, they said with one accord, 'He made us'. But he knew that he could not have heard them say even this if he had not known of God in other and more inward ways.[1] The science of religions is showing, I think, that even in the case of pagan and primitive religion, where the word 'God' has its plural, it was not by such arguments from nature, in howsoever primitive form, that the idea of the divine was reached. Christian faith does in fact praise God as Creator of all things, but such arguments from nature do not in themselves even begin to tell us what Christianity means by 'God'.

Does the word then mean the Source and Guardian of the moral law? That represents roughly the new approach proposed by Kant, the road of moral faith proposed in place of the speculative proofs which he found fallacious. This route looks at first far more promising; and Kant's conception can be so interpreted as to contain a great deal of truth. And yet if it is taken as an inferential argument from our moral convictions, as premises, to God the Moral Governor of the universe as conclusion, it does not give us what Christians mean by God. At best it would give us 'the moral and providential order'. If we took this as the essential meaning of the word, it would reduce the practice of religion to 'mere morality',

---

[1] Augustine, *Conf.*, X, vi.

and it would give us a thoroughly Pelagian conception of the life of faith. From the Christian point of view this would be a falsification of morality itself. To accept it would be to forget that there is a sense in which the Christian secret transcends morality altogether. It is Christianity that has discovered and exposed what we may call 'the paradox of moralism'[1]—that the attempt to be moral defeats itself, leads to 'Pharisaism' instead of real goodness. Christianity has a different method, because it has a different conception of God. Christianity means a much deeper mystery, a much greater marvel, when it uses the word 'God'.

What, then, does the word 'God' mean, in its true and full Christian use?

It means something so paradoxical that it is difficult to express in a few words. It means the One who at the same time makes absolute demands upon us and offers freely to *give* us all that He demands. It means the One who requires of us unlimited obedience and then supplies the obedience Himself. It means the One who calls us to work out our own salvation on the ground that 'it is He Himself who works both the willing and the working' in our hearts and lives. It is not that He bestows His favour, His grace, upon those who render obedience to His commands. Such divine giving in response to human obedience is a sub-Christian idea, alien to the New Testament; and indeed if God's grace had to wait for man's obedience, it would be kept waiting for ever. But the Christian, when he has rendered his fullest and freest obedience, knows well that somehow it was 'all of God', and he says: 'It was not I, but the grace of God which was with me.' This is the Creator-God who made us to be free personalities, and we know that we are most free and personal when He is most in possession of us. This is the God of the moral order who calls us every moment to exercise our full and responsible choice; but He also comes to dwell in us in such a way that we are raised altogether above the moral order into the liberty of the sons of God. That is what Christians mean by 'God'. It is highly paradoxical, but it is bound up with the whole

---

[1] Writers on ethics have often spoken of 'the paradox of hedonism'—the fact that the quest of happiness defeats itself. But they have not so often noticed what I call 'the paradox of moralism'—the fact that the quest of goodness defeats itself.

message of Christianity and the whole structure of the Christian life; and it follows inevitably if we take seriously the fundamental paradox: 'Not I, but the grace of God', as we are bound to do unless we are content to be Pelagians. It is God's very nature to give Himself in that way: to dwell in man in such a manner that man, by his own will choosing to do God's will (and in a sense it must depend on man's own choice) nevertheless is constrained to confess that it was 'all of God'.

Such is the Christian conception of God; and therefore it is with such a conception that we must work when we try to understand the Incarnation.

The question may well be asked at this point: Is this really the *distinctively* Christian conception of God? Do we not seem to have forgotten that the peculiarly Christian view of God is to be found in the doctrine of the Trinity? And if that is the case, ought not the Trinitarian conception to be our starting-point in Christology? To this I would reply: Are these two conceptions really different from each other? The conception of God that has worked itself out in the language of devotion in the foregoing pages—is it not identical with that which is expressed in doctrinal terms in the dogma of the Trinity? I shall return to this subject in the next chapter, but it seems necessary to say a word about it at this point. The Christian doctrine of the Trinity is not a mysterious mathematical statement about three-in-one, nor a metaphysical statement about a logically necessary triad. It may be difficult to understand the idea which Barth derives from Aquinas, that the numerical terms in the doctrine of the Trinity are to be taken metaphorically,[1] but the statement that God is three-in-one is virtually meaningless until we go on to indicate the relation of the three to the one concretely on a basis of the Gospel history and the Christian experience out of which the doctrine arose. What the doctrine of the Trinity really asserts is that it is God's very nature not only to create finite persons whom He could love, and to reveal and impart Himself to them, even to the point of incarnation (through His eternal Word) but also to extend this indwelling to those men who fail to obey Him, doing in them what they could not do themselves, supplying

---

[1] Karl Barth, *Doctrine of the Word of God*, p. 407.

to them the obedience which He requires them to render (through His Holy Spirit). All of this, says the dogma of the Trinity, is of the eternal nature and essence of God. He is Father, Son and Holy Spirit, and the Son and the Spirit are consubstantial with the Father. And this outgoing love of God, His self-giving, is not new nor occasional nor transient, but 'as it was in the beginning, is now, and ever shall be, world without end'. Surely this doctrine is the objective expression of the same great paradox which finds its subjective expression in the confession: 'Not I, but the grace of God.'

This is the God in whom Christians believe. And this apprehension of God seems to be distinctive of Christianity. I do not say that it was never in any measure foreshadowed, for if this is the very nature of God there would naturally be some foreshadowing of the paradox wherever there was any knowledge of God at all. But the full paradox is peculiar to the religion of the Incarnation. It may be asked: What of the paradox so deeply rooted in Indian religion where the divine Brahma so dwells in man that He is both the worshipped and the worshipper, not only the hearer of prayer but the prayer itself, not only the desired but also the desire, not only the goal but also the aspirant? Yet that is very different from the Christian conviction, and indeed completely misses the depth of the paradox, because it is pantheistic, giving us a religion of identity, in which human personality is a painful illusion and its true goal is absorption and annihilation. In such a system the true idea of incarnation is impossible, just as there is no room for the paradox which combines the fullest personal freedom with the fullest divine indwelling, 'I, yet not I, but the grace of God'. At the other extreme stands a system like Islam, and here also there is no room for the paradox, but for the opposite reason. Islam is too moralistic for such a paradox. Its God is too sheerly transcendent, the Lawgiver, but not the Gracegiver, not the indwelling source and author of the obedience which He demands. Thus Islam is repelled by the doctrine of the Trinity, and its conception of God leaves no room for an incarnation.

There is, then, something peculiar to Christianity in the paradoxical conception of God that we have been elaborating and that has its counterpart in what I have called the central paradox of

our Christian experience. That is, distinctively, what Christia.
mean by 'God'. And therefore when we try to understand th
Incarnation, when we ask how God could become man and what it
means, *that* is the God about whom we must ask the question.

But if so, then we have *ipso facto* begun to find an *answer* to the
question, the only kind of answer that we ought to expect. In that
case the doctrine that Jesus Christ is both God and Man is not
sheer mystification. We can begin to understand it. Not that the
reality so described becomes less wonderful. But it is not more
wonderful than the God in whom we believe. I am reminded of the
teaching we find in some of the Logos-theologians of the Patristic
age, especially Irenaeus, to the effect that, while God is in Himself
incomprehensible, unknowable, yet it is also His very nature to
reveal Himself to His creatures, even to the point of Incarnation,
because that is the natural activity of the Logos, and the Logos is
of the essence of God. I am reminded also of Karl Barth's remark,
that 'while God's becoming *man* is not a matter of course, yet it
can be justly considered I as the most natural of all natural occurrences, because it was *God* who became man in Jesus Christ'.[1]
It may be objected that thus to explain the Incarnation by showing how naturally it connects with the doctrine of the Trinity, or
with the paradoxical Christian conception of God, is no explanation at all, since these conceptions have themselves arisen out of the
Incarnation. In one sense this is perfectly true. But it is not dis-
concerting. For there is a sense in which we should not expect or
attempt to 'explain' the Incarnation. Our theological task is to
try to make sure that we know what we mean by it, what it means
and what it does not mean; to try to make sure that, while it remains the *mysterium Christi*, it is not sheer meaningless mystery,
but becomes a truly Christian paradox to us. And I am suggesting
that this can happen because in our own experience, however poor
and fragmentary, we know something of the paradoxical grace of
God, something of the God who was incarnate in Jesus.

Our two lines of argument have converged upon the one point,
with a view to such an understanding of the paradox of the
Incarnation.

---

[1] Karl Barth, *The Knowledge of God and the Service of God*, p. 72.

IV

True God and True Man

Let us try to trace more fully the connection and analogy between what I have called the paradox of grace and the paradox of the Incarnation.

Let us begin with the witness of the New Testament. It is plain that we find in the New Testament both the very highest claims for the divine revelation in Jesus and the very frankest recognition that He was a man. How far can we also find these two related to each other in a way that reminds us of the paradox by which a Christian says: 'I, . . . yet not I, but God'? A very great deal has been written by biblical scholars during the last century on the question as to what Jesus held and taught about Himself and His place in God's purpose, and a common phrase which figured as the title of many discussions a generation ago was 'the (messianic) self-consciousness of Jesus'. The phrase was doubtless legitimate and useful.[1] And yet it has a somewhat unnatural sound, because in the Jesus of the Gospels it is not 'self-consciousness' that strikes us, but God-consciousness. Throughout the story we get the impression of one who, with all His high claims, kept thinking far less of Himself than of the Father. Even in Him—or should we say, supremely in Him?—self-consciousness was swallowed up in His deep and humble and continual consciousness of God. When He worked cures, it was to His heavenly Father that He looked up for aid, and it was to God rather than to Himself that He expected people to give the glory when they were cured.[2] As regards goodness, He was not conscious of possessing it Himself independently, but looked away from Himself to God for it. When once a man addressed Him as 'Good Master', he replied: 'Why do you call me good? No one is

---

[1] It was, of course, a translation of *Selbstbewusstsein*, which in this kind of usage seems more at home in the German language than its translation does in the English.

[2] Mark vii, 34; v, 19; Luke xvii, 18.

good except God.'[1] If we take the reply seriously, we shall surely find in it the supreme instance of that peculiar kind of humility which Christianity brought into the world. It was not self-depreciation: it was rather a complete absence of the kind of self-consciousness which makes a man think of his own degree of merit, and a dominating sense of dependence on God. The Man in whom God was incarnate would claim nothing for Himself as a Man, but ascribed all glory to God.

It is, however, when we turn to the Fourth Gospel that we find on the lips of Jesus the most remarkable expressions of this central paradox of Christian experience. I cannot in this place discuss the question as to how far the great Johannine discourses give us the *ipsissima verba* of Jesus; but it is in any case sufficiently impressive that in the Gospel which gives us the most transcendently high Christology to be found in the New Testament, Christology is more than anywhere else interwoven with the paradoxical human confession: 'I, . . . yet not I, but the Father.' On the one hand there is Jesus making His human choice from moment to moment, a choice on which in a sense everything depends. 'He that sent me is with me: he hath not left me alone; for I do always the things that are pleasing to him.'[2] 'Therefore doth the Father love me, because I lay down my life, that I may take it again. No one taketh it away from me, but I lay it down of myself. I have power to lay it down, and I have power to take it again. This commandment received I from my Father.'[3] But on the other hand, all His words and all His choices depended on the Father. 'I can of myself do nothing: as I hear, I judge: and my judgment is righteous, because I seek not mine own will, but the will of him that sent me.'[4] 'Verily, verily, I say unto you, the Son can do nothing of himself, but what he seeth the Father doing: for what things soever he doeth, these the Son also doeth in like manner.'[5] 'My teaching is not mine, but his that sent me. . . . He that speaketh from himself seeketh his own glory: but he that seeketh the glory of him that sent him, the same

---

[1] Mark x, 17f.
[2] John viii, 29.
[3] John x, 17, 18.
[4] John v, 30.
[5] John v, 19.

is true, and no unrighteousness is in him.'[1] 'I am not come of myself, but he that sent me is true, whom ye know not. I know him; because I am from him, and he sent me.'[2] 'I spake not from myself; but the Father which sent me, he hath given me a commandment, what I should say, and what I should speak.'[3] 'The words that I say unto you I speak not from myself: but the Father abiding in me doeth his works.'[4]

In these remarkable passages we find Jesus making the very highest claims; but they are made in such a way that they sound rather like disclaimers. The higher they become, the more do they refer themselves to God, giving God all the glory. Though it is a real man that is speaking, they are not human claims at all: they do not claim anything for the human achievement, but ascribe it all to God. According to Barth, the holiness of Jesus means that He did not treat His own goodness as an independent thing, a heroic human attainment. His sinlessness consists in His renouncing all claim to ethical heroism. He did not set up at all as a man confronting God, but along with sinners—who do *not* take this attitude —He threw Himself solely on God's grace. The God-Man is the only man who claims nothing for Himself, but all for God.[5]

It hardly needs to be said the New Testament is conscious of a great gulf between what Christ is and what we are even when we are His people; and to some it may seem that this should exclude all analogy between His experience of God and ours. Especially it may occur to some that experience of the *grace* of God belongs to sinful men and does not enter at all into the mystery of divine Incarnation. According to Newman's hymn, 'God's presence and His very self, And essence all-divine', in the Incarnation is 'a higher gift than grace'. More than one critic[6] has made the comment that there is no higher gift than grace, since the grace of God is simply His personal and loving action upon us or within us; but it is perhaps not necessary to quarrel with Newman's meaning. It

---

[1] John vii, 16, 18.
[2] John vii, 28, 29.
[3] John xii, 49.
[4] John xiv, 10.
[5] This is but a rough summary of a whole paragraph in Barth's *Kirchliche Dogmatik*, I, ii, 171ff.
[6] E.g. N. P. Williams, *The Grace of God*, p. 110.

does not follow, however, that we must not think of Jesus as the recipient or object of the grace of God, or that we must not take the 'paradox of grace' as in any measure a pointer to the Incarnation. According to Thomas Aquinas, the grace given to Christ is twofold: *gratia habitualis*, given to Christ as man, like other men, and *gratia unionis*, given only to Christ;[1] but this seems an artificial distinction. It is relevant, however, to remember that the New Testament, while it speaks of the grace of God as given to Christ, speaks much more of the grace of Christ as given to us. And that indicates exactly the relation between His experience of God and ours, as conceived in the New Testament. Ours depends upon His. If God in some measure lives and acts in us, it is because first, and without measure, He lived and acted in Christ. And thus, further, the New Testament tends sometimes to say that as God dwells in Christ, so Christ dwells in us. St. Paul can express the paradox of grace by saying: 'I live; and yet no longer I, but *Christ* liveth in me';[2] as he can say to Christians: 'You are of Christ, and Christ is of God.'[3] But that is only a part of the truth, and St. Paul can also speak of Christian men sharing, in a sense and in a measure, Christ's relation to God. It is God's purpose that these men should 'be conformed to the image of his Son, that he might be the first-born among many brethren'.[4] In the Epistle to the Hebrews we find strong emphasis laid on the analogy between Christ's human experience and the experience of those men whom He saves. 'Both he that sanctifieth and they that are sanctified are all of one: for which cause he is not ashamed to call them brethren.'[5] In the Fourth Gospel the risen Christ speaks of the disciples as 'my brethren' and of God as 'my Father and your Father, and my God and your God'.[6] There also we find the purpose boldly expressed that all Christ's people should come to have the same kind of unity with Him, and through Him with the Father, as He has with the Father: 'That they may all be one; even as thou, Father, art in me, and I

---

[1] See Ottley, *The Doctrine of the Incarnation*, 4th ed., p. 527.
[2] Gal. ii, 20.
[3] 1 Cor. iii, 23.
[4] Rom. viii, 29. Cf. 'the first-born from the dead', Col. i, 18.
[5] Heb. ii, 11. Weymouth translates 'have all one Father'.
[6] John xx, 17.

in thee, that they also may be in us: that the world may believe that thou didst send me. And the glory which thou hast given me I have given unto them; that they may be one, even as we are one; I in them, and thou in me, that they may be perfected into one; that the world may know that thou didst send me, and lovedst them, even as thou lovedst me.'[1]

'He was made what we are', wrote Irenaeus, 'that He might make us what He is Himself.'[2]

If then Christ can be thus regarded as in some sense the proto-type of the Christian life, may we not find a feeble analogue of the incarnate life in the experience of those who are His 'many brethren', and particularly in the central paradox of their ex-perience: 'Not I, but the grace of God'? If this confession is true of the little broken fragments of good that are in our lives—if these must be described on the one hand as human achievements, and yet on the other hand, and in a deeper and prior sense, as *not* human achievements but things actually wrought by God—is it not the same *type* of paradox, taken at the absolute degree, that covers the whole ground of the life of Christ, of which we say that it was the life of a man and yet also, in a deeper and prior sense, the very life of God incarnate?

It seems plain that it is the presence of this paradox that has always made it so difficult to express the doctrine of the Incarna-tion without running into error on the one side or on the other, so as to lose either the divinity or the humanity. And it appears to me that the method of approach which I have indicated is a certain safeguard against these errors, because it can be a continual re-minder of the need of holding fast the two sides of the paradox and letting them correct each other. On the one hand, there was from the beginning the 'Adoptionist' or 'Ebionite' type of error, by which Jesus was regarded as a man who achieved such good-ness that God exalted him to divinity or quasi-divinity. The reason why the Church could not rest content with such a view was not because they objected to the idea of deification (for the Greek Fathers tended too much to conceive even of salvation as deifica-

---

[1] John xvii, 21–3.
[2] *Adv. haer.*, Bk. v, Pref. (quoted by Ottley).

tion) but because the Adoptionist Christology began with the human achievement of Jesus and brought God in at the end, so that it was a case of 'first man, then God' or a man becoming God, instead of 'first God, then man' or God becoming man. It was, of course, perfectly right to regard the life lived by Jesus as a human achievement. To deny that or to obscure or minimize it would be to fall into the opposite type of error, with Docetists, Apollinarians, and Monophysites. Jesus was a real man, subject to the conditions and limitations of humanity, with a human will that had to make its continual choices in face of life's temptations, and thus His goodness must be quite realistically regarded as a human achievement. But goodness in a human life, even in small proportions, is *never* simply a human achievement. To regard it as such would be pure Pelagianism. And 'no New Testament thinker could think of Jesus in Pelagian terms'.[1] All goodness in a human life is wrought by God. That is the other side, and somehow that side comes first, without destroying the human. And therefore the goodness of Jesus can ultimately be described only as the human side of a divine reality, which, so to say, was divine before it was human. The divine is always prevenient, so that however far back one may go in the life of Jesus, one can never reach a point that would meet the requirements of 'Adoptionism', just as one can never reach a point of which a 'Pelagian' account would be satisfactory. It is not adoption that we have to deal with, but Incarnation.

The whole problem of the Incarnation is contained in the old question, which can be asked in so many ways: Was Jesus divine because He lived a perfect life, or was He able to live a perfect life because He was divine? To put it otherwise: Did the Incarnation depend upon the daily human choices made by Jesus, or did He always choose aright because He was God incarnate? If our whole line of thought has been correct, this question does not present us with a genuine dilemma. It must, of course, be true that His choices were genuine human choices, and that in a sense everything depended upon them. 'He that sent me is with me; he hath not left me alone; for (or because) I do always the things that are pleasing

---

[1] Hoskyns and Davey, *The Riddle of the New Testament*, p. 255.

to him.'[1] All depended on those human choices from moment to moment. And yet as soon as we have said that, we must inevitably turn round and say something apparently opposite, remembering that in the last analysis such human choice is never prevenient or even co-operative, but wholly dependent on the divine prevenience. We must say that in the perfect life of Him who was 'always doing the things that are pleasing to God', this divine prevenience was nothing short of Incarnation, and He lived as He did because He was God incarnate. Thus the dilemma disappears when we frankly recognize that in the doctrine of the Incarnation there is a paradox which cannot be rationalized but which can in some small measure be understood in the light of the 'paradox of grace'. Somebody may wish to press the question in another form: Would any man who lived a perfect life be therefore and thereby God incarnate? But such a questioner would indeed be a Pelagian, showing by his very question that he regarded the human side of the achievement as the prevenient, the conditioning, the determinative. When we really accept the paradox of grace, when we really believe that every good thing in a man is wrought by God, when we have really understood the confession: 'I . . . yet not I, but God', and have taken that divine priority in earnest, the question loses its meaning, and, like the proposed dilemma, fades away into the paradox of the Incarnation. And if we take these things in earnest, we have, as it appears to me, at least an approach to the *mysterium Christi* which will enable us to combine the most transcendent claims of a full and high Christology with the frankest recognition of the humanity of the historical Jesus.

It seems certain that whatever restatement of Christology may be necessary in the modern world, it will be in the direction of fuller and ever fuller recognition of both these sides of the truth. On the one hand there will be no abatement, but rather, if it were possible, an enhancement, of the highest predicates that Christian faith has ever given to Jesus Christ as God incarnate.

> *The highest place that heaven affords*
> *Is His, is His by right:*
> *The King of kings and Lord of lords*
> *And heaven's eternal Light.*

---

[1] John viii, 29.

THE PARADOX OF THE INCARNATION

The Church must indeed break out continually into such lyrical notes to make up for the shortcomings of theological prose, and no expression can be too high. Nothing can be too high; and nothing can be too lowly or too human. Nothing can be too high, if only we save it from Docetic and Monophysite unreality by treating His life as in every sense a human life. A toned down Christology is absurd. It must be all or nothing—all or nothing on both the divine and the human side. That is the very extreme of paradox; but I have tried in this chapter to show how, as it seems to me, the derivative paradox which is the distinctive secret of the Christian life may help us to interpret in a truly Christian way the paradox of the Incarnation.

Chapter VI

THE INCARNATION AND THE TRINITY

In the foregoing chapter we reached a certain resting-place in our quest. But before we have rested long we find ourselves confronted with further questions. We have been trying to understand and interpret the historical episode of the Incarnation, the union of the divine and the human in Jesus in the days of His flesh, and I have suggested what seems to me a fruitful line of argument. But we are bound to ask how all this is related to what we may call the antecedents and the consequences of the Incarnation—to what the Church has always believed about the pre-existence of Christ as the eternal Son of God, and about the continued ministry of Christ and His presence with His people in every age through the Holy Spirit. This raises the whole question as to what we mean by the distinction between the Father and the Son, and what we mean by the further distinction of the Holy Spirit from the Father and the Son. In short, we are involved in a consideration of the meaning of the doctrine of the Trinity in its relation to the Incarnation.

I

Two Trends of Trinitarian Thought

There has been a good deal of thought in recent years on the doctrine of the Trinity, partly as a result of the 'return to dogma' and the strong reaction against the movement which reduced Christianity to 'the Jesus of history'. But it is a notable fact that recent interpretation of the doctrine, while professing on all hands to be deeply Trinitarian, takes two divergent if not opposite directions. In the one camp the tendency is in the direction of what in its extreme form might be accused of modalistic heresy. In the other the tendency is in the direction of what might be accused of verging on tritheism, because of its use of the 'social' analogy associated with the Cappadocian Fathers of the fourth century. This is manifestly an important divergence in the theology of our time, and we must briefly consider it.

(a) The outstanding representative of the first of these tendencies in recent theology is Karl Barth. He goes so far as to maintain that it is better to speak of three 'modes of being' in the Godhead than of three Persons, so that he might on a superficial view seem to be tending in a modalist or Sabellian direction. Now it has been a common enough thing in the modern world for theologians of various schools, but especially of the tradition that runs through Schleiermacher and Ritschl, to reduce the significance of the doctrine of the Trinity, softening its distinctions (even to the point of avowed Sabellianism, as in Schleiermacher's case) or belittling them as belonging to metaphysical speculation rather than to the original Gospel (as was the tendency in the Ritschlian school), and generally relegating the treatment of the subject to the closing sections of their systematic treatises. But it is far otherwise with Barth. With him the doctrine of the Trinity is not the epilogue to his dogmatics, but the starting-point, and indeed the broad foundation. It might almost be said that the whole of his immense Prolegomena (in two very large volumes) constitutes a treatise on the Trinity. This is a new turn for Protestant theology on the Continent, and it is highly significant. But it is all the more striking to find Barth, in spite of his return to dogma, suggesting that in the modern world, with its changed use of words, it is better to speak of three 'modes of being' in God than to continue to speak of three Persons.

Barth points out historically how the accepted term *hypostasis* in the East (even if safer than *prosōpon*) and the accepted term *persona* in the West (even if preferable to *substantia*, which would have seemed the natural translation of *hypostasis*) both presented difficulties, so that neither East nor West was really satisfied, though

they accepted the terms. He quotes with a frank expression of re-
lief St. Augustine's bold admission that the use of the term *persona*
in the doctrine of the Trinity was simply a 'necessity' or a 'manner
of speaking', adopted not for its own sake but because it was better
than saying nothing at all.[1] Barth quotes also the famous definition
of *persona* which was given by Boethius in the sixth century and
continued to be influential through the Middle Ages: *naturae
rationabilis individua substantia*, which really means an individual
rational being; and he goes on to point out how Aquinas in particular was conscious that this definition increased the difficulties
of the Trinitarian conception of three Persons in the Godhead.
But it is when we come to the quite modern concept of personality,
which, according to Barth, adds the attribute of *self-consciousness*,
that he feels the difficulty to be acute, because 'three Persons' in
the modern sense would mean three distinct centres of consciousness, three self-conscious personal beings, and this seems very near
to tritheism. Barth points out that in this situation there are two
courses open to theology if it is to retain the formula of 'three
Persons' at all. It may use the word in its modern sense, and conceive of God as actually consisting of three distinct individual
centres of consciousness. This is akin to the line of thought which
we are to consider presently. Or, on the other hand, theology may
ignore the modern concept of personality altogether, using the
word 'Person' in its ancient and medieval sense (which, however,
was not really clarified) and so continue without embarrassment to
speak of 'three Persons in one God'. But to Barth himself both of
these alternatives are so unsatisfactory that he prefers on the whole,
in spite of the departure from traditional usage and the danger of
misunderstanding, to drop the term 'Persons' in the doctrine of the
Trinity and to speak of three 'modes of being' in God. 'The God
who reveals Himself according to Scripture is One in three of His
own modes of existence, which consist in their mutual relationships, Father, Son, and Holy Spirit.'[2] 'The ancient concept of
Person, which is the only one in question here, has to-day become

---

[1] *Non ut illud diceretur sed ne taceretur omnino.*
[2] *The Doctrine of the Word of God* (Eng. trans. of *Kirchliche Dogmatik*, I, i),
p. 400.

obsolete. . . . Wherever ancient dogmatics, or Catholic dogmatics even to-day, speaks of "Persons", we prefer to call Father, Son, and Holy Spirit in God the three individual modes of existence of the one God, consisting in their mutual relationships.'[1] 'It is to the one single essence of God, which is not to be tripled by the doctrine of the Trinity, but emphatically to be recognized in its unity, that there also belongs what we call to-day the "personality" of God.'[2] Thus in the sense in which we speak of ourselves as persons, it is truer to think of God as one Person than as three. 'The problem is not whether God is a person, the problem is whether we are. Or shall we find among us men one whom in the full and real sense of this concept we can call a person? But God is really a Person, really a free subject.'[3] In other places Barth maintains that God is 'a Person in a way quite different from that in which we are persons'. This is 'just because He and He alone is a true, real and genuine person'.[4] Thus the doctrine of the Trinity really reminds us that God is 'personal in an incomprehensible way'; and indeed it is but a hint of 'inconceivable distinctions in God Himself',[5] and especially of the paradox of the revelation to man of a God who according to His essence cannot be revealed to man.[6] 'The Holy Spirit in particular, then, even were that possible in the case of Father and Son, could under no circumstances be regarded as a third 'person' in the modern sense of the concept. The Holy Spirit in particular is in a specially clear way what Father and Son also are, not a third spiritual subject, a third I, a third Lord alongside two others, but a third mode of existence of the one divine subject or Lord.'[7]

This may sound 'modalistic', but it is not Modalism in the heretical or Sabellian sense. There is no such implication in the use of the term, 'modes of existence',[8] and in fact Barth regards

---

[1] Ibid., pp. 420ff.

[2] Ibid., p. 403.

[3] Ibid., p. 157.

[4] *The Knowledge of God and the Service of God*, p. 31.

[5] *The Doctrine of the Word of God*, p. 427.

[6] Ibid., p. 431.

[7] Ibid., p. 537.

[8] The phrase 'modes of being' is part of the traditional orthodox terminology of Trinitarian doctrine, and was used in the Patristic age by the very school

Modalism as a grave error, and explains why. 'The doctrine of the Trinity means, as the denial of Modalism, the expressed declaration that those three elements are not foreign to the Godness of God. The relationship is not that we should have to seek the proper God beyond these three elements, in a higher being in which He was not the Father, the Son and the Spirit. The revelation of God, and therefore His being as Father, Son and Spirit, is not an economy foreign to His essence, limited as it were from above or from within, so that we should have to enquire about the hidden Fourth, in order really to enquire about God.'[1] Plainly Barth does regard the doctrine of the Trinity as standing for real distinctions in God, and, moreover, for the *kind* of distinctions on which orthodox belief has always insisted: the three Persons are not three *parts* of God, and yet they are not mere attributes, or shifting aspects, relative to our apprehension, or arbitrarily selected from among others, but are of the eternal being of the God who has revealed Himself to us in Christ and dwells in us by the Holy Spirit. It would be quite unfair to speak of this as Modalism. Nevertheless it is notable that Barth definitely prefers the term 'modes of being' to the term 'persons', and he may fairly be taken as standing for one of the two divergent contemporary tendencies in the interpretation of the doctrine of the Trinity.

(*b*) On the other hand there is the tendency, mainly among Anglican theologians, to sharpen the distinction between the Persons of the Trinity, and to go farther than theology has been accustomed to go in the direction of regarding them as distinct personal beings between whom there can be a 'social' relationship. In the Patristic age it was the Cappadocian Fathers, the two Gregories and Basil, that went farthest in this direction, illustrating the Trinity by the analogy of three individual men; and thus we might speak of the 'ultra-Cappadocian' movement in modern Trinitarian thought. This goes back for its inspiration very largely

---

that was sometimes accused of leaning towards tritheism (because of their use of the analogy of three individual men)—the Cappadocian Fathers. It is a translation of τρόποι ὑπάρξεως, which means that Father, Son and Holy Spirit are modes of the very *being* of God, not merely modes of revelation, τρόποι ἀποκαλύψεως. See Ottley, *Doctrine of the Incarnation*, 4th ed., pp. 363, 565ff., and *Essays on the Trinity and the Incarnation* (ed. Rawlinson), p. 285.

[1] Ibid., pp. 438f.

to the Gifford Lectures of Professor Clement C. J. Webb.[1] It is interesting that Webb starts from the definition of *persona* by Boethius as *naturae rationabilis individua substantia* which we found Barth quoting as historically important. It was in direct connection with Trinitarian doctrine that Boethius in the sixth century formulated this definition in a controversial work against the Nestorian and Eutychean heresies, and we found Barth asserting that the term '*persona*' as thus used in ancient and medieval theology has nothing directly to do with 'personality' in the modern sense. But Professor Webb makes no such separation between ancient '*persona*' and modern 'person'. 'The general history of the word Person with its derivatives in philosophical terminology may be said to have moved throughout on lines determined for it by the process whose result is summed up in the Boethian definition of *persona*.'[2] He assumes that when ancient or medieval divines discuss *persona* and when modern philosophers or theologians discuss 'person' or 'personality', they are really speaking of the same thing, though not without the concept having undergone some development. And thus he leads us to the admittedly surprising conclusion that it is historically quite unorthodox to speak of God as a Person, or even to speak of the Personality of God. Until quite modern times, he points out, only heretics would have used such expressions, and they did it in criticizing and rejecting the doctrine of the Trinity. Not that orthodox thought did not conceive God as personal. But it spoke of personality *in* God rather than the personality *of* God: it conceived of God as consisting of a unity of three personalities, not as one personality.[3] Moreover, Professor Webb

---

[1] See in particular, *God and Personality* (1918), Lectures II and III.

[2] Ibid., pp. 47ff., 54.

[3] Ibid., pp. 61ff. It is important to note that Barth also, and quite independently, in speaking of what we now call 'the personality of God', points out that 'the concept—not the thing designated by it, but the designation, the explicit assertion of God not as an It but as a He—was as foreign to the Fathers as to the medieval and post-Reformation scholastics'. But he goes on to give a somewhat different perspective from Webb's, as regards the reasons for their attitude and for the modern change from it. 'They always spoke—from our point of view, not theirs—too innocently and uncriticially of the *deitas*, of the *essentia divina*, etc., i.e. apparently of God as of a neuter. The concept of the "personality" of God . . . is a product of the struggle against modern naturalism and pantheism.' *The Doctrine of the Word of God*, p. 403.

does not only speak historically, but ranges himself with that Trinitarian tradition as he understands it, and thus would rather speak of personality in God, or of God as the unity of three Persons, than of God as a Person. 'It might seem then as though Divine Personality might be conceived as analogous to the Personality of a nation or state.'[1]

There can be no doubt about the influence that these ideas have had upon Anglican theology during the last quarter of a century, culminating in Professor Leonard Hodgson's very able and stimulating volume of Croall Lectures entitled *The Doctrine of the Trinity* (1943). It is easy to see how different this interpretation is from that which is offered by Barth, and to see that it is more in line with the analogies (of three distinct individual men alongside each other) used by the Cappadocian Fathers than with the analogies used by others of the Fathers, such as the root, the tree and the fruit, or the sun, the ray and the light, or the source, the stream and the estuary, or the intelligence, the memory and the will in the unity of a single mind. It might almost be said that a school of thought has sprung up around this 'social' interpretation of the Trinity. It has made us familiar with such phrases as 'the social life of the Blessed Trinity', based partly, no doubt, on the traditional idea common to all schools that the doctrine stands for the mutual love that exists eternally within the Godhead apart from the existence of any created beings that could be objects of the divine love. This is sometimes described as giving us something different both from the stark and lonely monotheism of Judaism and from the frank polytheism of pagan religion, a new and richer development in the thought of God, due to the Christian revelation, and making God social as well as personal. In the same circles this has frequently been regarded as having important consequences not only for worship but for Christian ethics, sociology and politics: because God is a Trinity in Unity, a social organism inspired by mutual love, in the faith of Christians, therefore Christianity can never be a merely individual gospel, but must have its social message too—there must be a Christian sociology.[2]

---

[1] Ibid., pp. 273-5. *Divine Personality and Human Life* (1920), p. 157.

[2] For further examples of this whole tendency in Anglican theology see the following: *Essays Catholic and Critical* (1926), especially the essays by L. S.

In all this there is no departure from orthodox tradition, but there is undoubtedly a one-sided emphasis, or a new development of *one* of the strains found in Trinitarian thought through the ages; if not actually, as I think Professor Hodgson would say, a rediscovery, in the light of modern thought, of what the doctrine of the Trinity has always really meant in the setting of the Christian religion. In any case the contrast between this and Barth's interpretation is plain. The one prefers to speak of one Person in three modes of being: the other school prefers to speak quite frankly of three Persons in the highest kind of personal and social unity.[1]

II

The Meaning of the Doctrine of the Trinity

I do not propose to attempt a settlement between the two types of Trinitarian interpretation that have been indicated. One writer on the subject has suggested that different approaches to the problem of the Trinity may be ultimate for different types of mind.[2] But it is important not to exaggerate the antithesis between the two schools of which I have spoken in this matter. It is not only the 'Cappadocians', ancient or modern, that can speak of mutual

---

Thornton and E. J. Bicknell; *Essays on the Trinity and the Incarnation* (1928), especially the essays by F. W. Green and L. Hodgson; Charles W. Lowry, *The Trinity and Christian Devotion* (1946).

[1] According to Barth, who shows no trace of acquaintance with the work of Professor Webb or the other Anglicans who follow him, two earlier attempts were made in modern German theology to interpret the Trinity as three separate Personalities in the modern sense. The first was by a Roman Catholic theologian, Anton Günther, and was actually condemned by Pope Pius IX in 1859. Barth summarizes his teaching thus: 'According to him the single Persons in the Trinity were single substances, three subjects thinking and willing for themselves, proceeding from each other and connected with each other and thus joined together in the unity of an absolute personality.' The other attempt in this direction was by the Protestant theologian Richard Grützmacher in 1910. He 'ascribed severally to Creator, Son, Spirit a special I-centre, with a special consciousness, will, and content. But according to him each individual of the three was also an absolute personality. . . .' Barth remarks that it is difficult not to call this doctrine tritheism. *Doctrine of the Word of God*, pp. 410ff.

[2] F. W. Green in *Essays on the Trinity and the Incarnation*, pp. 244–7.

relationships of love between the Persons of the Godhead. Barth can write: 'Even in the life of God within the Trinity, of course, the eternal generation of the Son or Logos is the expression of God's love, of His wish not to be alone. . . . The eternal generation of the Son by the Father itself asserts first and foremost that even apart from the world and us altogether God is not lonely: His love has its object in Himself.'[1] Barth can speak of 'the love of the Father to the Son, of the Son to the Father' and can say: 'This eternal *love in God Himself* is the Holy Spirit.'[2] And on the other hand, the Anglican writers who go farthest with the 'social' interpretation of the Trinity must not for a moment be suspected of verging upon tritheism or of neglecting the truth that God is One. Professor Hodgson, who has developed this line of thought more fully and with finer subtlety than any other writer, never suggests that the unity of a human social organism, the 'personality' of a society or a state, is anything like an adequate analogy of the divine unity. Rather does he regard the unity of the three Persons in God as a higher kind of unity than any other that we can imagine, and indeed as a mystery beyond our understanding. And yet I find it difficult to go the whole way with an interpretation which is, as it seems to me, so one-sided in its emphasis that it excludes certain familiar and traditional principles of Trinitarian doctrine. If we regard the three *personae* of the Trinity as quite distinct persons or personalities in the full modern sense, we seem to imply that they are *parts* of God, and it is difficult to remedy this by going on to speak of their being united in the highest conceivable kind of unity. If they are three distinct Persons, are they limited by each other, so that they are *finite* Persons? Or if that is rejected as intolerable, and it is maintained that each has the divine attribute of infinity, is it not very difficult to think of *three infinite Beings*, of the same essence, coexisting with each other as distinct entities? Yet I do not see how the interpretation in question can avoid that difficulty.

The Cappadocian Fathers indeed eased the situation by their doctrine of the *perichoresis*, circumincession, or mutual interpenetration of the three Persons, and by their doctrine that the whole of God is in *each* of the three Persons. But that means that

---

[1] Ibid., p. 158.
[2] *Credo* (Eng. trans.), p. 136.

while those Fathers could speak of the Trinity under the analogy of three individual men, they used the analogy only in a very limited measure, and did not go the whole way with the idea that the Persons are three distinct personalities in a 'social' unity even of the highest kind, as is indeed indicated by the fact that they could also speak of the three Persons as God's three 'modes of existence'. Moreover they emphasized the identity of operation of the three Persons. St. Basil wrote: 'The Father and the Son and the Holy Ghost alike sanctify, quicken, enlighten, comfort, and effect all else of the same kind. . . . So likewise all other operations are equally wrought in the saints by the Father, the Son and the Holy Ghost.'[1] He was also, perhaps, the first to suggest that the numbers One and Three are not to be taken in a hard and fast and literal sense. 'St. Basil refuses, in fact, to apply to the Deity any numerical ideas at all, as implying a limitation which has no place in God. If it is folly to say that God is Three, it is equally foolish to say that He is One in number. If this divine simplicity exists in modes of being ($\tau\rho\acute{o}\pi o\iota$ $\acute{v}\pi\acute{a}\rho\xi\epsilon\omega s$), these are not three in relation to each other, so that we can, as it were, count them, one, two, three; but the Father one, the Son one, the Spirit one.'[2]

It is plain that all these qualifications were made because of the difficulties and dangers that would be involved in conceiving quite literally of three distinct individual personalities coexisting in God. It is also plain that these qualifications alter the whole situation, so that the resultant doctrine, while very different from a cold and transcendental Jewish monotheism, is also very different from the idea of God consisting of three distinct persons in the modern sense, one of whom could be simply identified with Jesus of Nazareth. Such an idea is surely an over-simplification—perhaps we should say an over-rationalization—and the reality is a much deeper mystery. It was easy for the ancient Arians, with their 'common-sense' theology, to get the distinction between the Father and the Son quite clear cut; and we ought to remember that what started the whole Arian controversy was that Arius, with his sharp dis-

---

[1] Basil, Ep. clxxxix, 7. Quoted by Ottley, *Doctrine of the Incarnation*, p. 364.

[2] F. W. Green in *Essays on the Trinity and the Incarnation*, pp. 284f. Cf. the following by the Jesuit Father Przywara: 'The doctrine of the Trinity has nothing to do with a numerical "one" and "three".' *Polarity* (Eng trans.), p. 71.

tinctions, accused his quite orthodox bishop of Sabellianism because he did not so sharply distinguish the Persons. It was much more difficult for profounder thinkers to state their doctrine of the relation of the Persons. The Arians were so crudely literal as to argue that if the Son had been co-eternal with the Father, then He would not have been a Son but a Brother![1] But to their orthodox opponents the matter was not so simple and clear cut, because they were more conscious of a deep mystery. One Athanasian argument was that if the Son did not exist with the Father from all eternity, that would mean that once God was without His Wisdom and Glory, that once the Father had no Word or Reason. It is worth while to quote from the well-known passage attributed to Athanasius, in which, citing the Old Testament passages about God being the fountain of life, the fountain of living waters, the fountain of wisdom, he identifies this life and wisdom with the Son or Logos. 'Is it not then irreligious to say, "Once the Son was not"? For it is all one with saying, "Once the fountain was dry, destitute of life and wisdom". But it would then cease to be a fountain; for what begetteth not from itself is not a fountain.'[2] These are, doubtless, mere figures of speech suggested by particular passages of the Old Testament. But this manner of speech is characteristic of a certain strain in Patristic theology, and not least of the theology of Tertullian,[3] who was so bitterly opposed to the Modalist conception of the Trinity. It has, of course, to be balanced by a more personalistic mode of speech, and by far the most definitive terminology was that of 'the Father and the Son', which from the Council of Nicaea onwards superseded the Logos terminology. It is even more important in the modern world to emphasize this truth that God is always and wholly and in every respect *personal*. Nothing in God is impersonal. His Word is personal. His Spirit is personal. Personality in God must indeed be a very different thing from personality in us. But that is because we are far from being perfectly personal. God is the only perfectly personal Being. So when Christians speak of any one of the *personae* of God, Father, Son or Holy Spirit, they do not say 'It', but 'He' and 'Him'. Yet when they speak of the

---

[1] Athanasius, *Orations against the Arians*, I, v.
[2] Ibid., I, vi.
[3] See Tertullian, *Adversus Praxean*.

Triune God, they do not say 'They' and 'Them'. God is three 'Persons', but He is also the infinite and universal Person in three 'modes of existence'. Both ways of expression are needed. And I do not see how theology can safely or successfully take the formula of three Persons and rationalize it into a Christian philosophy which conceives of a symmetrical triad of three distinct personalities in the modern sense co-existing in a higher unity. That appears to me to be an over-simplification of a mystery, or an over-rationalization of a paradox.

In the preceding chapter I suggested that the meaning of the doctrine of the Trinity may be closely connected with that highly paradoxical conception of God which comes to the Christian in his consciousness of 'the paradox of grace'. Let me now try to elaborate that suggestion. It strikes me as a curious fact that if the question were put to a mixed selection of theologians: 'What is the distinctively Christian conception of God, which came into the world as something relatively new through Christianity?' two apparently quite different methods of answering would appear in different quarters. Some would proceed to answer by extracting from the Synoptic Gospels the distinctive teaching of Jesus about God, as compared with what prophets or wise men had said before Him, and from this would go on to its explication in the rest of the New Testament, showing what kind of God St. Paul and St. John believed in. There would thus emerge an account of the 'character' of God as holy and loving beyond measure, taking the initiative in seeking men before they seek Him, infinitely merciful and redemptive. But others, quite as a matter of course, would take what seems an entirely different line, and answer: 'The new and distinctively Christian conception of God is the Trinitarian conception, Father, Son and Holy Spirit in one God.' Which of these is the true answer? What I am suggesting is that the two are not really divergent but convergent and ultimately identical. The first needs to be crystallized into the second, and the second needs to absorb the first.

The God in whom Christians believe is, as we have seen, not merely the Creator, the Lawgiver, the wise and righteous Moral Governor, but something far more wonderful: He is the One who *gives* us what He demands of us, *provides* the obedience that He requires; so that we are constrained to acknowledge what I have called the paradox of grace, expressed in the confession: 'I . . . yet not I, but the grace of God.' This is a paradox because the ascription of all the glory to God for anything good that is in us does not imply any destruction of our freedom as human personalities, but precisely the reverse: our actions are never more truly free and personal and human, they are never more truly our own, than when they are wrought in us by God. But the whole experience of this paradox, which covers only those fragments of our lives in which there is something good, has come into our lives through One in whom it covered the whole of His life, so that His life was the very life of God Himself, and yet was at the same time in the fullest sense the life of a man. Jesus Christ is the One in whom human selfhood fully came to its own and lived its fullest life, as human life ought to be lived, because His human selfhood was wholly yielded to God, so that His whole life was the life of God. That was the one life which was wholly divine and wholly human. He lived His life in such a way that it was the life of God incarnate; but also, since the initiative is always with God, He lived it as He did *because* it was the life of God incarnate. And thus through Him there came to those who knew Him a new revelation of God.

But what happened through Him did not come to an end when 'the days of His flesh' ended, though His disciples thought it would and were appalled at the prospect of His being taken from them. Very soon afterwards they made two great discoveries. They discovered, first, that the divine Presence of which they had become aware while their Master was with them in the flesh had come back to them, and was going to continue, in a far deeper and more marvellous way, in a way that was independent of His actual presence in the flesh, though not independent of His *having* lived on earth in the flesh. It was the same, and yet different, for it was as though their Master had now drawn them into something of that union with God which had been His secret, and now they know God for themselves and He has taken possession of them. And their second discovery was that this experience, which depended entirely on Jesus, need not be confined to those who had known Jesus in the flesh. It could come to anybody anywhere through the story of Jesus and their witness to its meaning. They went hither and thither and told the story; and the thing kept happening. It was a new experience of God, and it lifted people out of themselves, and above the moral struggle, into a spontaneous goodness which claimed no credit for itself but gave all the glory to God. This was something new in mankind's knowledge of God. It could not have come if Jesus had not lived. It all depended on Him. And yet it was different from the experience of knowing Jesus in the flesh—not less, but greater, deeper, more universal, more transforming. It was a further stage, which could not have come while Jesus was present in the flesh; so that it was actually 'expedient' for His followers that His earthly life should end, in order that this might come.

What was it? His followers remembered how they had often read a prophecy of a coming age when God would pour out His Spirit not merely on occasional outstanding men like the prophets, but on all sorts of ordinary people.[1] They remembered also things which their Master had said about God giving His Spirit to them for their needs. And they said: This is what the prophet Joel foretold,[2] this is what Jesus promised. This is the Holy Spirit, giving back to us for ever all that we thought we should lose, and much more; reminding us of all that Jesus taught us, helping us to understand it better, carrying us farther still, teaching us new truth, giving us the presence of Christ in a new and greater way, to dwell in our hearts and to do in us and for us what we could not do ourselves. Thus they could say, thenceforth, concerning any good that was in their lives: Not I, but the grace of God that was with me. Not I, but Christ that dwelleth in me. It is not we that speak, but the Spirit of our Father that speaketh in us.

Thus the paradoxical Christian knowledge of God inevitably came to be expressed in the Trinitarian form: God the Father, God the Son, and God the Holy Spirit, three in one. Not in the sense of three successive parts played by God, or three successive phases of His being, as the Modalists of the third century sometimes said; for God was and is ever the same, and it is the same Holy Spirit who inspired the Old Testament prophets that can take the things of Christ and show them to us. Nor, again, in the sense of a symmetrical triad of Persons with quite separable functions. We do not exhaust the truth of the matter by saying that while God the

---

[1] Joel ii, 28f.
[2] Acts ii, 16ff.

Father reigns eternally on high, God the Son was incarnate in Jesus on earth, and God the Holy Spirit dwells in us. The New Testament can also speak of God the Father dwelling in Christ, and of the Holy Spirit being given to Christ; and it can speak of God the Father dwelling in us and we in Him, and of Christ dwelling in us, and we in Him. All this seems impossible to systematize, and indeed it does not make sense until we remember the historical facts and experiences out of which it arose, and attempt to relate them to the eternal God. When we do that, the doctrine of the Trinity sums up the Gospel by telling us that the God of grace, who was revealed through the Incarnation and Pentecost as the One who paradoxically works in us what He demands of us, is the same from all eternity and for ever more; so that where men of old sang: 'Not unto us, O Lord, not unto us, but unto Thy name be the glory', Christians can sing: 'Glory be to the Father, and to the Son, and the Holy Ghost: as it was in the beginning, is now, and ever shall be, world without end.'

III

The Background of the Incarnation

Having thus considered the relation of the doctrine of the Trinity to the 'paradox of grace' which I took as our clue to the meaning of the Incarnation, we are now in a position to take up the questions that I mentioned at the beginning of this chapter. The first of these is the question of what might be called the background of the Incarnation, or the relation of that historical episode to the pre-existent or eternally existent Son of God. When we confess 'one Lord Jesus Christ, the only-begotten Son of God, begotten of His Father before all worlds . . . who for us men and for our salvation came down from heaven and was made flesh and was made man', what are we asserting? Obviously we are using symbols, including a spatial metaphor, and are striving to express in our inadequate words the relation of the temporal and the eternal. But what is the truth that we are trying to express? 'When the fullness of the time came, God sent forth his Son, born of a woman, born under the law.'[1] What does that mean? In what sense was the life that Jesus lived on earth, with its human choices from moment to moment, determined by 'heavenly' antecedents, as the life of the eternal Son of God who became man 'in the fullness of the time'?

Right through the Patristic Age and the Middle Ages the question was frequently asked whether the Incarnation was in any way contingent upon happenings in the course of human life on earth, and whether it would have taken place at all, or in the same manner and conditions, if man had not sinned. This question in its more usual forms will be touched on in our next chapter. But one form of it is highly relevant to the present point. Why did the Incarnation take place just at the time it did? In what sense was that 'the fullness of the time'? Why could it not happen earlier? Why was it at so late a point in the long history of the human race that God sent His Son for its salvation? Since God was always working, and never left Himself without a witness among men, why such long delay in the coming of this full revelation and redemption? These questions may be foolish, or at least they may be largely unanswerable. But here is a partial answer that was sometimes given: that through all the earlier ages of mankind God was preparing for the Incarnation and paving the way for it in the world —'paving the way of faith for us, that we might more easily believe that the Son of God had descended into the world'. It was to this end that the Son of God 'condescended to converse with men, from Adam down to the patriarchs and prophets'.[2] And then, when man was ready to receive it, the full revelation came. Thus we may say that God was continually pressing through into human life in every age, so far as man would allow, and the reason why the Incarnation did not take place earlier is because man was not sufficiently receptive. Since man is not a puppet and cannot be saved against his will, there is a sense in which God cannot go faster with His revelation than man will let Him. That is what gives a tragic note to the 'sacred history' of ancient Israel. Israel was a 'chosen people', chosen by God not because they deserved it or had earned their fitness for it, but that God might make them fit and

---

[1] Gal. iv, 4.
[2] Tertullian, *Adversus Praxean*, c. 16 (Souter's trans.).

use them for His saving purpose in the world, since the initiative is always with God. Yet on the other hand there is a sense in which His choice and His use of them were conditioned by the fitness of their response, because God could not use Israel as His slave but only as His son. And it is precisely because of their obtuseness, their intractability, that His purpose had to work so slowly. He had to wait for men who would be responsive, 'stretching out His hands all day long to a disobedient and contrary people'. That must be true even of His purpose of Incarnation, and so it may be said that the Incarnation did not come earlier in human history because man was not ready to make a full response.

Therefore when at last God broke through into human life with full revelation and became incarnate, must we not say that in a sense it was because here at last a Man was perfectly receptive? If the life of our Lord is to be conceived as a truly human life, subject to the hazards of all human life on earth, we must indeed say that the Incarnation of the Divine Word in Him was conditioned by His continual response. If it was a real Incarnation, not to be explained away in the docetic manner, it depended in a sense upon His free human choice from moment to moment. 'He that sent me is with me; he hath not left me alone; because I do always the things that are pleasing to him.'[1] 'Therefore doth the Father love me, because I lay down my life, that I might take it again.'[2] On this verse Professor Leonard Hodgson has commented: 'There is no getting away from the plain meaning of the verse. It represents the Father's love for the Son as conditional on His fulfilling His vocation. But the thought of the love of the Father for the Son as being in any sense conditional is beyond Christian imagination. Only, in silent and wondering reverence, we can listen to the words as spoken by our Lord.'[3]

Yet there is more to be said. That is indeed a side of the truth to which we must do full justice unless we are content to let our Lord's earthly life be reduced to an unreal show. But as soon as we have said these things, we remember that, by the inevitable paradox, the other side is also true, and even with a deeper and

---

[1] John viii, 29.
[2] John x, 17.
[3] Leonard Hodgson, *And was made Man*, p. 200.

prior truth, so that the sayings just quoted might be reversed and be equally valid—'I do always the things that are pleasing to Him, because He is with me and hath not left me alone.' The divine is always prevenient. And so from the human life of Jesus on earth we are, paradoxically but inevitably, led back to its divine origin and eternal background in heaven, on which it all depended. 'When the fullness of the time was come, God sent forth his Son', and He who was 'born of a woman, born under the law', lived as He did because He was the Son of God.

In that sense it is impossible to do justice to the truth of the Incarnation without speaking of it as the coming into history of the eternally pre-existent Son of God. This does not mean, it need hardly be said, anything like a conscious continuity of life and memory between Jesus of Nazareth and the pre-existent Son. Nor are we to think of the human personality of Jesus of Nazareth as having had any heavenly and eternal pre-existence. The Church has never taught that the human element in Jesus, His manhood, is consubstantial or co-eternal with God, but that it is consubstantial with ourselves and belongs to the order of created things. But it was the eternal Word, the eternal Son, very God of very God, that was incarnate in Jesus. And the initiative is always with the divine; so that we are bound to say: 'God sent forth His Son', and He 'came down from heaven and was made flesh and was made man'. It is of this eternal and heavenly background of the Incarnation that St. Paul is thinking when he says: 'Ye know the grace of our Lord Jesus Christ, that, though he was rich, yet for your sakes he became poor';[1] and again when he speaks of 'Christ Jesus, who, being in the form of God, counted it not a prize to be on an equality with God, but emptied himself, taking the form of a servant, being made in the likeness of men'.[2] And St. John: 'God so loved the world that he gave his only-begotten Son',[3] and 'Herein was the love of God manifested in us, that God hath sent his only-begotten Son into the world, that we might live through him'.[4] These verses deal with the relation between the temporal and

---

[1] 2 Cor. viii, 9.
[2] Phil. ii, 6, 7. I am aware that some scholars interpret this differently.
[3] John iii, 16.
[4] 1 John iv, 9.

the eternal, the relation of the historical Incarnation on earth to its eternal and heavenly antecedents, and therefore they are obviously figurative and symbolic in their expressions. But we are bound to use such expressions in order to do justice to the divine priority and initiative and condescension, and even sacrifice, in the Incarnation. We are bound to use them in such a way as to confess that while the life lived by Jesus was wholly human, that which was incarnate in Him was of the essence of God, the very Son of the Father, very God of very God. Thus the doctrine of the Trinity, which inevitably arose out of the historical Incarnation, gives us its eternal background in the only possible terms.

IV

The Legacy of the Incarnation

If Christianity has always had something to say about the heavenly antecedents of the Incarnation, about the pre-existent Christ, it has always had even more to say about the sequel to the Incarnation, about the risen and glorified Christ who is 'on the right hand of the Father' and who also dwells with and in His people on earth until the end of the world. How is all this related to the line of thought that we have been following? If God was incarnate in a real Man who lived a fully and genuinely human life on earth, where is that Man now? The days of His flesh are long past, but are we still to think of Him as living a human life in what we call heaven, united with God by that divine indwelling which, as we saw, does not destroy human nature and personality but consummates it? Or is all that over and done with, so that now we have to think only of the divine Son, the second Person of the Trinity, who once assumed human nature for a brief period of thirty years and lived as a Man among men, but who has now left that behind? Are we to say that His humanity ended with the days of His flesh on earth?

A great many would-be orthodox people will without a moment's thought say: Yes, all that was left behind. But the voice of the Church has clearly and consistently said: No, it was not left behind: the humanity of Christ continued and is permanent. He, 'being the eternal Son of God, became man, and so was and continueth to be, God and man in two distinct natures and one person for ever'.[1] Doubtless this answer raises further questions which are exceedingly difficult to deal with, and which we may not be able to answer at all so long as we 'see through a glass darkly' in this present life on earth. But it is easy to see that the opposite answer would be a betrayal of the whole meaning and reality of the Incarnation, as the Church decided unequivocally in the year 451 at the Council of Chalcedon. This was, of course, part of the doctrine of the two distinct natures, the divine and the human, united in the one Person of Christ, which was first quite clearly defined in the Chalcedonian formula. This formula has been sharply criticized in the modern world, as making an unnatural dualism in the Christ whom we know from the Gospel story,[2] and the criticism is not unjust. We should not naturally express the truth in those terms to-day. But the two-nature doctrine was obviously intended to safeguard the complete recognition of the humanity of Christ, as against Eutyches and the Monophysites. If Chalcedon insisted on two distinct natures in Christ, it was because those who said 'one nature', fusing the divine and the human into one, really meant that the human was lost in the divine. They did not really believe in the humanity of the life that Jesus lived on earth. Much less could they entertain the idea of His being still human in His heavenly state after the days of His flesh were past. And whenever people find that idea surprising, is it not because they have misconceived the meaning of the Incarnation itself, thinking of it as a mere theophany, by which the Son of God appeared for a short time on earth in the guise of mortal flesh, and then returned to heaven, no longer human because He never was human except in the sense of inhabiting a human body? That is very different from the doctrine of the Incarnation. If we believe in the Incarnation, we cannot possibly say that Jesus ceased to be human when He departed from this world.

But when we go on to ask further questions about His life in glory, about the conditions of His continued humanity, about the

---

[1] *Westminster Shorter Catechism*, 21.

[2] E.g. by H. R. Mackintosh, *Doctrine of the Person of Jesus Christ*, pp. 293-9.

sense in which He is still a Man, and about the relationships that
are involved, we have obviously entered a region in which many
questions can be asked that cannot be answered. Perhaps indeed
the only questions in this whole region that we can ever expect to
be able to answer are those which directly concern the life of faith
—questions that are not speculative but practical, about the relationships that are possible in the actual present between Christ and
ourselves. And here again it seems plain that the only possible
answer to our questions is to be found in the doctrine of the Trinity.

In the early days of Christianity, the question must often have
been asked: What can make up to us for the loss of the actual
presence of Jesus on earth? How can a precious memory take the
place of His presence for those of us who once knew Him in the
flesh? And how can an old story, given by others at second hand,
avail for those of us who never knew Him in the flesh at all? As we
read chapters fourteen to seventeen of the Fourth Gospel we can
almost hear those questions being asked. But in these and many
other chapters of the New Testament we can also quite unmistakably hear them being answered. The Church was clear about the
answer. It derived from Pentecost, and amounted to this: that
Christians need not be content with either an old story at second
hand or a precious memory of the past, and those who never knew
Jesus in the flesh are at no disadvantage as compared with those
who did; because the divine Presence which He brought into the
world goes on for ever in the hearts of His people through the Holy
Spirit. It seems clear that this is why the doctrine of the Holy
Spirit becomes so vitally important in the New Testament. It was
not absent from the Old Testament, but now there is a new reason
for its prominence. A new thing had come into the world with Jesus
Christ, God manifest in the flesh; and the new thing, while dependent on Him, was not confined to the days of His flesh or to
those who had known Him in the flesh: it is available in an even
fuller form to everybody, everywhere, and in every age, through
the Holy Spirit. If we go on to ask whether there is any difference
between having God's presence with us, having Christ dwelling in
us, and being filled with the Holy Spirit, we are bound to answer
that the New Testament makes no clear distinction. It is not that
no distinction is made between the Father, the Son, and the Holy

Spirit; but all three come at every point into the full Christian experience of God. It is not a case of three separate experiences: it is all one.[1] The God who was incarnate in Christ is still present with us and in us through the Holy Spirit. And yet there is very good reason for the threefold distinction, and indeed it is indispensable, as the only way in which the peculiarly Christian apprehension of God could be expressed. The Incarnation of God in Christ made a permanent difference in man's knowledge of God, and we know God now as the Father of our Lord Jesus Christ. Yet our knowledge of God is not just the same as His. Ours is dependent on His. And not dependent merely as a pupil depends on his teacher. Nor again in the sense that our knowledge of God is at second hand. For the Holy Spirit who from Pentecost onwards showed the disciples the real meaning of what Christ had been and said, and thus led them into the new knowledge of God for themselves, does the like for us. Or, to put it otherwise, the God who was incarnate in Christ dwells in us through the Holy Spirit; and that is the secret of the Christian life.[2]

So we come back to the paradox that we have taken throughout as our guiding-thread, the paradox of grace, which in the lives of Christians is a result and reflection of the Incarnation, raising them above 'mere morality' into a new kind of goodness which they confess is not their own but God's. 'Their ability to do good works is

---

[1] For this point I may be allowed to refer to what I wrote a good many years ago about those chapters of the Fourth Gospel, in my *Faith in God*, pp. 261ff.

[2] That great missionary, Temple Gairdner of Cairo, whose life-work it was to give the Christian message to Mohammedans in face of their antagonism to any Trinitarian conception of God, wrote some deeply interesting words on this subject out of his experience. After reminding us that the Mohammedans themselves have a kind of borrowed doctrine of the Holy Spirit, a heavenly being quite distinct from Allah, he speaks of the missionary's task of showing them that the Holy Spirit 'is not a sort of second and inferior deity, but is God in our hearts'. 'The glorious truth is that the Christian synthesis yields a true monotheism, which the Muslim dilemma does not.' He goes on to say that what Christianity, with its doctrine of the Trinity, is really up against in facing Islam is the Mohammedan conviction that God is unknowable. And as regards Christ and the Holy Spirit: 'The Spirit of God, which was in Him, and which through Him is the divine means of grace to-day', 'we have nothing else to give the Muslim unless we give this.' (See the Report of the Jerusalem meeting of the World Missionary Council in 1928, entitled *The Christian Message*, pp. 264ff., 279ff.)

not at all of themselves, but wholly from the Spirit of Christ. And that they may be enabled thereunto, besides the graces they have already received, there is required an actual influence of the same Holy Spirit to work in them to will and to do of his good pleasure.'[1] Plainly it is this paradox, with the conception of God which it implies, and with its dependence on Jesus Christ, that is summed up in the doctrine of the Trinity.

Therefore it seems to me that the Trinitarian approach to God must always be important for Christian worship, as a safeguard against our worshipping an idol of our imaginations instead of the true God. It is somewhat surprising to find Professor Emil Brunner writing as follows: 'The doctrine of the Trinity is a theological doctrine, not a scriptural proclamation ($\kappa\acute{\eta}\rho\upsilon\gamma\mu\alpha$). It is not a message to be preached. It is a defensive doctrine, which would not have been necessary at all if the two fundamental statements of the Christian creed had been allowed to stand: God alone can save, and Christ alone is the divine salvation.'[2] If the doctrine of the Trinity is not a message to be preached, would Brunner also say that it is not of importance for Christian worship and devotion? That would seem to follow; and so it remains merely a 'theological' doctrine. I should be inclined to say almost the opposite. Of course I do not deny that it is a theological doctrine, but this seems to be the point at which the ubiquitous paradox of religious thinking reaches its climax, and theology *exit in mysterium*. As I have already indicated, I do not see how this doctrine, with its symbolical expressions, can be fully rationalized and conceptualized and worked out into a philosophical theology. But it seems to me to be an indispensable summing-up of the Christian Gospel for the life of worship. This is where the recent Anglican treatment of the doctrine of the Trinity, which I have had to criticize theologically, seems to me to be thoroughly sound and indeed highly important. There has been a kind of rediscovery of the fact that Trinitarian doctrine is not merely of theological interest but is vital to the life of faith and devotion.[3] In the third Chapter I maintained that unless

---

[1] *Westminster Conf. of Faith*, xvi, 3.
[2] Emil Brunner, *The Mediator*, p. 276.
[3] E.g. the last of the seven lectures in Prof. Leonard Hodgson's *The Doctrine of the Trinity*, is on 'Trinitarian Religion'. And in Dr. Charles W. Lowry's book,

we have a Christology our whole conception of God is impoverished or even perverted, and now I might say the same thing about the doctrine of the Trinity. To those who know and accept the whole Christian story, this doctrine is a symbolical epitome of the truth about God, and its constant use in our worship helps to secure that we are drawing near to God as He really is—the God who was incarnate in Jesus Christ.

The Trinity and Christian Devotion, the last two of six chapters are on 'Devotion and the Trinity' and 'Worship, Action and the Trinity'. Both of these books make the point very strongly that the life of faith must be based quite definitely on the Trinitarian apprehension of God.

Chapter VII

WHY ATONEMENT?

I

Cur Deus Homo?

It is often said that in the modern world the besetting question about the Christian faith or about any statement of it is not 'Is it true', but 'Is it relevant?' However tired we may be of the word 'relevance', there is some point in this remark. In past ages, and especially at certain periods, it has been a common enough experience for devout souls in Christendom to find themselves doubting what they had been taught to believe, but it has usually been a painful experience, because without religious belief life seemed to have no taste or meaning, and they heartily wished they could recover their faith. But now something new seems to have appeared: there seem to be many people, especially of the younger generation, whose perplexity is not as to whether religious beliefs can be true, but as to whether it makes any difference. Does it matter to me, in the actual business of living, whether the mysterious being called God really exists, or whether I believe in His existence, any more than it matters whether I know of the existence of some distant star which is not visible to the naked eye? And more particularly, many men of to-day, after listening to an elaborate argument about the Incarnation, designed to make it intelligible and credible that God was incarnate in a man who lived in Palestine nineteen centuries ago, will ask: Why is it so important? In what way should I be the better of believing in it?

If such blank questioning is widespread, this is doubtless an indication of the extent to which Christendom has moved away from an even elementary knowledge of Christian teaching; and it also suggests that we who are Christians have not been giving a very good account of what we believe. But the questions themselves are perfectly real and reasonable, and they must be answered. The questions of the Wherefore and the Why of the Incarnation and of its bearing on actual human need, if they are now being asked with a new note of bewilderment, are nevertheless very similar to those that were continually being asked and debated by divines in the Patristic age and through the Middle Ages. Why did God become man? For what purpose did Christ come down from heaven?[1] These were the simplest forms of the question. But the inquiry was pursued much farther, because it seemed that the answers might affect the whole problem of the meaning of the Incarnation. Was the Incarnation part of God's original and eternal plan for mankind, as the true end and crown of creation? Or was it made necessary only by the Fall of Man and the consequent need of redemption? Would Christ have come if Adam had not sinned?[2] If man had not fallen, would the Incarnation perhaps have taken place in a different way and under different conditions? Or was it simply in order to die on the Cross for human salvation that Christ came at all? And was it necessary that human salvation should be accomplished by that one method? Could not God have saved man in some other way, perhaps in a less costly way, by a mere fiat of His will? All of these points were debated in the Middle Ages, and even if the asking of the more hypothetical questions was sometimes deprecated, they were asked because they seemed to have a bearing not only upon human salvation but upon the interpretation of the Incarnation itself. Calvin deprecated the asking of curious questions as to whether God would have become man if there had been no Fall, on the characteristic ground that we know from Scripture that Christ actually did come in order to redeem us from sin, and that is enough.[3]

To us the more speculative of the questions mentioned above, if not completely unreal, will at least appear to be among those un-

---

[1] *Cur Deus Homo? Ad quid Christus descendebat?*
[2] *Utrum Christus venisset si Adam non peccasset.*
[3] Calvin, *Instit.*, Bk. ii, chap. xii, secs. 4–6.

answerable questions about which it is best to profess a *docta ignorantia*. But it is different when we come to the question as to how the Incarnation, and the belief in it, actually affect human salvation. That is a question which any theory of the Incarnation must be prepared to answer and must find to be crucial. We may hesitate to accept all the implications of Melanchthon's famous saying that to know Christ is simply to know His benefits, lest we should land ourselves in a Ritschlian Christology of mere value-judgments. But any knowledge of Christ, or any Christology, which cannot show how it makes a vital difference, and brings 'saving benefits' to our human situation, must be more than suspect. The *Heidelberg Catechism* asks at one decisive point, 'But what doth it help thee now, that thou believest all this?'[1] This question of 'saving benefits' may well be used, as in principle it has regularly been used since the days of the Fathers, to test any proposed interpretation of the Incarnation and to draw out its meaning. If your Christology is true, what difference does it make? How are we the better off, in the actual business of living, for having such a Christ?

Now I have already given a partial answer to these questions by showing how our Christology affects our whole conception of God. The doctrine of the Incarnation properly understood, gives us the Christian apprehension of God, with all its saving power; leads us, in short, to the Trinitarian conception, which is the true basis for sound Christian living. But this is not a sufficient answer. If the central tradition of Christian theology through the centuries has been right, the full answer cannot be given without a consideration of the whole problem of sin and forgiveness, atonement and reconciliation. There can be no doubt that this is what the Christian witness has said from the beginning. 'Faithful is the saying, and worthy of all acceptation, that Christ Jesus came into the world to save sinners.'[2] 'Verily the Son of Man came . . . to give his life a ransom for many.'[3] God 'sent his Son to be the propitia-

---

[1] '*Was hilft es dir aber nun, wenn du dies Alles glaubest?*' *Heidelberg Catechism*, Q. 59. Karl Barth uses this question from the Catechism effectively in introducing his treatment of the Forgiveness of Sins in his *Credo*.

[2] 1 Tim. i, 15.

[3] St. Mark x, 45.

tion for our sins'.[1] It is true that some of the Greek Fathers seem to give less emphasis than was given by the New Testament and by Latin Christianity to the thought of salvation from sin through the death of Christ, and that they sometimes think of God as assuming human nature in order to transform it by illumination and so make it immortal. But the thought of Christ having come into the world to die for our sins was never very far away. Thus Christology was continually passing into Soteriology, and throughout the whole Christian tradition the supreme human exigency to which the doctrine of the Incarnation had to be related and made relevant has been the need of salvation from sin, the forgiveness of sins.

But at the same time it is beyond dispute that to a great many modern minds even within Christendom this exigency itself is largely unreal. Not only will they question the whole idea of an 'atonement' that must be made, or can be made, for human wrongdoing in order that it may be forgiven: they will go much farther still. They will wish to ask whether the message of the forgiveness of sins is itself in any way 'relevant' to the human situation to-day. And the answer cannot be taken for granted. Why do we need to have our sins forgiven? What difference does that make? If we are to be radical, we must answer that question. We must try to understand what the forgiveness of sins means in the Christian life, and to exhibit it as something real and vital, and from that work backwards to the question of Atonement and its connection with the Incarnation.

II

The Need of Divine Forgiveness

It is a commonplace to say that the sense of sin and of the need of forgiveness is largely strange to the modern mind. The distinguished scientist of last generation who remarked that the higher man of to-day is not troubling about his sins may not have meant what he was taken to mean, but his *obiter dictum* was quoted to the

---

[1] 1 John iv, 10.

point of weariness because it seemed to give expression to a widespread attitude. Since then two world wars, with the accompanying revelations of human wickedness, may have somewhat altered the scene, but Dr. Reinhold Niebuhr, who knows his world so well, could still in 1939 speak of 'the complacent conscience of modern man' as the one thing common to all modern views of human nature. 'The universality of this easy conscience among moderns is the more surprising since it continues to express itself almost as unqualifiedly in a period of social decay as in the eighteenth- and nineteenth-century heyday of a bourgeois culture.' He quotes a contemporary writer who dismisses the sense of sin as 'a psychopathic aspect of adolescent mentality'.[1] This utterance comes, he says, from 'a particularly vapid modern social scientist', yet it illustrates a common attitude. Apart, however, from theorists altogether, there is a modern inability to understand the sense of sin and especially the meaning and the need of divine forgiveness. 'Why', many a serious-minded man will ask, consciously or unconsciously, 'should I brood over my sins and the need of having them forgiven? If my forefathers did so, it seems to have been because they were troubled about the *punishment* of their misdeeds in this world or the next. But it is not the penalty that matters most, but the wrongdoing in itself. And that now belongs to the past and cannot be changed by "penitential tears" or any other process. Therefore why waste time on "crying over spilt milk"? (Fichte said: "I have no time for penitence.")[2] It is the future that matters now. No one can "atone" for my misdeeds except myself, and I can do it only by leaving them behind, making any possible reparation to any whom I may have wronged, and then forgetting the past and going blithely on to better things. Therefore I will not trouble about my sins and their forgiveness.'

To many a modern mind all this sounds true and wholesome, and of course it would make nonsense of the whole Christian message of salvation. But is it really true and wholesome? Would it work? It seems to me to be extraordinarily naïve and unrealistic. It betrays a profound ignorance of human nature, and even, as we shall presently see, of modern psychology. For the fact is that if we

---

[1] R. Niebuhr, *The Nature and Destiny of Man*, vol. i, p 100.
[2] Quoted by H. R. Mackintosh, *Types of Modern Theology*, p. 232.

are serious-minded and morally earnest we shall quite inevitably
brood over our moral failures unless we have some deeper secret of
dealing with them. I am not maintaining that we *ought* to brood
over them, but simply that we shall. It may not do us any good,
it may be a waste of time, it may even be a hindrance to our going
on to better things; but none of these considerations in themselves
can save us from brooding over our misdeeds if we are taking life
in earnest. The advice, 'Don't worry', is always futile, even when
accompanied by the assurance that worry does far more harm than
good, unless it is also accompanied by some prescription for overcoming worry. If I set my heart on riches or honour or anything
else, and miss or lose the beloved object, I shall inevitably feel
sorrow and disappointment in exact proportion to the strength of
my desire and the place it occupied in my life. And if my moral
ideal, my quest of the good, takes first place, then I shall be more
troubled about my misdeeds, my moral failures, than about anything else in the world. It is idle to talk of forgetting them quickly
and going on blithely to better things. For if I can treat them thus
lightheartedly and go on my way rejoicing without a qualm or
pang, then undoubtedly I shall not go on to better things, but to
the same things over again. I shall repeat my old sins, world without end, because I do not greatly care about right and wrong, I
do not take these issues very seriously. If I did, I should be gravely
troubled.

Must we then, after all, conclude that the modern mind, when it
is serious, is gravely troubled about its sins? Has the typical decent
'modern' man after all a sense of sin? No, I do not think that he
has. But I should like to suggest that he has a kind of *moralistic
substitute* for the sense of sin, and that this much less wholesome
substitute is the chief cause of that perennial *malaise* which surely
underlies the superficial complacency of the modern mind.

If 'sense of sin' is to the modern man a piece of unmeaning
theological jargon, there is another kind of jargon which he
readily understands, that of the new psychology; and it provides
a phrase which every schoolboy knows, and which may help me to
explain what I mean by the moralistic substitute: the phrase
'inferiority complex'. It seems to me that a great many persons in
the world to-day have something like a repressed 'moral-in-

feriority complex' or 'moral-failure complex'. They do not confess their sins to God or man, but they have an uneasy dissatisfaction with themselves and with what they have made of their moral opportunity. They do not consciously accuse themselves, for they have a protective pride which is highly characteristic of the whole situation. Their companions might never suspect that there was any dissatisfaction, but rather the reverse; for the inferiority complex, as the psychologists tell us, easily passes over, by a process of over-compensation, into the superiority complex, which is but the other side of the same state of mind. The dissatisfaction may be with one's own personal character and conduct, or it may involve an obscure sense of complicity in the great public evils that have brought such tragedy to our age, but in either case it is largely repressed and subconscious. A man is secretly sick of his unworthy past, but he does not know what to do with it, and therefore cannot face it. The sense of it becomes a repressed complex, festering uneasily under the surface, with the effect of confusing the whole moral outlook, paralysing moral endeavour, inhibiting every attempt at a new beginning. It would doubtless be a gross exaggeration to describe such a condition in all cases as one of repressed complexes, in the exact psychological sense, with definitely 'psychopathic' results. Perhaps I am merely borrowing a convenient set of terms. Yet it is, after all, a matter of degree, and it may not be too much to suggest that there is something pathological in the *malaise* of which I have been speaking. Thus it is not the sense of sin that is 'psychopathic', but the moralistic substitute, which develops in an age of unbelief under the surface of a secularistic complacency. 'Under the perpetual smile of modernity', says Niebuhr, 'there is a grimace of disillusion and cynicism',[1] and there may also, in the less superficial minds, be what I have called the 'moral-failure complex' with its morally paralysing effect.

Now, everybody knows that the modern psychology which has discovered repressed complexes to be the cause of so much *malaise* has also prescribed a simple cure. It consists in dragging up the complex into the light of day. Very often it turns out that it had a trivial origin, in some unpleasant experience long forgotten,

---

[1] Op. cit., p. 129.

perhaps a sudden fright or a harsh rebuff experienced in child-hood, the memory of which was repressed by an unconscious de-fence-mechanism until it grew into a morbid complex beneath the surface of consciousness. As soon as it is discovered and dragged up into full consciousness, it can be calmly faced, it loses its terror, which had no real foundation, and the mind is healed.

But it is plain that this is not true of the kind of trouble which I have ventured to call the 'moral-failure complex'. For in this case the *malaise* has a real foundation, which is not trivial or inno-cent but solid and evil: the fact of moral failure, the fact that a man has disobeyed his conscience, betrayed his ideals, tarnished his character, lost his battle. These are hard facts, and the sting is not taken out of them when they are faced in the light of day. That makes them look worse instead of better. So it seems plain that the technique of psycho-analysis cannot in itself meet this situation and liberate the will for a new beginning. What then is the solution of this desperate problem?

There is no solution so long as we remain on the level of 'mere morality'. There is no solution until we allow the whole situation to be transformed by an orientation towards God. A moralist, as such, can never forgive himself. That is where we see most plainly the bankruptcy of the attempt to have morality without the life of faith. The endeavour is sure to defeat itself, because it is self-centred instead of God-centred, which is the very root of evil. And the more earnest it becomes, the more hopeless does it be-come, because it has no way of dealing with its failures. The poor moralist is too proud to forgive himself, and so self-righteousness and self-despair meet together and are one, hindering the soul's salvation.

> O son, thou hast not true humility;
> . . . for what is this
> Thou thoughtest of thy prowess and thy sins?
> Thou hast not lost thyself to save thyself.[1]

The situation is quite different when the soul is orientated towards God. Then morality is no longer 'mere morality', but

---

[1] Tennyson, *The Holy Grail.*

takes its place, transformed and wholesome, as part of the whole life of faith. Then the consciousness of moral failure becomes something different: it becomes a sense of sin against God, a sense of having disobeyed the will of God, of having betrayed the love of God. Then it is no longer a case of merely dragging our repressions up into the light of day, but rather: 'Thou hast set our iniquities before thee, our secret sins in the light of thy countenance.' That makes the situation worse than ever. But also better than ever, with a quite new possibility, because of the divine forgiveness. A moral law cannot forgive, and the moral consciousness cannot forgive itself. But these are abstractions, and the concrete reality is God, whose love, continually claiming us, is what we so inadequately call the moral law. This love does not give us up even when we betray it, but keeps pressing upon us with the offer of forgiveness. And if we have come to be so orientated towards God that we are more concerned about Him than about our own characters, then we can accept His forgiveness and find release and a new beginning.

It was, I think, from one of F. W. Robertson's sermons that I learnt this lesson many years ago, and I will cite a passage, which begins with a sentence quoted with strong disapproval from Newman. ' "A true penitent", says Mr. Newman, "never forgives himself." O false estimate of the Gospel of Christ and of the heart of man! A proud remorse does not forgive itself the forfeiture of its own dignity; but it is the very beauty of the penitence which is according to God, that at last the sinner, realizing God's forgiveness, does learn to forgive himself. . . . This is the great peculiar feature of this sorrow: God is there, accordingly self is less prominent. It is not a microscopic self-examination, nor a mourning in which self is ever uppermost: *my* character gone; the greatness of *my* sin; the forfeiture of *my* salvation. The thought of God absorbs all that.'[1] And here is a similar testimony, from a very different quarter, about the penitence of the Christian: 'His sorrow for sin is not a mortified, humiliated, angry disgust with himself. It is a humble hopeful sorrow, always "turning into joy". . . . "But I am unworthy of joy; I am willing to work and suffer if need be as a

---

[1] From the sermon on *The Power of Sorrow* (*Sermons*, Third Series).

sinner. I don't look for joy." That is a sentiment true for a pagan, but it contradicts the whole Creed of the Catholic Church. "I believe in the Holy Catholic Church, the communion of saints, the forgiveness of sins." '[1]

I have been trying to show the 'modern' man, in his own terms, that the consciousness of sin against God and of the divine forgiveness, instead of being morbid or unpractical, is the ultimate secret of wholesome living and far more conducive to it than the moralistic substitute which belongs to a secular age. Why is it that such maladies as neurasthenia, 'nervous breakdown', are so common in our modern world? Is it entirely unconnected with the fact that there are now so many serious-minded people who have no belief in God, who are trying to have morality without religion? Because they have no God, they have no saving secret for dealing with their moral failures. They cannot lightly shake off the memory of them, because they are in earnest; yet they cannot really face the memory, because they know nothing of divine forgiveness; and so their memory of failure, instead of becoming a wholesome sense of sin which can lead to forgiveness, is unconsciously repressed until it becomes a morbid complex, with paralysing effects. Their sorrow is 'the sorrow of the world, which worketh death'. It needs to be turned into the 'godly sorrow' which 'worketh repentance unto salvation and bringeth no regret',[2] because it leads to forgiveness. That is what brings liberation and renewal, sometimes (psychiatrists tell us) to the body as well as to the mind and will.[3] As for the true life of the Christian, it is a life in which those morbid 'moral-failure complexes' need never develop, not because he is never troubled about his sins, but be-

---

[1] *Spiritual Letters of Father Congreve*, p. 11.

[2] 2 Cor. vii, 10. This is the text from which F. W. Robertson preached the sermon quoted above.

[3] One of my theological teachers used to quote what an Edinburgh psychiatrist said: 'I always send my patients to hear Dr. —— preach, because he preaches the doctrine of the forgiveness of sins.' To this I may add the following testimony from Dr. Leslie Weatherhead: 'After fifteen years of psychological study and practice as a minister in the Christian Church, he hopes that he is not presumptuous in saying that he can quote case after case in which the received idea of the forgiveness of sins has resolved the conflicts in men's minds, and led to the complete disappearance of disabling physical symptoms.' See *Times Literary Supplement*, 7th March 1935.

cause he continually uses the liberating secret, confessing his sins with sorrow every day and receiving God's forgiveness and the grace of a new beginning. 'If we say that we have no sin, we deceive ourselves, and the truth is not in us.' We are using an 'escape-mechanism' and running away from reality. But 'if we confess our sins, he is faithful and righteous to forgive us our sins, and to cleanse us from all unrighteousness'.[1]

III

Forgiveness and Punishment

How is this forgiveness related to the actual punishments that we have brought upon ourselves and others by our sins, and that apparently continue to operate after we have accepted God's pardon? We cannot escape that question, and a consideration of it may shed still further light upon the Christian experience. Take the case of a man who by a sinful course of living has brought upon himself physical disease and disability, or loss of employment and prospects, with severe privation. He must indeed regard this as the divine punishment of his sin. Yet when he sincerely repents and accepts God's forgiveness and 'turns over a new leaf', those evil consequences of his old sins may still pursue him in his new life and may even continue as long as he lives. How is he to regard them now? Is God, who has 'abundantly pardoned' his former sins, and 'remembers them no more', still punishing him for them? I am aware that some theologians answer that question in the affirmative, maintaining that the divine forgiveness has nothing to do with remission of punishment. But I find it very difficult to take that position. So long as the sinner was hiding himself from God, these evil consequences were indeed his punishment. They looked black enough under the shadow of that cloud of sin, though even then God's love, hidden behind the cloud, was seeking his good. But now that he is forgiven and is living in the light of divine love, these things are no longer punishments, though he brought them upon

---

[1] 1 John i, 8, 9.

himself by his sin and still has to bear them. The real punishment lay not in the sufferings themselves, but in the alienation from God, and the frown of His wrath, of which they are inevitably and rightly taken as expressions. Once the reconciliation has come, the sufferings are the same and yet different. There is nothing particularly difficult or novel in this idea that the same things become quite different in meaning when they come to us in the light of the divine love. And it is not merely a question of words, whether we speak of 'punishment' or not: it concerns the whole spirit of the Christian life. If a man's sins are forgiven, that is an end of them; and now the suffering they have left as their legacy is simply part of his lot, a divine discipline perhaps, but not a divine punishment. It is part of the situation which, in the providence of God, he has to face, his share of the cross of humanity; and it is God's will that he should face it blithely, not with proud and bitter remorse, refusing to forgive himself, as if he had not received God's forgiveness, but with faith and hope, just as he has to face other troubles not due to his own fault, and as all true men have to do.

But let us suppose that the man's wrongdoing has involved suffering and disaster for other people. That is the hardest part. Let us suppose that he has brought material and even moral and spiritual ruin to other lives alongside his own, and that he sees this go on even though he is himself forgiven and is leading a new life. What good is even God's forgiveness to such a man in such a case? How could he even accept it honourably? Ought he then to go softly all his days in the bitterness of his soul, reproaching himself with gloomy remorse, brooding wretchedly over the ruin he has caused, living in the spirit of a convict working off a life-sentence with a very black mark against him? Is that the truly Christian way of facing the situation?

One must speak carefully at a point where misunderstanding is so easy. But I cannot believe that the bitter way described is the truly Christian way. It is certainly true that the man must make reparation to those whom he has ruined, to the utmost of his ability and at whatever cost; and if he tried to shake off this responsibility lightly, he would merely show that he had not truly come to repentance or begun to understand the divine forgiveness. If he has really understood and accepted it, his chief endeavour for the rest of his days will be to put right what he has put wrong in the lives of his fellows. That will come before everything else, and the stress of it will always be a chastening discipline. But he must not set about it in a glum and bitter frame of mind, working like a galley-slave under the lash of a tormented conscience, as if he had not been forgiven at all. That will not help, but hinder, his work of reparation in the lives of his fellows. 'If we are sinners forgiven', wrote Father Congreve again, 'we ought to behave as forgiven, welcomed home, crowned with wonderful love in Christ, and so cheer and encourage all about us.'[1] The man is forgiven, and now the evil he has caused in other lives is part of the world's great mass of evil, which all true men must help to bear, with God's gracious aid. It was caused by his sin, but even that is not the most important fact about it now. After all, we ought, all of us, to be in some measure feeling the whole of the world's woe, as a burden for which we have a corporate responsibility. We human beings cannot feel it all equally, or visualize it all continually, or we should go mad, like the man mentioned in Kierkegaard's *Journals* who went mad through thinking continually of the revolution of the earth upon its axis! We are bound to be more keenly concerned, each one, with that portion of the world's woe which our own situation presents most plainly to us; and especially with any part of it that is directly due to our own past misdeeds and that calls for active reparation. But as regards feeling, mood and temper, is there not a danger of our making *too* sharp a distinction between the woe that we have caused and the rest of the world's woe, as if the former really mattered more? It all matters equally to God, and it all matters equally to the victims, whether we or others have caused it, and however we may feel about it. And when we refuse to see it thus, may it not be that we are still thinking too much of ourselves, our own merit and demerit, instead of having our souls orientated in the truly Christian way towards God and towards our fellowmen in God? May it not be a persistent relic of the self-

---

[1] Op. cit., p. 12. Cf. the following, from George Macdonald: 'Can one ever bring up arrears of duty? Can one ever make up for wrong done? Will not heaven be an endless repentance? It would need a book to answer the first two of these questions. To the last of them I answer, "Yes—but a glad repentance".' (*Alec Forbes of Howglen*, vol. i, chap. xxv.)

centredness which is the essence of sin, and even of the pride which is its most deadly form, because it will not accept the forgiveness of sins; the pride that makes us refuse 'justification by faith' and choose 'justification by works'? The Christian way is the very opposite. It sets us free for the service of God and man by delivering us from ourselves. And so its ultimate confession, as we have been seeing throughout these chapters, is: Not I, but the grace of God.

It seems to me that this is very near the heart of the new secret that Paul discovered in becoming a Christian. He had all his life been trying to save himself, to win God's favour by keeping His law and being a good man. But he knew in the bottom of his heart that he was not succeeding, though he could not face the fact: and so there was in his life a great deal of what we should call 'unresolved conflict'.[1] Then in his conversion he learned that he had been making a grand mistake: he had been viewing reconciliation with God from the wrong end. He discovered that God's love for us does not depend on our being worthy of it. We could never possibly earn His love by our own goodness, and when we try we make a very bad business even of our goodness, becoming at the best self-righteous 'Pharisees' such as Jesus disliked (Paul was a Pharisee). But we do not need to earn God's love: He loves us already 'while we are yet sinners'.[2] It is He that takes the initiative in reconciliation. He has done it in Christ, and it is for us to accept as a free gift what we could never earn or deserve. And then comes release and a new quality of life. 'And not only so', writes Paul, who has his own memories of having 'persecuted the Church of God and made havoc of it', doing perhaps irreparable harm in the world, 'but we also rejoice in God through our Lord Jesus Christ, through whom we have now received the reconciliation'.[3] He, the former persecutor, is not fit to be called an apostle. 'But by the grace of God I am what I am: and his grace which was bestowed

---

[1] The evidence for these statements may be found in his letters (see Gal. ii, 18–21; Rom. vii, 9–23; Phil. iii, 4–9) as well as in the speeches attributed to him in Acts (see especially Acts xxvi, 14, 'It is hard for thee to kick against the goad').

[2] Rom. v, 8.

[3] Rom. v, 11.

on me was not in vain; but I laboured more abundantly than they all: yet not I, but the grace of God which was with me.'[1]

All this discussion, apparently so digressive, of the nature of the experience of divine forgiveness, has been necessary in the argument against the complacency of the 'modern man', by way of showing the bankruptcy of a morality which attempts to dispense with the forgiveness of sins. 'Why speak of divine forgiveness? Surely a man must atone for his own sins by immediately leaving them behind.' I have tried to show how that is just what he cannot do. His attempts defeat themselves, and there is no solution of his moral problem until God comes in. 'All for sin could not atone: Thou must save and Thou alone.' Martin Luther somewhere in dealing with this matter refers to Horace's rule of dramatic art, that a God must not be introduced into the action unless the plot has got into such a tangle that only a God could unravel it.[2] Well, says Calvin, human sin is such a tangle.[8] Only God can deal with our sins.

IV

But Why Atonement?

At this point of my argument the modern man, with whom I began the discussion in this chapter, will inevitably wish to ask: But why do you speak of *atonement* at all? Is not forgiveness enough? He might indeed point out—and other critics might agree with him from other points of view—that I seem in this matter to have cut the ground from under my own feet by maintaining that God loves us equally through all our sins, that His love in no wise depends on our being worthy of it, but is eternally seeking us for our good, and that His forgiveness is free to all who will accept it. If that is indeed what Paul discovered in becoming a Christian, how could he afterwards work out a theology in terms of redemption, propitiation, reconciliation, through the blood of Christ?

---

[1] I Cor. xv, 10.

[2] '*Nec deus intersit nisi dignus vindice nodus inciderit.*'—HORACE, *De arte poetica*, 191 f.

[3] Unfortunately I do not know where Luther says this.

What room is there for an atoning sacrifice? Does not God's free forgiveness cover everything?

That position has often been taken in the modern world, even by theologians, usually perhaps in violent reaction against falsely crude and sub-Christian theories of atonement. Here are two examples, both from the school of what is commonly named 'Liberal Protestantism' on the continent of Europe. Paul Wernle of Basel wrote: 'How miserably all those finely constructed theories of sacrifice and vicarious atonement crumble to pieces before this faith in the love of God our Father, who so gladly pardons! The one parable of the Prodigal Son wipes them all off the slate.'[1] And Wilhelm Bousset of Göttingen wrote: 'The sin which you have committed no one can atone for instead of you, neither man nor God. . . . Sin and guilt can only be removed by the voluntary moral and personal act of one God, who forgives sin and remits guilt.' These utterances sound so reasonable that it is no wonder if the 'modern man' now asks me: How can you still speak of the need of atonement? Do you not, after all, believe in the eternal love of God seeking out sinners to forgive them freely?

In reply to this I will ask another question: Is there no difference between a good-natured indulgence and a costly reconciliation? There is an immense moral and spiritual difference between the two. And which of them are we to attribute to the love of God? Does the whole process of reconciliation cost Him nothing? Is His forgiveness facile and cheap? And if it were, or if we accepted it as such, would it have the liberating power, to set us free for a new and better life?

When we speak of God's free love toward us, continuing unchanged through all our sin, and eternally ready to forgive us, there is always the danger that this should be taken to mean that God is willing to pass lightly over our sins because they do not matter much to Him; that it is all a matter of easy routine, about which we need not be greatly concerned and need not greatly wonder. The classical expression of this is in the oft-quoted words of the dying Heine: 'God will forgive me: that is His business.'[2]

---

[1] Wernle, *The Beginnings of Christianity* (Eng. trans.), I, p. 109.
[2] '*Dieu me pardonnera: c'est son métier.*' *Souvenirs de la vie intime de Henri Heine*, by Princess della Rocca, (Paris, 1881), p. 125.

This illustrates a real danger of misunderstanding the doctrine of divine forgiveness in a way which would make the whole idea morally unwholesome. It is as if God were to be regarded as indulgent and good-natured, making as little as possible of our misdeeds, glossing over our delinquencies. Frederick Faber's hymn about the kind Shepherd and the frightened sheep has one verse which runs:

> *There is no place where earth's sorrows*
> *Are more felt than up in heaven:*
> *There is no place where earth's failings*
> *Have such kindly judgment given.*

After the simple truth of the first two lines the third and fourth lines always seem to me to make a very weak anti-climax, with the total effect of suggesting that God feels our sorrows much more deeply than our sins, and that His attitude to our sins can be described as mere 'kindly judgment'! Is God's love for sinners simply 'kindly judgment'? Nay, it is 'a consuming fire'. He cannot take our sins lightly or treat them with indulgence. 'The love that draws us nearer Thee is hot with wrath to them.' God must be inexorable towards our sins; not because He is just, but because He is loving; not in spite of His love, but because of His love; not because His love is limited but because it is unlimited, and because, as George Macdonald said, 'nothing is inexorable but love'.[1]

We may, I think, find at least a faint analogy of this in the love of a true friend who receives a grave wrong but who generously forgives. If I play my friend false behind his back in a weak moment, basely betraying his confidence, and he discovers it, will he pass over it lightly, without any painful explanation and restoration? If he is a shallow soul, and not a very true friend, he may treat the matter in that light way, for the sake of comfortable relations, because he does not care very deeply for me. But he cannot do that if he is a good man and a true friend who loves me deeply. It is not that he will be slow to forgive me; but his forgiveness will not be a

---

[1] Cf. this, from one of Macdonald's novels, with reference to God: 'He will forgive anything, but he will pass nothing.' Cf. also these words of Mélanie Calvat, shepherdess of La Salette: 'The love of God is without mercy.' Quoted by Raïssa Maritain. *Adventures in Grace*, p. 136.

good-natured indulgence. It will come out of an inexorable fire of love which I shall shrink from facing. I shall be far more afraid to meet him and look him in the face than I should be if he were a shallow friend. So great a thing is his forgiveness.

But if these things are true, it is also true that in the whole great process of forgiveness it is my friend that has the hardest part to play. It is he that bears the brunt. He suffers more than I. Not because he is the person that has been wronged: nay, it is the shame of what I have done that weighs most on him. He bears my shame as if it were his own, because of his great love for me. He bears more of the agony than I, because he is a better man and loves more deeply. And it is out of all this noble anguish that his forgiveness comes. All that is what lies behind it.

How much more deeply all these things must be true of God, both in His judgment of our sins and in His 'atonement' for them! My human friend, whom I have wronged, knows that, after all, he is not the ultimate judge of my conduct. He will keep reminding himself that his judgment is fallible and apt to be one-sided, he will guard against being misled by his own *amour propre*, he knows the deceitfulness of his own heart so much better than he can know mine, and he will make all possible allowances. Even then he must be faithful with me if he loves me. But God loves me perfectly and knows me perfectly—far better than I can know or love myself. If I have been disloyal to Him, as I have in all my misdeeds, I have been disloyal to the infinite Love which is the heart of the universe, which is the source and end of my existence, and the very meaning of the 'moral law' which I have broken. There can be nothing more inexorable than such a love. If I have betrayed it, that is the ultimate betrayal. That is what has to be wiped out, and such an 'atonement' must be the most difficult, the most supernatural, the costliest thing in the world.

But also—if we may follow the analogy farther—it is God that bears the cost. Our reconciliation is infinitely costly to Him. Not in the sense that it is difficult for Him to forgive us, as it would be difficult for a Shylock, who has to be induced not to insist upon his pound of flesh; not in the sense that He is inhibited from forgiving, by some hard necessity outside His own nature, so that there has to be an 'expiation' before God can act mercifully. It is His very nature to love and to forgive. He could do no other, and He has to wait for nothing but our response. Yet the forgiveness is not an easy amnesty, such as a good-natured tyrant might give with a stroke of his pen. It comes from the heart of a love that has borne our sins, and because the love is infinite, the passion is infinite too. 'Who suffers more than God?' asks Piers Plowman. There is an atonement, an expiation, in the heart of God Himself, and out of this comes the forgiveness of our sins.

It is from the sacrificial system of ancient Israel that we have inherited the whole terminology of atonement, expiation, propitiation, reconciliation; and it seems to me that after a long and puzzling story we find that system reaching in the Christianity of the New Testament a climax in which it is completely transformed into the idea of an atonement in which *God alone bears the cost*. The whole subject of sacrifice in ancient Israel is both complicated and controversial, but I must sketch the broad facts on which I base this statement.

The initial function of sin-offerings and guilt-offerings in Israel was the wiping out of ceremonial offences. In saying this, I do not imply anything as to the earliest meaning and purpose of sacrifices in Israel, or as to the point of time when they first came to be connected with the removal of sin and guilt; for both of these are controversial matters. But it may safely be said that when sacrifice did come to be regarded as a means of expiating offences, it was not the great and wilful moral offences, such as flagrant breaches of the Decalogue, that were in question, but the ritual offences which might be committed either unwittingly or through carelessness and without any very evil intent. These could be wiped out through the appropriate sacrifices. But for the remission of great and deliberate sins of dishonesty, violence, and the like, there was no such provision: God might indeed in some cases be induced to be merciful, but that would be something exceptional, on which nobody could count; and, in general, sinners must simply take their punishment. It is, of course, important to realize that this did not mean final and everlasting punishment in the next world, for the whole of that eschatological prospect of judgment was beyond the horizon. The punishment was in this world. For some great offences there was a civic punishment, inflicted according to the legal code. For others God would punish with misfortune, perhaps even to the third or fourth generation; sometimes with defeat in war and national calamity, if the offence were rather corporate than individual.

But in the great Prophetic movement which began in the eighth century B.C. two new notes appeared, and they are indeed among the glories of the prophetic message. First, the prophets began to proclaim, with immense conviction, that it is the moral offences (as we should call them) that really matter: injustice, dishonesty, bribery, perjury, oppression, violence, cruelty. These are the *real* sins, and so long as these go on, even if they keep on the safe side of the law, as they can so easily do under respectable disguises, God cares not at all for the most correct and profuse offerings and sacrifices: nay, He hates them and is disgusted with them, He will not accept them, or look with any favour on those who offer them. And the other new note was this: God will freely forgive even the greatest sins, if only the sinners will repent and turn from their evil ways. Nothing else is needed, no expiation, no offerings, for God has everything already. Sincere repentance is enough, and a real turning from sin to God; and then the sinner can count on God's mercy. 'Let the wicked forsake his way, and the unrighteous man his thoughts: and let him return unto the Lord, and he will have mercy upon him; and to our God, for he will abundantly pardon.'[1]

Now a student of the history of Israel, finding these two new and epoch-making messages emerging in the Prophetic movement, might expect to find the whole sacrificial system soon afterwards coming to an end, either by an official discontinuance or by a slow languishing into decay. But instead of this we find that in the Post-Exilic period the sacrificial system became more elaborate than ever, with more emphasis than ever on sin- and guilt-offerings, and not only in relation to ceremonial offences, but now with full and regular provision for the sacrificial expiation of *all* the sins of the people. Various explanations of this may be given. It may very well be that the great prophets themselves never meant that the sacrifices could be dispensed with altogether (this is a controversial point among specialists). Or it may be that there was always a gulf

---

[1] Isa. lv, 7.

between the prophetic and the priestly tradition in this matter, though I think scholars now maintain that this has been greatly exaggerated. It may very well be also that as time went on the problem of sin and forgiveness and the need of expiation became more acute to the devout mind: because continuing national calamity seemed to speak of the divine displeasure; because with a deepening sense of the meaning of sin people felt that they were never able to make a perfect repentance and were slipping back into sin every day; and perhaps because there was also a deepening sense of the meaning of punishment as alienation from God, and an extension of its meaning beyond this world under the influence of the apocalyptic movement. All this might lead to a more earnest use of the sacrificial cultus, even by those who had best learnt the prophetic message of repentance and forgiveness. And so we come to the beginning of the Christian era.

Now when we turn from that long story to the Christianity of the New Testament, we find this extraordinary climax. On the one hand we find the Prophetic message of absolutely free forgiveness to the penitent sinner carried much farther than ever, with a definite extension that has been recognized even by Jewish scholars as surpassing anything ever taught by prophet or rabbi before.[1] We find Jesus teaching that God not only freely forgives the sinner who turns to him in repentance, but goes out in quest of the sinner who has *not* repented, as a shepherd goes out into the wilderness to find the one lost sheep. On the other hand we also find the New Testament writers speaking of the long sacrificial tradition as having at last found its climax and fulfilment; but in such a way that its meaning is completely transformed, because now it is God Himself that makes the sacrifice. All the old terms are used, which we translate as sacrifice, offering, expiation, propitiation, atonement, reconciliation, and which meant so much to every Israelite who had a sense of sin. But now they have received a radically new interpretation,[2] not only because they are applied figuratively to that Christian sacrifice which was not in the literal sense a sacrifice at all, but because it is ultimately God Himself that is regarded as bearing the brunt and paying the price. That is the

---

[1] See chap. iii above (p. 63).
[2] This will be taken up more fully in the next chapter.

remarkable witness, in many different forms, of the New Testament. Here is the 'reconciliation' which wipes out our trespasses, but we contribute nothing to the process: 'It is all of God',[1] who provides the means Himself. Just as Abraham 'did not spare his beloved son' but was ready to sacrifice him for God, so God 'did not spare his own Son, but gave him up (we might almost translate "sacrificed him") for us all.'[2] Here is the sin-offering, but now the victim and the priest are one, and they are none other than the eternal Son of God, through whom He made the worlds, 'the effulgence of his glory and the impress of his substance'.[3] Here also is the lamb sacrificed for the sins of men; but this Lamb is 'in the midst of the throne of God', this 'Lamb of God that taketh away the sin of the world' is none other than the eternal Word, the eternal God, by whom all things were made.[4]

Thus the two strains that we distinguished, from the age of the Prophets onwards, become one in their Christian climax: the strain that tells of God's readiness to pardon freely and abundantly, and that which persistently speaks of the need of costly atonement. God's forgiveness, as now understood in the New Testament, outruns all human attempts at expiation, because the expiation is made in the heart and life of God Himself, the Divine Shepherd, who goes out into the wilderness in quest of the lost sheep. As I have already in this discussion quoted one simple popular hymn about the Divine Shepherd, I may be permitted to quote some imaginative lines from another.

> '*Although the road be rough and steep,*
> *I go to the desert to find my sheep.*'
> *But none of the ransomed ever knew*
> *How deep were the waters crossed,*
> *Nor how dark was the night that the Lord passed through*
> *Ere he found the sheep that was lost.*

---

[1] 2 Cor. v, 18.

[2] Rom. viii, 32. It is important to note that in the LXX of Gen. xxii, 16, it is the same Greek word that is used of Abraham, not 'sparing' Isaac. As regards the Pauline passage, in the context of which he is talking of 'justification', ought we perhaps to translate the remainder of the verse: 'Will he not also with him *forgive* us everything?'—a meaning which the Greek (χαρίσεται) can easily bear?

[3] Heb. i, 1–3.

[4] Rev. vii, 17; John i, 1, 2, 29.

That is the atonement for our sins that takes place in the very heart and life of God, because He is infinite love; and it is out of that costly atonement that forgiveness and release come to us.

I have tried in this chapter to show how the endeavour after the good life becomes bankrupt without the message of the forgiveness of sins, and how this in turn must rest on a doctrine of divine atonement. But this has been only a preparation for what comes next, and the reader must now be impatient to ask: How is all this connected with the Cross of Christ? It is indeed high time for us to deal with that question, so much debated for many centuries, though we can do no more than endeavour to see whether the issues are becoming any clearer. This will occupy us in the next chapter.

Chapter VIII

THE LAMB OF GOD

St. Anselm has sometimes been accused of beginning at the wrong end in his study of the Atonement,[1] because he began by exhibiting in an abstract way the exigency of the situation which called for such a divine atonement before proceeding very belatedly to contemplate the actual provision made by God in Jesus Christ. I may be accused of making the same mistake. But though I should then be in very good company, I think it would be truer to say that I have tried to exhibit the Christian experience of reconciliation in order to work back from it to a consideration of that which made it possible, the Cross and Passion of Christ.

I

Why did Jesus Die?

If we are to understand the relation between divine Atonement and the Cross of Christ, we must surely begin by turning to the Gospel story and to the Jesus of history. The men who shaped the tradition and wrote the story down in the four Gospels devoted an altogether disproportionate amount of their space to the passion and death of their Master, because to them and their fellow-Christians this was of supreme importance. But they also took a great deal of trouble to prepare for that climax by giving vivid and

---

[1] In his *Cur Deus Homo?*

elaborate reminiscences of the words and deeds of Jesus throughout His public career, as these had been preserved in the tradition, because the meaning of the Cross could not be understood without some knowledge and understanding of the person who died on it. And if we say, with the voice of the Christian ages, that Jesus died for sinners, it will be well for us to realize at the outset that this is profoundly true, not merely as a matter of theological interpretation, concerning the overruling purpose of God, but also in a purely historical sense, in respect of Jesus' personal relations with the sinners in ancient Galilee.

It has often been remarked that the question, *Why did Jesus die?* embraces several distinct questions.[1] It may mean: Why was He condemned to death by the Roman Procurator? or: Why did the Jewish authorities contrive to get Him condemned? It may also mean the theological question: What was the ultimate purpose of the death of Jesus in the divine economy, the providence of God? Or again it may mean: In what sense and for what reason did Jesus Himself 'lay down His life' on the Cross? All of these questions, though not unconnected, can be distinguished from each other, and it is especially important to see that the last two are two different questions. It is true, I believe, that Jesus accepted the Cross as from the will and purpose of God. But it was by human faith that He did it, not by the superhuman knowledge which can 'declare the end from the beginning'. And as it would be artificial to think of Him as setting forth from the beginning with the clear consciousness that He had come into the world to die a violent death for human salvation, it would be equally artificial to think of Him as forming the *intention*, at any point in His career, of being condemned to death.[2] The evidence of the Gospels leaves no room for such an idea of Jesus' plans, though it has sometimes been entertained by modern writers. The Gospels were written at a time when Christians could look back and glory in the Cross as ordained by the purpose of God; but they do not conceal the fact that to Jesus Himself, when He looked forward and saw that it was likely, and even

---

[1] This is worked out in detail in Dr. A. B. Macaulay's penetrating volume of Cunningham Lectures, *The Death of Christ* (1938).

[2] Cf. A. B. Macaulay: 'The voluntariness of His death is totally misconceived if He be represented as inviting it.' Op. cit., p. 114.

when He embraced it by faith, it appeared as an unspeakable tragedy, and that up to the last night He hoped and prayed that it might not come.

At the same time, it is important to realize, Jesus did not die as a helpless victim: He could have escaped, and He went on with His eyes open. Not only in the Galilean days, but even in Jerusalem almost up to the last, He could have steered clear of the trouble and danger by changing His course. If He had been content to give up His troublesome activities and retire into private life, the authorities would doubtless have been glad to let Him do it: indeed that was precisely what, by opposition and intimidation of various kinds, they tried to make Him do. It would have saved them a great deal of trouble. And He would have saved His life. That was the choice He had to face. But though even His own disciples would have liked Him to take a safe course—which added greatly to the stress of the choice [1]—He could not hesitate. 'He that saveth his life shall lose it': so He had taught. He *could* have saved His own life, but it would have meant the loss of all that He had lived for. So He would not turn aside from the path that was leading Him to suffering, shame and death.

What then was the path that He would not give up though He should have to die for it? What did He die for? What brought Him to such an end? In a word, it was, more than anything else, His attitude to 'sinners'.

In the preceding chapter I spoke of Paul's discovery that God loves sinners, not waiting for them to earn His love or become worthy of it, but loving them while they are still sinners. Where did that revolutionary discovery come from? What was its ultimate source? Whatever may have been the process by which it came home to Paul in his conversion, it seems indubitable that the discovery came in the first instance from the plain story of how Jesus, as He moved about Galilee, had taken people's breath away by showing Himself a 'friend of sinners'. There is nothing more unmistakable or better authenticated in the Gospel records than this: that the Rabbi from Nazareth astonished and alienated people by His habit of intercourse with men and women of doubtful char-

---

[1] See Mark viii, 31-5.

acter and by His attitude to them. He was friendly towards them, would go to their houses and talk familiarly with them. He appeared to be more interested in these people than in anybody else, and He practically said that God was too. He said that His own mission was not to the 'righteous' people but to 'sinners'; and the supreme examples in the world's literature of the experience of the divine forgiveness are to be found in the stories of how Jesus said to such men and women individually: 'Thy sins are forgiven: go and sin no more.' Not that He regarded the 'righteous' people, the Scribes and Pharisees, as being without sin. They might be even worse in God's eyes than the 'publicans and sinners'. They also were sinners and needed to repent. And when He spoke such scarifying words to them about their sins, was it not, in the last analysis, because He loved them too and would fain bring them to repentance? But they could not tolerate His words and His ways—His words to themselves and His ways with the 'publicans and sinners'. (Neither could Paul the Pharisee when he first heard of these things: this was doubtless partly why he hated the new 'Way', though he afterwards came to class himself among the 'sinners'). Jesus seemed to be subverting all rules by lumping together the good and the bad that they might all depend on God's mercy; and this was at least one of the main things that got Him into trouble with the leaders of His people. But He would not be turned aside by their opposition, for what they so disliked was of the very essence of what He knew He had to do. So He went straight on as the 'friend of sinners', and got deeper and deeper into trouble, until in the end He was condemned to death.

We can hardly do more than reverently conjecture as to how far it was given Him by faith to grasp the divine purpose that would use His death for the salvation of sinners, though there are various indications in the Gospels that He applied to Himself the Deutero-Isaianic prophecy of the Suffering Servant. But quite apart from that, and from all subsequent theological interpretations, it is true in the plainest historical sense that He died for sinners: it was His love for them that brought Him to the Cross.[1] Moreover when we

---

[1] This whole thesis is developed impressively in the first chapter of Dr. D. M. Ross's *The Cross of Christ* (1928), a book that deserves to be much better known than it is.

speak of the 'passion' of Jesus, we are not speaking merely of His dying, but of the whole course of suffering of which that was the climax, and not only physical suffering, but also and indeed chiefly the spiritual agony of the entire situation. He wept not for Himself but for the sons and daughters of Jerusalem who were rejecting Him. It was the contemplation of that immense moral and spiritual tragedy that made the situation almost unbearably terrible to Jesus. In that most literal and immediate sense His love was bearing their sins at infinite cost as He approached the Cross. That was the passion of Christ: and all this is even more important than the question as to how far He interpreted His coming death. For it is entirely congruous with the whole meaning and method of the Incarnation that He who, on the ultimate interpretation, died 'for the sins of the whole world' should in His own consciousness be mainly concerned with those sinners who were His immediate environment, the 'lost sheep of the house of Israel' in His own time.

II

The Cross and the Love of God

The crucifixion of Jesus set men thinking more than anything else that has ever happened in the life of the human race. And the most remarkable fact in the whole history of religious thought is this: that when the early Christians looked back and pondered on the dreadful thing that had happened, it made them think of the redeeming love of God.

Not simply of the love of Jesus, but of the love of God.

One might have expected them rather to lose all faith in the love of God, for the crucifixion might well seem to be the final *reductio ad absurdum* of the belief that the world is governed by a gracious providence. If in the religious history of Israel we find men continually being staggered by the spectacle of the sufferings of the good and the triumph of the forces of evil, if we find a psalmist confessing that he almost lost his foothold altogether when he saw things happening so, we should have expected to find all this doubt and rebellion increased a hundredfold in the minds of the followers of Jesus when they contemplated the unspeakably dreadful thing that had been done to their Lord and Master. If God was good, how could He have allowed such a thing to happen? There could be no doubt about the goodness of Jesus, or of His love for men: that had been made plainer than ever. But how could they believe any longer in the love of God? Would they not renounce God, and take Jesus as their Prometheus, who had brought warmth and light into their lives and then suffered crucifixion for what He had done, under the sky of a remote and angry God?

If the followers of Jesus did not feel like that, was it because the tragedy of the crucifixion was soon followed by the experiences of Easter morning? That was certainly all-important, determining the whole substance and tone of the early Christian message. But even then we might have expected something very different from what we find, and something very much less. We should have expected to find the resurrection regarded as reversing a tragic defeat, righting a dreadful wrong, by snatching Jesus back from the powers of evil which had had their way and worked their will upon Him. That was indeed one way of regarding it: the crucifixion *was* a dreadful wrong, and it had been brought about not merely by wicked men, but by demonic forces of evil, the 'rulers of this Age' who had 'crucified the Lord of Glory'. Yet the followers of Jesus had more than that to say about the crucifixion. Apparently from the very earliest days of the Church they maintained that somehow it had also been brought about by the purpose of God, and, moreover, by His merciful purpose of sending forgiveness to sinners—a forgiveness which could even embrace the men who had crucified Jesus. [1] We cannot trace the steps of the process by which this conviction was reached. The whole teaching of Jesus Himself must have contributed largely, though it is difficult to say how far He had prepared the way by speaking specifically of the significance of His death. As I have said, there is good reason for holding that as He saw His death approaching He applied to Himself the words of Deutero-Isaiah about the death of

---

[1] The evidence for this may be found in Acts ii, 23, 38f.; iii, 17–19, 26; iv, 27f, and in 1 Cor. xv, 3, where we have St. Paul's evidence as to what was passed on to him by those who were Christians before him.

the Servant of the Lord, which do not seem ever to have been applied to the Messiah before.[1] Certainly the primitive Christian community began at a very early date to use that passage in its thinking and preaching about Jesus, and it may have played an important part in the development of a theology of the Atonement. But however that development may have come about, there is no doubt that when we come to the main types of New Testament teaching, the Pauline and the Johannine, we find the death of Jesus not only connected with a divine purpose, but quite expressly and even confidently traced to the working of the love of God. Moreover, this is conceived as a sacrificial love. It is not a case merely of a gracious action or a gracious gift; it is something infinitely costly, a giving up by God of His only Son in the process of dealing with our sins, so great is His love towards us. In one place St. Paul speaks of how rare a thing it is for anyone to be ready to lay down his life even for a good man who deserved it: and then when he goes on to speak of Christ laying down His life for sinners, we should have expected him to take this as proving signally the love of *Christ*. But instead of that we find him, without any explanation, taking it as a signal proof of the love of *God*. 'God commendeth *his own* love towards us, in that, while we were yet sinners, Christ died for us.'[2] He 'did not spare his own Son, but gave him up for us all'.[3] And in Johannine language: 'God so loved the world that he gave his only begotten Son',[4] and 'herein is love, not that we loved God, but that he loved us, and sent his Son to be the propitiation for our sins'.[5]

Throughout the whole of this New Testament material there is no trace of any contrast between the wrath of God and the love of Christ, or of the idea that God's attitude to sinners had to be changed by the sacrifice of Christ from wrath and justice to love and mercy. There is ample use of the terminology of the Jewish sacrificial system, but it is highly doubtful whether even in the Old Testament period the purpose of the sin-offerings was to change

[1] Isa. liii.
[2] Rom. v, 8.
[3] Rom. viii, 32.
[4] John iii, 16.
[5] 1 John iv, 10.

God's atttude in that sense. A great deal of confusion has been caused by the fact that the English word 'atonement' has moved away from the sense it had when the Bible was translated, viz., reconciliation. The Hebrew word which lies behind it originally meant 'covering' or 'wiping out', and it may have included the idea of an 'expiation' that had to be made before the sinner could be acquitted, but it certainly did not imply anything like propitiation of an angry God. For, as scholars have pointed out,[1] it is always God Himself who is regarded, in the Old Testament, as having appointed the ritual of sin-offering, in His desire for reconciliation. That is highly important. Man has, of course, to provide the offering (the victim or other material) and to carry out the ritual, but it is God that has provided this means of reconciliation, taking this merciful initiative because He does not desire the death of a sinner but his restoration.

But when we come to the New Testament, we can go much farther than this. For the Greek word used ($\kappa\alpha\tau\alpha\lambda\lambda\alpha\gamma\acute{\eta}$) to correspond with the Old Testament 'atonement', means simply 'reconciliation'.[2] Moreover, the New Testament does not speak of God being reconciled to man, but of man being reconciled to God, and of God as the Reconciler, taking the initiative in Christ to that end.[3] There are indeed three passages, one Pauline and two Johannine, where we find another word in the English Bible: 'propitiation'. As regards the Johannine passages, it is clear that the word ($\acute{\iota}\lambda\alpha\sigma\mu\acute{o}\varsigma$) does not mean anything like the appeasing of an angry God, for the *love* of God is the starting-point. 'Herein is love, not that we loved God but that he loved us and sent his Son to be the propitiation for our sins.'[4] The Pauline passage has been much discussed by commentators. 'Being justified freely by his grace, through the redemption that is in Christ Jesus, whom God hath set forth as a propitiation ($\acute{\iota}\lambda\alpha\sigma\tau\acute{\eta}\rho\iota\sigma\nu$) through faith, by his blood. . . .'[5] Professor C. H. Dodd, who has made a careful study

---

[1] See e.g. A. C. Welch, *Prophet and Priest in Old Israel*, p. 139.

[2] In the A.V. it is only once translated 'atonement', in Rom. v, 11, and even there it becomes 'reconciliation', in line with all the rest of the passage, in the R.V.

[3] See especially 2 Cor. v, 18f.

[4] 1 John iv, 10. The other passage is ii, 2.

[5] Rom. iii, 24f.

of the word, assures us that the rendering 'propitiation' is misleading, being in accord with pagan usage but foreign to Biblical usage, and that the real meaning of the passage is that God has set forth Christ as 'a means by which guilt is annulled' or even 'a means by which sin is forgiven'.[1] It is just possible that the Greek word ought here to be given the meaning that it regularly bears in the Septuagint (and which also appears in Heb. ix, 5), and that we should translate it simply as 'mercy-seat' or 'place of forgiveness'.

But however we translate those terms borrowed from the Jewish sacrificial system, it is quite plain that in the New Testament they undergo a transformation of meaning because of the really extraordinary setting which is now given to them. We saw that even in the Old Testament usage the pagan meanings had been left behind because it was God Himself who was regarded as having mercifully appointed the ritual of expiation, though man had of course to supply the victim. But this is the amazing new fact that emerges when we come to the New Testament: that God even provides the victim that is offered, and the victim is His own Son, the Only-begotten. In short, 'it is *all* of God': the desire to forgive and reconcile, the appointing of means, the provision of the victim as it were from His own bosom at infinite cost. It all takes place within the very life of God Himself: for if we take the Christology of the New Testament at its highest we can only say that 'God was in Christ' in that great atoning sacrifice, and even that the Priest and the Victim both were none other than God. There is in the New Testament no uniformity of conception as to *how* this sacrifice brings about the reconciliation, and indeed some of its interpretations of the meaning of the Cross are in terms drawn from quite other realms than that of the sacrificial system. But in whatever way the process of salvation through the Cross is conceived, God's merciful attitude towards sinners is never regarded as the *result* of the process, but as its cause and source.[2] It all took place because

---

[1] See C. H. Dodd's *Romans* (Moffatt Commentary) in loc. What Professor Dodd says is based on a careful study of the background of the term.

[2] In Rom. iii, 24ff., there does seem to be a suggestion that God's attitude to human sin was different after the Cross from what it had been before. But if the suggestion is there, what is suggested is not that there was a change from wrath

God so loved the world. Its background is the eternal love of God. This does not mean that there is no place for the idea of the 'wrath' of God, or that 'the Wrath' from which we are saved is something impersonal and apart from God in New Testament thought, as Professor Dodd suggests.[1] But His wrath must not be regarded as something which has to be 'propitiated' and so changed into love and mercy, but rather as being identical with the consuming fire of inexorable divine love in relation to our sins. 'The wrath of God', writes Brunner, 'is not the ultimate reality; it is the divine reality which corresponds to sin. But it is not the essential reality of God. In Himself God is love.' And the revelation in Christ is 'the place where the love of God breaks through the wrath of God. This revelation of the divine mystery of love in the midst of the reality of wrath is the "propitiation" (ἱλασμός).'[2] Moreover there is in the New Testament a remarkable identification of the love of Christ which led Him to the Cross and the love of God which sent or gave Him. The identification is the more striking because it is made so tacitly. It does not appear as a theological consequence of an actual identification of Christ with God, for St. Paul's Christology had hardly got so far as that in express formulation. But when he is speaking of the great reconciliation, he runs ahead of his Christology and speaks of the love of Christ and the love of God almost interchangeably. 'Who shall separate us from the love of Christ?' he asks, in one great passage; and then in his eloquent answer he speaks of 'the love of God which was in Christ Jesus our Lord'.[3] There was no distinction: the two were one and the same thing. In discoursing of the love that was shown in the Cross of Christ the New Testament is never able to stop short of tracing it up-stream to the eternal love of God dealing sacrificially with the sins of the world.

---

to mercy, but rather, as Dr. Vincent Taylor points out, that there was a change from forbearance to righteousness, from mere 'passing over' to 'justifying'. What Dr. Taylor says further on this point is well worth reading. See *The Atonement in New Testament Thought*, pp. 133f.

[1] C. H. Dodd, op. cit., pp. 20ff.

[2] Emil Brunner, *The Mediator*, pp. 519ff.

[3] Rom. viii, 35ff.

III

Historical and Eternal Atonement

In the preceding chapter we reached the conclusion that the whole Christian life rests upon a doctrine of the forgiveness of sins which implies a redemptive sin-bearing, a costly atonement, in the heart of God. But of course it was not by any mere 'implication' that such a divine sin-bearing was conceived: the idea arose out of the historical event that we have been considering in this chapter, the death of Jesus Christ, in which the New Testament found the redeeming love of God. What are we now to say about the relation between this historical atonement and the eternal sin-bearing of the divine Love? To reduce the importance of the historical event would be contrary to every instinct of Christian faith; and yet it seems impossible to say that the divine sin-bearing was confined to that moment of time, or is anything less than eternal.

Here we are confronted with a problem with which theology is continually beset, that of the relation between time and eternity. We are accustomed to say that while we finite creatures are subject to temporality in our experience, living always in a present moment which is between the remembered past and the unlived future, God 'inhabits eternity', living in an eternal present, in which past, present and future are all one. But we must be careful. There is a danger that we should come to think of the life of God as simply *timeless*, out of all relation to time, as an abstraction is timeless, or in a sense which would imply that time is a mere illusion from which God is free. If we think of the eternity of God in such ways, then to speak of an eternal atonement in the heart of God for human sin will be likely to mean something like the resolution of all contradictions in a timeless Absolute, in a sense that would obscure the reality of evil, and that would reduce the historical episode of the Cross to a merely accidental symbol of a timeless truth. But when we say that God lives in eternity, not in time, we ought to mean something different. We ought to mean, not that God has no relation to time and no experience of it (which would imply *either* that time is a sheer illusion *or* that God's experience falls short of that aspect of reality!) but that, while embracing time in His experience, while knowing past, present and future, God is not confined, as we are, within the limits of temporality and successiveness, but transcends these limits, so that He can experience past, present and future all in one. If He is 'a God who *does* things', a living God, we must think of Him as having the positive kind of eternity which has a direct 'vertical' relation to each moment of our temporal experience; and when we speak of His activity we are bound to use temporal expressions, verbs with past, present and future tenses, though we know that they are inadequate, because the eternal reality is beyond anything that we can imagine or express.

And thus when we speak of divine Atonement we will not hesitate to say that God was uniquely present in the passion and death of Jesus, making Atonement, 'reconciling the world unto Himself'. As God was incarnate in Jesus, so we may say that the divine Atonement was incarnate in the passion of Jesus. And if we then go on to speak of an eternal Atonement in the very being and life of God, it is not by way of reducing the significance of the historical moment of the Incarnation, but by way of realizing the relation of the living God to every other historical moment. God's reconciling work cannot be confined to any one moment of history. We cannot say that God was unforgiving until Christ came and died on Calvary; nor can we forget that God's work of reconciliation still goes on in every age in the lives of sinful men, whose sins He still bears. 'The Atonement', says Brunner, 'is not history. The Atonement, the expiation of human guilt, the covering of sin through His sacrifice is not anything which can be conceived from the point of view of history. This event does not belong to the historical plane. It is super-history, it lies in the dimension which no historian knows in so far as he is a mere historian.'[1] Brunner does not mean that the historical episode of the passion of Christ is of limited importance, but that the mystery of divine Atonement involved in it is not one of those empirical factors with which historical science can reckon. It is not that the historical episode is a mere symbol of something 'timeless': it is actually a part (the incarnate part) of the

---

[1] Brunner, op. cit., p. 504.

eternal divine sin-bearing. But it would be quite false to think of *any* moment of human history as having no direct relation to this divine sin-bearing, which transcends the temporality of past, present and future, without destroying it. There has never been an age when it would have been true to say that God was not carrying the load of the sins of His people and thus making atonement and offering forgiveness. 'In his love and in his pity he redeemed them, and he bare them and carried them all the days of old', even when they 'grieved his holy Spirit'.[1] That is the truth of the picture of 'the Lamb slain from the foundation of the world'.[2] And beside it we may place Pascal's complementary picture: 'Jesus will be in agony until the end of the world.'[3] These pictures give us one side of the truth. And if this eternal aspect has not had a large place in traditional doctrine, it is doubtless partly because of the danger of reducing the importance of the historical episode, but also partly because false ideas of propitiation obscured the truth that the Atonement is something within the life of God, wrought by God Himself, and applied by Him to men in every age.

It is deeply interesting to note that there was a genuine recognition of this in the old Protestant tradition. It was an old theological problem whether and how the believing souls in Israel before the coming of Christ actually had their sins forgiven and received the benefits of the Atonement which was prefigured by the types and sacrifices of the old dispensation. The medieval teaching was that those ordinances did not actually *communicate* to believers in Israel the benefits which they foreshadowed. The benefits of the Atonement were not yet available because the sacrifice on Calvary had not yet been made. Therefore the Old Testament believers could not pass into the bliss of heaven when they died, but had to remain in the *limbus patrum* until Christ, after His atoning death, descended to release them and take them to heaven. But Reformed theology rejected all that, and taught that Old Testament believers had

---

[1] Isa. lxiii, 9, 10.

[2] Rev. xiii, 8. I am, of course, aware that a comparison of this verse with Rev. xvii, 8, makes it highly doubtful whether the usual translation, which I have used, is correct. I do not base any argument on it, but I quote it partly because its traditional use in this connection comes up a page or two later.

[3] Pascal, *Pensées* (ed. Brunschvicg), 553.

no such waiting. Though Christ had not yet come and suffered and died, they could already by faith have the full benefits of His Atonement: they not only looked forward to it, but actually received, as truly as we do, the forgiveness and salvation which it brought.[1] The old Reformed divines doubtless conceived this as a *proleptic* appropriation of the benefits, through a faith that looked forward to Christ. Yet what could this mean except that the divine work of reconciliation was already present, that in some sense God was already making atonement, and the same atonement which was afterwards to appear on the plane of history in the Cross of Christ? There is more than a hint of this in the Westminster Confession of 1647. 'Although the work of redemption was not actually wrought by Christ till after his incarnation, yet the virtue, efficacy and benefits thereof were communicated unto the elect in all ages successively from the beginning of the world, in and by those promises, types, and sacrifices, wherein he was revealed and signified to be the Seed of the woman, which should bruise the serpent's head, and *the Lamb slain from the beginning of the world, being yesterday and to-day the same, and for ever.*'[2] I need not discuss whether the one side or the other was right in that controversy, as we should hardly formulate the question in the same way. But surely the Protestant answer reveals a sound theological judgment, even in its somewhat unexpected use of the notion of the Lamb eternally slain. For we must believe that the faithful in Israel did, in their measure and according to their lights, receive the divine reconciliation; and whether or not they should be conceived as looking *forward* in this matter, it would obviously be absurd to say that *God* had to look

---

[1] St. Augustine had said: 'The sacraments of the New Testament give salvation: the sacraments of the Old Testament promised a Saviour.' Calvin maintains that the scholastics misinterpreted this, and he writes: 'The scholastic dogma . . . by which the difference between the sacraments of the old and the new dispensation is made so great, that the former did nothing but shadow forth the grace of God, while the latter actually confer it, must be altogether exploded'. (*Inst.* IV, xiv, 23.) The Old Testament believers 'both had and knew Christ the Mediator, by whom they were united to God, and made capable of receiving his promises'. 'Who will presume to represent the Jews as destitute of Christ, when we know that they were parties to the Gospel covenant, which has its only foundation in Christ?' (Ibid., II, x, 4.)

[2] *Westminster Confession of Faith*, chap. viii, § 6 (my italics). Cf. chap vii § 5; chap. xi, § 6; chap. xxvii, § 5.

forward to the historical Atonement in order to be able to forgive
and save! The work of atonement is His own work, incarnate in the
Passion of Jesus Christ because it is 'eternal in the heavens' in the
very life of God—the love of God bearing the sin of the world.[1]
'There was a cross in the heart of God', wrote Charles Allen Dinsmore, 'before there was one planted on the green hill outside
Jerusalem.'[2]

As regards the idea that the divine sin-bearing, the atoning
work, which appeared in history once for all on Calvary, goes on
ever since in the heavenly sphere, there are hints of this in the
Christian tradition from the beginning. When Paul at his conversion hears the voice of Christ saying: 'I am Jesus whom thou
persecutest', and when the Epistle to the Hebrews speaks of apos-
tates as 'crucifying the Son of God afresh for themselves and putting him to open shame',[3] there is the idea that Christ still suffers
at the hands of men though His historical Passion is past and over.
Deissmann pointed out that when St. Paul speaks of 'Christ crucified', the participle he uses is not in the aorist but in the perfect
tense (not σταυρωθείς but ἐσταυρωμένος) which means not
'Christ who was once crucified' but 'Christ who is crucified' or
'Christ who has been crucified and bears the marks upon Him still'
(perhaps we might even say, 'Christ on the Cross'). Dr. H. G.
Wood, who refers to this, quotes also from the Fourth Gospel:

---

[1] Canon J. K. Mozley (*Doctrine of the Atonement*, p. 90 and note) says that
Dean Inge, who advocated a doctrine of eternal atonement, and Dr. Denney,
who criticized him, both seem to confuse two meanings of that phrase (*a*)
'eternal atonement viewed as an eternal truth', and (*b*) 'eternal atonement as
implying something which has been part of God's eternal purpose'. Dr. Mozley
himself holds, I understand, that the second is the only sound meaning. He says:
'Atonement is no afterthought, since God knows that it will be required. No
questions as to the relation of the historical to the eternal, of temporal fact and
supratemporal reality, need be raised.' But this seems to me to simplify the
matter unduly. 'God knows that it will be required': required by whom, or by
what? It is not anything outside God's own nature that requires it, and it is
only God that can accomplish it. Surely, then, it must in the last analysis be an
eternal work of atonement, supratemporal as the life of God is, but not 'timeless' as an abstraction is; appearing incarnate once, but touching every point
of history, and going on as long as sins continue to be committed and there are
sinners to be reconciled.

[2] C. A. Dinsmore, *Atonement in Literature and Life*, p. 232.

[3] Heb. vi, 6.

'He showed them his hands and his side', which gives the idea of Christ's risen body as still bearing the marks of the wounds.[1] But far more important is the idea worked out in the Epistle to the Hebrews and carried further in the catholic tradition, that the atoning work of Christ, as Priest and Victim in one, is not confined to His Passion on earth and did not end with His death on the Cross. That work on Calvary was indeed a finished work, a perfect sacrifice made once for all on earth. Yet it was the beginning of a priesthood which goes on for ever in the unseen realm, in heaven, in the Holy Place beyond the Veil, into which our High Priest entered through death, and where he 'ever liveth to make intercession for us', being continually 'touched with the feeling of our infirmities'. I do not think this Epistle contains the idea of the atoning *sacrifice* of Christ being repeated or continued by Him in the heavenly realm, but it certainly is full of the idea that His work as High Priest goes on for ever in heaven and that He can still enter into our trials and temptations because He passed through such experiences Himself.

But all of this has received a further interpretation in the theology of the catholic tradition, particularly in the doctrine of the eucharistic sacrifice, which has often been perverted into something sub-Christian, but which at its best has certainly not minimized the 'once-for-all-ness' of the 'finished work of Christ' on Calvary, but rather made it fundamental. There has been a considerable development of this kind within recent years in Anglican circles, with a new emphasis on the idea of the continued exercise by Christ of His priestly office in heaven, and its representation on earth in the Eucharist. As long ago as 1901 Bishop Gore wrote: 'In the Epistle to the Hebrews all that goes before the ascension is the preparation of Christ for His priestly work. His work as the great high priest, and His entrance into at least the effectiveness of His office, begins with His entrance into the true holy of holies, in the power of His own blood once for all surrendered in death. . . . It is at the entrance into heaven, and not upon the cross, that He accomplishes His atonement for us, according to the Epistle to the Hebrews, and His work as high priest, which

---

[1] H. G. Wood, *Christianity and History*, p. 212.

begins with His entrance into heaven, is perpetual. His propitiation and His intercession are identical: and both consist in His "appearing" or presenting Himself for us.' And Gore finds the Church of the early centuries teaching that in the eucharistic sacrifice 'God has united the offerings of the church to the ever-living sacrifice of the great High Priest in the heavenly sanctuary'. [1] 'We offer on the earthly altar', wrote Canon Holmes, 'the same sacrifice that is being perpetually offered on the Heavenly Altar.' [2] 'The Eucharist', wrote Canon Quick, '. . . is the perpetual externalization in human ritual of the self-offering of Christ, which was once for all in fact externalized on Calvary, but is ever real in the inward and heavenly sphere.' 'In the Eucharist . . . we make before God an offering which is one with Christ's present and eternal offering of Himself.' [3] A similar line of thought was pursued by Bishop Hicks, with special emphasis on the thesis that in the Old Testament sacrifices it was not the *death* of the victim in itself that was supposed to be effectual, but rather the *life*, set free by the act of sacrifice upon the altar and thus offered to God. 'The death is vital to the sacrifice, because it sets free the blood, which is the life. But the victim is, in a true sense, operative, not as dead, but as alive "as it had been slain": not as νεκρόν but ὡς ἐσφαγμένον.' [4] And so the sacrificial death of Christ on the Cross is not the end of His atoning work, but makes possible His entry into the heavenly sphere where His self-offering goes on for ever.

Very similar is the following from Professor Arseniev of the Eastern Orthodox Church. In the Eucharist 'we are raised above our human, earthly plane to contemplate the perpetual self-offering of the Lamb of God before the face of the Father. He suffered once on earth and He offers continually His death to the Father on the heavenly altar. . . . Our Eucharist is the true representation of His true and continuous sacrifice, once for all time offered on the earth—on Golgotha, and perpetually presented

[1] Charles Gore, *The Body of Christ*, pp. 212, 252f.
[2] E. E. Holmes, *The Church, Her Books and Her Sacraments*, p. 87 (quoted by Arseniev).
[3] O. C. Quick, *The Christian Sacraments*, pp. 198, 200.
[4] F. C. N. Hicks, *The Fullness of Sacrifice*, p. 18.

to the Father on our behalf in Eternity.'[1] It is deeply interesting, in this connection, to learn that in modern Orthodox theology, especially among the Russians, there has developed the idea that the divine *kenosis*, self-emptying or humiliation was not confined to the historical Passion or even to the Incarnation, but is something eternal in the life of God. It was apparently from the Kenotic school in Protestantism that Russian Orthodox thinkers first borrowed *kenosis* as an important theological concept. While criticizing the Protestant use of the idea,[2] they have used it in their own way, maintaining that divine *kenosis* is involved in the whole divine conflict with evil, in the very act of creation, and even in the life of the Trinity. But here is what concerns our present argument: 'The *kenosis* of Christ is still going on. As far as there is evil in the world, the Lamb is still slain. Christ is still humbling Himself and waiting for the decision of man's freedom.'[3]

I have brought together these various statements from such diverse quarters, not to endorse all that they say, but to illustrate the widespread sense, among those who make the historical Cross quite central, that the divine Atonement cannot be confined within any one moment of time, but, so far as it can be described in temporal terms at all, is as old and as endless as the sin with which it deals. 'The Lamb slain from the foundation of the world.' 'Jesus will be in agony until the end of the world.' 'Behold the Lamb of God which taketh away the sin of the world.'

IV

Objective and Subjective Atonement

What, then, is the divine Atonement, which is thus both historical and eternal? Is it an 'objective' reality, something done by

---

[1] Nicholas Arseniev in *The Ministry and Sacraments* (edited by Headlam and Dunkerley), p. 86.

[2] See above, chap. iv, p. 97 footnote.

[3] Gorodetzky, *The Humiliated Christ in Modern Russian Thought*, p. 171. This book gives an account of the whole movement, mentioning as its main representatives Vladimir Soloviev, M. M. Tareev and Sergius Bulgakov.

Christ, something ordained and accepted by God, in 'expiation' of human sin, quite apart from our knowledge of it and its effect upon us? Or is it a 'subjective' process, a reconciling of us to God through a persuasion in our hearts that there is no obstacle, a realizing of His eternal love? Surely these two aspects cannot be separated at all, though the attempt has often been made to classify atonement-theories in that way. In theological argument on this subject we are apt to forget that we are dealing with a realm of personal relationships and nothing else. If we use the terminology of an ancient sacrificial system, we should remember that in the last analysis the only offering we can make to God is the offering of ourselves in faith and love. What Jesus offered to God was Himself. But to offer oneself thus to God means at the same time to love men without limit, and so to carry the load of their sins. That is what Jesus did, in a passion which included physical suffering, social persecution and obloquy, even to the point of a shameful death, and above all the spiritual agony of seeing other lives go wrong. But if, on the deepest interpretation, this was not only an offering made by a man to God, but also a sacrifice made by God Himself, then it is part of the sacrifice that God is continually making, because He is infinite Love confronted with human sin. And it is an *expiatory* sacrifice, because sin is a dreadfully real thing which love cannot tolerate or lightly pass over, and it is only out of the suffering of such inexorable love that true forgiveness, as distinct from an indulgent amnesty, could ever come. That is the objective process of atonement that goes on in the very life of God.

All this may seem to conflict with the traditional doctrine of the divine impassibility, and perhaps the prevalence of that doctrine, which excludes all suffering from the divine nature, is one of the factors that have hindered the acceptance of such ideas as I have been developing. But it is hard to see how a rigid acceptance of the doctrine can leave room for any belief in costly divine sin-bearing at all, even in the incarnate life. There is little help in the traditional solution, that while the impassible God bore suffering in His incarnate life, it was not God the Father but God the Son that suffered, and He suffered not in His divine but in His human nature; for that leaves us asking whether it was really *God* that suffered, and if not, how we can say that God bore our sins. I cannot but think (in spite of Baron von Hügel's impressive protest [1]) that there is some truth in the widespread modern tendency to modify the impassibility doctrine. Perhaps we can conserve both sides of the truth by saying, paradoxically, that while there is suffering (for human sin) in the life of God, it is eternally swallowed up in victory and blessedness, and that is how God 'expiates' our sins, as only God could do.

In this connection it is not irrelevant to remember that St. Paul connects the atoning work of Christ very closely not only with His Cross and passion, but also with His Resurrection, His victory, His risen life. If, as we saw, the important points for the author of *Hebrews* are the death and the ascension, the vital points for St. Paul in this connection are the death and the resurrection, and very closely joined together. Christ 'was delivered up for our offences and raised again for our justification'.[2] 'Who shall lay anything to the charge of God's elect? It is God that justifieth. Who is he that shall condemn? It is Christ Jesus that died, yea, rather, that was raised from the dead. . . .'[3] 'Not having a righteousness of my own, even that which is of the law, but that which is through faith in Christ, the righteousness which is of God by faith; that I may know him, and the power of his resurrection and the fellowship of his sufferings, being conformed unto his death, if by any means I might attain unto the resurrection of the dead.'[4] When we contemplate the story of Jesus we are bound to speak of the suffering and the victory as successive phases; and so does St. Paul: 'Christ being raised from the dead dieth no more; death no more hath dominion over him. For the death that he died, he died unto sin once; but the life that he liveth, he liveth unto God.'[5] But the same chapter gives us Paul's mystical doctrine of the union of the believer with the dying and rising Christ; with the implication that in some sense the passion and the resurrection are not simply episodes in the past, but are, both together, a

---

[1] See his essay on 'Suffering and God', in the Second Series of his *Essays and Addresses.*

[2] Rom. iv, 25.

[3] Rom. viii, 33f.

[4] Phil. iii, 9–11.

[5] Rom. vi, 9f.

present reality, an eternal conflict with evil which is also an eternal victory.

This brings us very close to the 'Christus Victor' conception of the Atonement which is advocated by Bishop Aulén as being the truly classic Christian view, and as holding the hope of the future, though at some periods it has been obscured.[1] According to this view, the Atonement is essentially, from start to finish, the costly but victorious conflict of God Himself, in Christ, with the forces of evil. This is a cosmic warfare against a very real enemy, and it involves divine self-sacrifice, but it is thereby triumphant over evil, with an eternal victory which is ever-present as well as past. Bishop Aulén is well aware that this 'classic' view has usually been expressed in highly dramatic and pictorial terms which cannot remain stereotyped for the future, but he is also sure that in this realm the truth can never be forced into a purely rational scheme or get rid of its tremendous paradoxes. It is plain that the New Testament, in dealing with this whole matter, while freely using figures drawn from the ancient system of sacrifices, does not confine itself to such imagery, but uses many other figures too. It is doubtless impossible to speak of such things without using symbolic language. But it is good to let one figure of speech correct and supplement another, and to remind ourselves that all of these are but attempts to exhibit the love of God dealing with the sin of the world and overcoming it as only love can do. That is the 'objective' work of atonement.

But since it is neither a 'material' nor a 'legal' victory, neither a battle conducted outside human life altogether nor a transaction completed as it were behind our backs or before we were born, but a spiritual process in the realm of personal relationships, the objective work cannot be separated from its subjective aspect by which it becomes a reality in the hearts and lives of men. And

---

[1] Bishop Aulén's book in its English translation is entitled *Christus Victor* (1931). It will occur to readers of his book that the 'classic' view, as expounded by Aulén, stresses the 'cosmic' aspect of the Atonement more than I have done. 'The classic type regards sin as an objective power standing behind men, and the Atonement as the triumph of God over sin, death and the devil.' But Aulén also emphasizes that the 'classic' view gives the most *personal* conception of sin, and that it is the 'Latin' type of theory that really tends to obscure the personal relationship between God and the sinner.

this happens above all through the story of the Cross of Christ, the point in human history where we find the actual outcropping of the divine Atonement. That is what brings us individually back to God. 'God was in Christ, reconciling the world unto himself; . . . we beseech you on behalf of Christ, be ye reconciled to God.'[1]

That is the only kind of answer that can be given to the questions with which we began our seventh chapter, as to why God became man, and what difference the Incarnation makes. We cannot answer speculative questions as to what might have been, what God might or might not have done; and we certainly dare not say that God *could* not have been merciful but for the Cross of Christ. But we can now say about the Incarnation not only that it gives us the Christian view of God, but also that it gives us that outcropping of divine atonement in human history which makes His mercy effectual for our salvation. The Christian message tells us that God was incarnate in Jesus, and that His sin-bearing was incarnate in the Passion of Jesus. His love is inexorable towards our sins, just because it is infinite love and sin is its opposite (self-centredness, lovelessness); and for the same reason it persists indefatigably through all our sinning. That is how He bears our sins. And that is how He overcomes them. That is the costly 'expiation' out of which forgiveness comes. And the story of that, as it was incarnate in Jesus, is what gives us the liberation which leads to a new life. For that story, with the Christian interpretation of it, makes us willing to bring our sins to God, to see them in His light, and to accept from Him the forgiveness which we could never earn. That brings release and a new beginning. And that leads to a new kind of goodness, not the 'Pharisaic' kind, which grows in those who try to save themselves and take credit to themselves for having (as they may think) achieved it; but the Christian kind, which is never conscious of its own merit but only of God's mercy. That is the very secret of the Christian character.

In an earlier chapter I spoke at some length of how the religion of the Incarnation has given rise to a new and highly paradoxical consciousness in the religious experience of mankind, which is expressed in the typical Christian confession: Not I, but the grace of

---

[1] 2 Cor. v, 19f.

God. But we can now see that more than the Incarnation was needed to awaken in us sinful men and women the sense of that paradox of grace. It is because the religion of the Incarnation became also the religion of Atonement that it has been able to do this. It is because 'God was in Christ, reconciling the world unto himself, *not reckoning unto them their trespasses*'. When we receive that message, and accept the forgiveness of our sins, then we begin to be set free from ourselves. Because God does not reckon unto us our trespasses, we will not reckon unto us our virtues. Our confession will be: Not I, but the grace of God.

Chapter IX

EPILOGUE: THE BODY OF CHRIST

This short chapter is but an epilogue, added because it seems necessary to view in retrospect not only the track that we have followed, by way of summarizing the argument, but the whole landscape which it traversed, and to do it from the vantage-point of the Church of Christ, since it is the Church that has to tell the story.

The 'sacred story' begins with God's eternal purpose for man, as faith perceives it. His eternal purpose was that mankind should be 'one body', with the unity of a perfect organism: a higher kind of organism, indeed, than any that we know (so that the very word 'organism' is inadequate if not misleading), a free and harmonious fellowship of persons united in the love of God. In such a perfect community each individual would have the fullest and highest freedom—without which there can be no true fellowship. But they would not be 'individualistic' in spirit: if they were, their personalities would be starved and cramped, since the true life of personality is in close fellowship. Moreover, fellowship with God and fellowship with men cannot be separated in human life—can hardly even be distinguished. Thus the true life of mankind is found in the corporate enjoyment of God, a life of complete community with God and man. That is true human nature, created in the image of God. That is God's plan for mankind: that it should be 'one body'.

But something has gone wrong. The organism has somehow failed to function as one body. It has come to be divided into countless little bits of life, each person trying to be a quite independent cell, a self-sufficient atom, dancing on a pattern of its own, instead of joining in the great communal game of universal love. Each person makes himself the centre of his universe, caring little for the fellowship of the whole, but seeing things from his selfish point of view; becoming his own God, and worshipping himself. That is the universal aberration symbolized in the 'myth' of the Fall of Man (it is the kind of thing that can only be described in a 'myth', since we cannot conceive it as an event that occurred at a particular date in human history on earth, but as something supra-historical, infecting all our history). In the story of Eden the serpent says to the woman: 'Ye shall be as gods.' That is the temptation to which mankind has succumbed: we have put ourselves, each one individually, in the centre of our universe, where God ought to be. And when persons do that, it separates them both from God and from each other. That is what is wrong with mankind. That is original sin.

Into that heritage every new child is born, and by it he is shaped from the start, so that as he grows into a self-conscious moral personality in the interplay with his human environment, he is already infected with the evil. And all our actual sins are the working out of that heritage. For the very essence of sin is self-centredness, refusal of divine and human community, absorption in oneself, which kills true individuality and destroys the soul. As Martin Luther put it, the 'natural man' (i.e. man fallen from his true nature and unredeemed from his spoilt sinful nature) is *incurvatus in se*, 'bent inwards upon himself',[1] instead of looking away from himself towards God and his fellows in love. That is what sin is, and all our sins can be reduced to that, even what we call the sins of the flesh. The evil comes not from the instincts and appetites connected with the body in themselves: these are part of the human nature that God has given us. The sins of the flesh come from this: that we care *more* for the body (our own bodies) than for 'the Body', the community for which God has created us; so that we are ready to use our own and other people's bodies for our own passing pleasure, instead of giving ourselves, soul and

---

[1] I owe this to Bishop Aulén.

body, to the love of God and man, which can use and consecrate both soul and body.

If we might make bold to view this matter in another 'myth' or divine emblem, I would tell a tale of God calling His human children to form a great circle for the playing of His game. In that circle we ought all to be standing, linked together with lovingly joined hands, facing towards the Light in the centre, which is God ('the Love that moves the sun and the other stars'); seeing our fellow creatures all round the circle in the light of that central Love, which shines on them and beautifies their faces; and joining with them in the dance of God's great game, the rhythm of love universal. But instead of that, we have, each one, turned our backs upon God and the circle of our fellows, and faced the other way, so that we can see neither the Light at the centre nor the faces on the circumference. And indeed in that position it is difficult even to join hands with our fellows! Therefore instead of playing God's game we play, each one, our own selfish little game, like the perverse children Jesus saw in the market-place, who would not join in the dance with their companions. Each one of us wishes to be the centre, and there is blind confusion, and not even any true *knowledge* of God or of our neighbours. That is what is wrong with mankind. Of course a man is not really happy in that attitude and situation, since he was created for community with God and man. Moreover, the light of God is still shining from the true centre upon his back, though not on his face. It throws his own shadow on the ground in front of him, and the shadow is contorted into grotesque shapes with every movement that he makes, until his whole world looks queer and unfriendly (it is indeed a fallen world, a ruined world). He knows, dimly or clearly, that all is not well. Perhaps he tries to *make* himself happy by pursuing his dance more furiously, but then his shadow dances still more mockingly, and things are worse than ever. For, as moralists have so often said, the quest of happiness defeats itself. Perhaps he even tries to mend matters by making himself *good*. But again he does not succeed. For, though this is not so obvious to moralists, the quest of goodness also defeats itself. The whole procedure of trying to improve our own characters keeps us thinking about ourselves. It is self-centred, and self-centredness is the very thing from which we need to be saved, because it is the essence of sin. That method fails, and failure brings discouragement and moral paralysis. Or if we ever begin to succeed in improving ourselves, or even to think we are succeeding, then we congratulate ourselves secretly on our achievement, which is the very worst kind of self-centredness—self-righteousness and pride. So instead of becoming saints, we become 'Pharisees'. (I have left our 'myth' behind: it has served its purpose, and I must not ride it to death.)

If that is what is wrong with the world, it is difficult to see how it could be put right. It seems impossible to change ourselves from being interested mainly in ourselves to being concerned with God and our fellows, because the more we try, the more are we concentrating on ourselves. How could we save ourselves *from* ourselves? We need to be drawn *out of* ourselves into the life of unselfish community: and how could we possibly do that?

But God has never given mankind up. He has always had His purpose. And (so far as we can venture to describe the divine plan in human history) His method of saving mankind has been like this. Thousands of years ago He started a new community, a little one at first, in order that it might be the nucleus of a new mankind. It was the People of Israel, the 'chosen People'. It consisted of ordinary men and women, who were sinners like the rest of mankind. But God drew them into a kind of compact, a 'Covenant', as they called it; and so they became in a special sense God's community, or (as they sometimes called it when they spoke Greek) the *Ecclesia* of God.[1] It was not that He was going to treat them as pampered favourites: far from it! He chose them, not for their own selfish sakes, but (though they did not usually realize it) for His great purpose of saving mankind. This would make high demands upon them (God would have to be stricter with them than with any other people[2]), but it would be worth while. For they would find their own salvation in being used for the salvation of mankind. Thus they would be a redeemed and redeeming community, through which all the world would be drawn back out of its disintegration into the life of community with God and man, and so the nucleus would grow into a new mankind.

---

[1] As in the Septuagint.
[2] Amos iii, 1, 2.

But Israel would not learn the lesson or rise to the occasion. Israel took its vocation in a selfish sense, and would not go far enough with the great purpose of God. Only a few men here and there, only a 'faithful remnant', proved to be willing and ready. Israel as a whole would not understand, and missed the opportunity of being the nucleus of a universal community of God.

And then God, whose 'counsel standeth for ever', who would not give mankind up, created a new nucleus for humanity by becoming incarnate Himself in a man of that race of Israel that had been so disappointing. This man Jesus, living in the midst of disintegrated sinful humanity, and subject to all its temptations, lived the kind of life that God meant all men to live. He was content to lose Himself entirely in the life of God and the life of His fellow-men, living without reserve the life of community, which is the very life of God Himself, though there was no community that would live it with Him, or even tolerate His living of it. He gathered around Him a dozen plain men, to make a beginning with them, though they hardly understood Him at all. They could not believe that 'the man who preserves his life will lose it', though they saw that their Master was not 'preserving' His life. He claimed nothing for Himself, not even life; and eventually His venture did cost Him His life. The people could not stand it, they got Him condemned to death. Even His chosen disciples deserted Him. He Himself was now all that was left of the 'faithful remnant' of the People of God, and He died on a cross, forsaken and alone.

But God had not given mankind up, and His purpose was not defeated.

A few weeks later, in that same city of Jerusalem where Jesus was condemned and crucified, we can see the most marvellous community that the world has ever known. It consists of those disciples of Jesus, now reunited, and a host of others with them, living in the warmest and closest fellowship, and growing in numbers every day and hour: the Church of Christ. Where has it sprung from? What has happened in that tragic and apostate city? How have those disciples been drawn out of themselves into this marvellous new fellowship, drawn out of the fallen pride of their dreadful failure, out of the inveterate and cowardly selfishness of their human nature, into the love of God and man? How had the impossible thing happened to them, or begun to happen? If we had asked them, they would have told us that their Master was not dead but alive, and even present with them. God had brought Him safely through death and raised Him up, and given Him back to them in an unseen way through what they called the Holy Spirit; and this had made them into a new community, with a wonderful solidarity which they called 'the fellowship of the Holy Spirit' and which God was using to draw other people in. But they would have told us something even stranger: that it was not only their Master's resurrection or His living Spirit that was doing such marvellous things—His very crucifixion, which had so scandalized and scattered them, had a great deal to do with it, and was indeed at the heart of the secret. For now, looking back, they could see that this was actually the love of God dealing with the sins of men, offering them forgiveness and a new beginning if only they would come and accept it. That was what had broken down their self-centred pride (which is always the real trouble, separating us both from God and from each other) and made them willing to come back into fellowship, not as good and worthy men who had a right, but as sinners all alike in need of mercy. Others were drawn in, and the community grew; and they kept thinking and saying ever more and more stupendous things about the man Jesus and His crucifixion: that this was God's sacrifice of His own Son for the salvation of men; that this was the eternal divine Word becoming incarnate and suffering as the Lamb of God that bears the sin of the world. This was the love of God Himself, exposing itself to the consequences of human sin, coming all the way in quest of sinners. These things made even Pharisees content to call themselves sinners and as such to enter the new community. It was indeed a new kind of community: a society of sinners forgiven, with the Cross as its badge, and every member confessing: 'Not I, but the grace of God.' That breaks down the barriers between man and man, and the members come to love each other because God first loved them and drew them out of themselves into the unity of 'one body'. That is the new People of God, the new Israel, the *Ecclesia*, the Body of Christ, the Church.

And this is the nucleus of a new humanity. It can never be content to remain a remnant, because its spirit is the spirit of divine love: not only towards its own members but towards all men. Its members will be interested not only in men's souls but in all that concerns their bodies too, all their material and social welfare, because God in His love came right into our material world, His Word was made flesh. It will transcend all barriers of class and race and nation, because from the standpoint of the Community of the Cross there is no difference: all are sinners and all can be saved. This new and universal community was created by what God did in Jesus Christ, and is based on nothing else: and through it God draws other men into community, and so saves the world. This, we can now say, is what God was preparing the world for when He chose and called the People of Israel. They did not know it, but God knew it; and as St. Paul said, this was God's great secret, the 'mystery' which had been laid up for countless ages but was now revealed: that 'Israel' would be transformed into a universal community, based not on Hebrew race but on faith in Jesus Christ, open to all men, the nucleus of a new mankind, the Israel of God. It is the Body of Christ. It shares in the sufferings, as it keeps the Festival, of the Broken Body. And it cannot be content until all men have been drawn into its fellowship, even if the perfect consummation must lie beyond the bounds of terrestrial history. It can never be content until mankind is truly 'one body' according to the eternal purpose of God—'till we all attain unto the unity of the faith and of the knowledge of the Son of God, unto a full-grown man, unto the measure of the stature of the fullness of Christ: that we may be no longer children [refusing to play God's game because we want to play our own] . . . but maintaining the truth may by love grow up wholly unto him who is the Head, even Christ: from whom all the body, fitly framed and knit together through that which every joint supplieth, according to the working in due measure of each several part, maketh the increase of the body unto the building up of itself in love.'[1]

Thus the Church is God's instrument of reconciliation through the ages. And to that end the perennial function of the Church is to proclaim, by Word and Sacrament and by its whole life, the

[1] Eph. iv, 13–16.

EPILOGUE: THE BODY OF CHRIST

message of what God has done in Jesus Christ. It is the Church, and it is only the Church, that can tell the story, the 'sacred history', because it is a confession and a testimony among men: TO WIT, THAT GOD WAS IN CHRIST, RECONCILING THE WORLD UNTO HIMSELF, NOT IMPUTING THEIR TRESPASSES UNTO THEM, AND HATH COMMITTED UNTO US THE WORD OF RECONCILIATION.

INDEX

INDEX